SIX SIGMA FOR THE
NEXT MILLENNIUM

Also available from ASQ Quality Press:

The Certified Six Sigma Black Belt Handbook
Donald W. Benbow and T.M. Kubiak

Applied Data Analysis for Process Improvement: A Practical Guide to Six Sigma Black Belt Statistics
James L. Lamprecht

Business Performance through Lean Six Sigma: Linking the Knowledge Worker, the Twelve Pillars, and Baldrige
James T. Schutta

Design for Six Sigma as Strategic Experimentation: Planning, Designing, and Building World-Class Products and Services
H.E. Cook

Applied Statistics for the Six Sigma Green Belt
Bhisham C. Gupta and H. Fred Walker

The Six Sigma Path to Leadership: Observations from the Trenches
David H. Treichler

Lean-Six Sigma for Healthcare: A Senior Leader Guide to Improving Cost and Throughput
Chip Caldwell, Jim Brexler, and Tom Gillem

The Manager's Guide to Six Sigma in Healthcare: Practical Tips and Tools for Improvement
Robert Barry and Amy C. Smith

Stop Rising Healthcare Costs Using Toyota Lean Production Methods: 38 Steps for Improvement
Robert Chalice

Six Sigma Project Management: A Pocket Guide
Jeffrey N. Lowenthal

Six Sigma for the Shop Floor: A Pocket Guide
Roderick A. Munro

Six Sigma for the Office: A Pocket Guide
Roderick A. Munro

To request a complimentary catalog of ASQ Quality Press publications, call 800-248-1946, or visit our Web site at http://qualitypress.asq.org.

Six Sigma for the Next Millennium

A CSSBB Guidebook

Kim H. Pries

ASQ Quality Press
Milwaukee, Wisconsin

American Society for Quality, Quality Press, Milwaukee 53203
© 2006 by American Society for Quality
All rights reserved. Published 2005
Printed in the United States of America

12 11 10 09 08 07 06 05   5 4 3 2 1

Library of Congress Cataloging-in-Publication Data

Pries, Kim H., 1955–
   Six sigma for the next millennium : a CSSBB guidebook / Kim H. Pries.
      p. cm.
   Includes bibliographical references and index.
   ISBN-13: 978-0-87389-656-6 (alk. paper)
   1. Six sigma (Quality control standard)   2. Total quality management.
   3. Quality control.   I. Title.
   HD62.15.P75 2005
   658.4'013—dc22

                    2005018863

Publisher: William A. Tony
Acquisitions Editor: Annemieke Hytinen
Project Editor: Paul O'Mara
Production Administrator: Randall Benson

ASQ Mission: The American Society for Quality advances individual, organizational, and community excellence worldwide through learning, quality improvement, and knowledge exchange.

Attention Bookstores, Wholesalers, Schools, and Corporations: ASQ Quality Press books, videotapes, audiotapes, and software are available at quantity discounts with bulk purchases for business, educational, or instructional use. For information, please contact ASQ Quality Press at 800-248-1946, or write to ASQ Quality Press, P.O. Box 3005, Milwaukee, WI 53201-3005.

To place orders or to request a free copy of the ASQ Quality Press Publications Catalog, including ASQ membership information, call 800-248-1946. Visit our Web site at www.asq.org or http://qualitypress.asq.org.

Quality Press
600 N. Plankinton Avenue
Milwaukee, Wisconsin 53203
Call toll free 800-248-1946
Fax 414-272-1734
www.asq.org
http://qualitypress.asq.org
http://standardsgroup.asq.org
E-mail: authors@asq.org

♾ Printed on acid-free paper

Contents

List of Figures and Tables

Preface

THE SIX SIGMA BLACK BELT BODY OF KNOWLEDGE

ASQ defines the Six Sigma Black Belt Body of Knowledge on its Web site, http://www.asq.org. The Body of Knowledge prescribes the minimum amount of information expected for the Black Belt certificate. It performs the additional function of defining a body of knowledge for all kinds of Black Belts, many of which are so designated without any kind of formal examination. In response to a questionnaire sent out several years ago by ASQ, I pleaded with them to "clean up" the Black Belt situation. Although many Black Belts have earned their titles through hard work, innovative projects, and teamwork, others have simply acquired the designation by sitting through some classroom exercises and lectures and completing a few poorly executed projects. (I have seen this myself!)

I believe it is critical to the future of Six Sigma and belt designations that they have meaning based on the two main items that ASQ requires:

1. Satisfactory results from the formal examination

2. Proof of successful completion of two projects, including executive sign-off on the form

The benefit of this approach is that it supports both sides of the Black Belt experience: the need for substantial technical knowledge and the practical experience to make a difference.

The Purpose of This Book

This book is designed to walk the reader through the Body of Knowledge at about a medium level of detail—it follows the order of the Body of Knowledge exactly. At the end of each subsection, I have provided one or two titles for further reading. These are works that I own personally and that I have used both for work and for formal examination study. The market now has a plethora of books claiming some relation to Six Sigma. Unfortunately, very few of them support the Body of Knowledge explicitly.

What I have tried to do in this work is to supply the Black Belt candidate with enough information to pursue the ASQ Certified Six Sigma Black Belt examination aggressively, either using the material in the book or using the indicated ancillary works. I have used a prototype version of this book when teaching the certification class for the professional education program at our local university.

ACKNOWLEDGMENTS

I would like to acknowledge support from the following individuals and organizations.

Christine Bayly at MINITAB graciously allowed me to plunder examples and other riches contained in this easy-to-use, yet profoundly powerful statistical software. MINITAB is always my weapon of choice when assessing problems from the statistical point of view.

Sue Darby at Air Academy Associates also allowed me to provide some examples using Air Academy's SPC XL software. The software arm of Air Academy took the route of using an existing tool—Microsoft Excel—and adding powerful functionality to the basic program through the use of the plug-in concept. SPC XL is not just a plug-in; it is an application that just happens to use Excel.

Christin La Grange at SmartDraw was very supportive. Nearly every graphic that did not come from a statistical program came from SmartDraw Suite Edition, version 7. The Suite Edition provides substantial graphical support for business process analyses with templates and numerous examples.

Jim Spiller at Critical Tools provides a significant improvement to the functionality of Microsoft Project with two plug-ins that remedy deficiencies in the base product: WBS Chart Pro creates excellent graphical representations of work breakdown structures and PERT Chart Expert replaces the abysmal network diagrams created by Project.

Virginia Systems provides tools for Adobe InDesign and other publishing programs that allow the user to create dynamic footnotes/endnotes, cross-references, sequential numeration, and professional-quality indexing. Adobe has created a master publishing tool with Adobe InDesign as well as Illustrator, Photoshop, and Acrobat. These tools work as a team to get the job done.

Of course, I own legal copies of all of these tools. I do not have business interest in any of the aforementioned companies.

I have also received support from people at my own company, Stoneridge Corporation: Stoneridge Electronics Group vice president Mark Tervalon, and Transportation Electronics Division general manager and vice president Shah A. Raza.

I would also like to thank my wife, Janise, for patiently tolerating my long weekends, days, and nights at the keyboard while working on this book.

Section I
Enterprise-Wide Deployment
(9 Questions)

Contents

A. Enterprise View

1. VALUE OF SIX SIGMA

Organization Value

So who cares about Six Sigma?

You do. Your company does. Your customers definitely do.

One of the major differences between Six Sigma and all previous quality initiatives is the emphasis on the bottom line. In concert with the obvious advantages of improving the bottom line is the concern for alignment with company goals—not just total quality because it sounds like a noble aspiration.

Additionally, Six Sigma has been the first real quality initiative to effectively divorce the participants from the formal quality department. This is not to say that quality managers, engineers, and auditors cannot participate, but that you do not have to be one of these in order to be a Six Sigma Black Belt, Green Belt, or Champion.

At General Electric, executive management considered the Six Sigma initiative to be important enough to make it a component of line managers' compensations. Jack Welch of General Electric made it clear that Six Sigma participation was a requirement for managers and a smart long-term career move.

Six Sigma Philosophy

The deployment and implementation of Six Sigma requires that management shift from talk to action, from slogans to data, from opinions to experimentation and control. The Six Sigma strategy spells out the drivers of the program, the implementers, and the quality tools and systems for improvement, and underlines the need for reliable measure of progress in various domains:

- Customer satisfaction

- Organization profitability

- Human resources

- Quality

Six Sigma Goals

Six Sigma solves business problems (not just quality problems) in order to promote profitability and growth. Marketplace requirements are wed to business outputs in an aggressive program designed to transform the enterprise into a highly aligned, profit-making organization.

Below the enterprise level, Six Sigma methods reduce variation, improve product quality, shorten the product development life cycle, accelerate business transactions, and improve overall service. Some benefits of using Six Sigma are:

1. Improvement of significant processes

2. Improvement of the "bottom line"

3. Alignment of participants and their activities with overall corporate goals

4. Provision of a suite of systematic approaches to improvement, problem-solving, and sustainment

5. Management of projects

6. Enhancement of staff capabilities

7. Emphasis on measurements and results

8. Improvements to corporate marketing

9. Enhancement in the use of statistical analysis

10. Development of focused products

11. Improvement of market share

12. Improvement in customer retention

Six Sigma Definition

From the preceding discussion, we can say that Six Sigma is a:

- Business philosophy oriented to the bottom line

- Suite of systematic techniques for product and process improvement

- Project-oriented toolbox

- Data-dependent family of procedures

- Highly statistical process

- Buzzword

- Reality at some firms

- Fantasy at other firms

- Form of total quality management (TQM)

- New version of TQM

- Management attribute with a bottom-line incentive

- Simple, easy-to-remember algorithm

- Focused form of project

- Method with many tools

- Process typically weak on sampling methods (remember that Six Sigma is oriented around projects and *not* ongoing techniques like incoming inspection, where sampling reigns—although Six Sigma methods can be used to improve the inspection scenario)

The point is that to some extent Six Sigma has become a management panacea. It is important to understand that Six Sigma really is more than a buzzword, that a systematic array of powerful tools is at the disposal of the Black Belt, and that real improvement can occur.

The following are some successes in Six Sigma implementation.

Six Sigma Successes

Motorola

- Started in 1987, based on a set of rules put together by Bill Smith of Motorola (hence the occasional reference to Smith as the father of Six Sigma)

- Spearheaded by Dr. Mikel Harry, among others

- Supported by Robert Galvin, chairman of Motorola

- Invented the terminology

General Electric

- Largest initiative—even larger than Motorola

- Encompassed divisions of General Electric

- Even GE Capital, a financing division, participated, developing a subtechnique known as "transactional" Six Sigma

- Reportedly saved GE $5 billion

Allied Signal

- Initiated by Larry Bossidy, a former General Electric executive

- Saves Allied about $600 million per year

- Began the first real implementations of Design for Six Sigma (DFSS) with corresponding reductions in development times

Stoneridge Corporation

- Successfully launched a multidivisional Six Sigma initiative

- Provided training at all levels

- Implemented DFSS as well as Define, Measure, Analyze, Improve, and Control (DMAIC)

- Developed systemwide supplier-input-process-output-customer (SIPOC) analysis of all phases of the enterprise

2. BUSINESS SYSTEMS AND PROCESSES

A company's core (non-support) processes may consist of the following:

- Marketing and sales

- Operations/production/manufacturing

- Procurement

- Customer service

Support processes may consist of the following:

- Research and development (engineering) if the company is a design house

- Human resources

- Accounting

- Materials

- Warehousing

- Logistics

A business system specifies how these core processes are related. In many cases, the various portions of the business system will be interlinked through a massive computer database called an Enterprise Resource Planning (ERP) system, the successor to Manufacturing Resource Planning (MRP-2) systems. Suppliers for ERP products include SAP, Oracle/PeopleSoft, GEAC, Baan, and J. G. Edwards.

The ERP system gives the Information Technology (IT) department a significant amount of responsibility and power. Also, those who live by the massive all-in-one system die by the massive all-in-one system. Distributed ERP systems are poised to reduce risk by disallowing systemwide downtime. Additional modules to a big ERP system can provide:

- A human resources information system (HRIS)

- Capacity resource planning (CRP)

- Job routings

- Work center costing information

- Distribution Resource Planning (DRP)

Figure I.1 shows a simple model of a business hierarchy. Clearly, the organization chart can be expanded to the small department level. Notice that Six Sigma teams do *not* appear in this diagram; nor would they appear in a more detailed diagram. Six Sigma teams are typically formed for the purpose of solving a specific problem and achieving well-specified results; they exist for four to six months. Note that the quality function has a dotted line to the corporation. This reporting system allows the quality function substantial authority at the subcorporation (divisional) level.

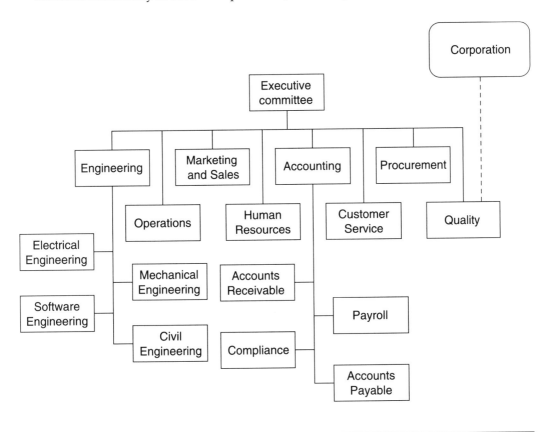

Figure I.1   Simple organization chart for an enterprise.

Understanding Business Systems and Processes

Businesses do not simply fit into nice hierarchies—they are composed of processes within processes within processes. If the business is ISO 9001:2000 certified, it will have documented these processes and defined all the inputs and outputs. Figure I.2 shows one possible high-level process for a business.

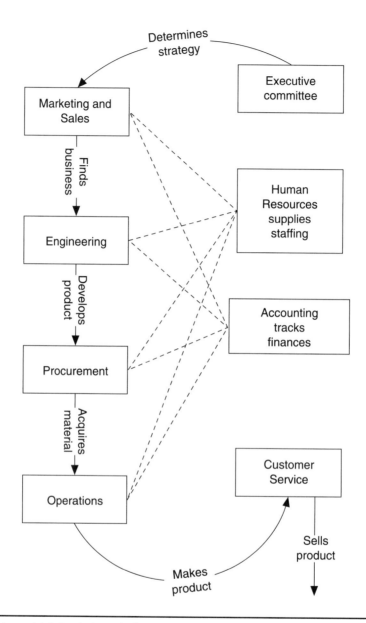

Figure I.2   A very high-level view of a business process.

We can define a set of core processes (accounting, marketing, IT, and so on) and define a high-level process. In turn, each step of this high-level process can be broken down further into subprocesses until some atomic level is reached where we can no longer sensibly decompose the functional hierarchy.

Interrelationships Among Business Systems and Processes

Every process or system has the following components (at a minimum):

- A supply source, which can supply a service, a product, or another process, which provides

- An input or set of inputs (which can be services or products), going into

- A process that transforms the inputs into

- An output or set of outputs, which is

- Consumed by a customer (a process *sink*)

Suppliers can be internal or external and the same idea follows with customers. Each process will have stakeholders, which consist of *any* party affected by the process. Again, see Figure I.2, which shows a very high-level process for a business. Once again, we could break this diagram down into subprocesses. The point here is that all organizations have some kind of process flow. ISO 9001:2000-certified companies always have these processes documented. The supporting documents for ISO 9001:2000 and ISO/TS 16949 (the automotive version of ISO 9001:2000) use some nonstandard process diagrams. Any diagram that can show flow clearly may be used, including such disparate formats as IDEF0 (FIPS-183) and value-stream mapping.

The SIPOC diagram in Figure I.3 shows the relationships from the "source" to the "sink." A Six Sigma Black Belt SIPOC diagram has much more detail than this one.

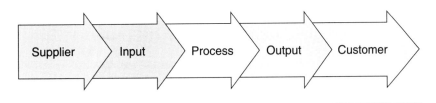

Figure I.3   The sequence of steps in a SIPOC diagram.

3. PROCESS INPUTS, OUTPUTS, AND FEEDBACK

Process Inputs

As mentioned in the previous section, process inputs are provided by a supplier, who can be internal or external to the enterprise. We can define more significant inputs to be key process input variables (KPIVs) or key process inputs (KPIs). Inputs are equivalent to stimuli in behavioral psychology or causes in cause-and-effect analyses. Inputs move away from a supplier and, ultimately, toward a customer. They come from sources.

Process Outputs

Outputs are the product of a process. Outputs are always responses or behaviors. Analogously with the inputs, we can define key process output variables (KPOVs) or key process outputs (KPOs). Outputs always move toward a customer (or consumer) or a sink (opposite of a source) if we think of activity and products as a flow. A simple mathematical relation of outputs to inputs is $y = f(x)$, where x represents the inputs and y represents at least one output. The function itself clearly represents the transformations caused by the process.

Process Feedback

Feedback occurs in a process when a portion of the output signal is captured and routed back to a comparator (decision-making device). The comparator allows the process to correct for error. The error or output noise can be cumulative error (integrated value) or instantaneous error (derivative value) based on some criteria that allow response. If the threshold for response is set too low, the system displays nervousness and measurement will show what is called jitter. If the threshold for response is set too high, the system displays a lack of responsiveness and may in fact become lost.

A response does not become feedback unless the control system routes the data back to a decision-making point and the system uses this data to affect the next action of the system.

Control System Impact on Enterprise System

In an enterprise, the control systems can be internal auditing from accounting or quality, monthly reviews, personnel evaluations, or reporting to higher levels of the corporation. A well-designed control system may lend itself to homeostasis—that is, the tendency to remain in dynamic equilibrium around some mean state. In other words, if the control system overcontrols, the enterprise may display substantial resistance to change, which is the antithesis of the breakthrough improvements desired during the deployment and sustainment of Six Sigma in the enterprise.

Figure I.4 shows a generic representation of a control system. Don't get concerned about unfamiliar terminology in this diagram. The important concept is that feedback is not simply a response, but a determinant for the signal that controls the process. Measurement must occur after perturbations or drift in order to bring the process back on target. The perturbation may be input noise (a random signal).

Some people find the process "turtle" or "octopus" diagram[1] shown in Figure I.5 to be a simpler representation. Each inner circle represents a function. The large oval represents an enterprise or some larger function. A similar type of hierarchical diagram is the data flow diagram often used by software engineers, where each bubble represents an activity and the "U" flows represent data flow.

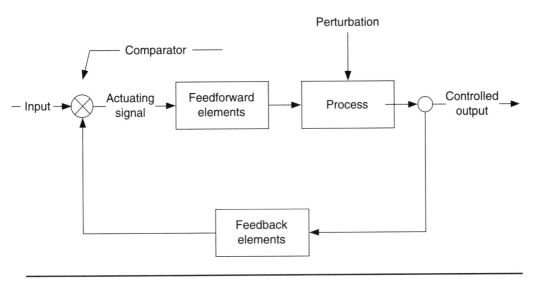

Figure I.4   A simple control system representation.

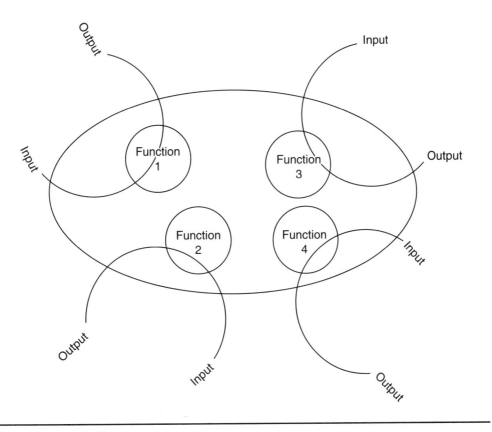

Figure I.5   A turtle diagram.

FURTHER READING

Eckes, George. 2001. *Making Six Sigma Last: Managing the Balance Between Cultural and Technical Change.* New York: John Wiley & Sons.

———. 2001. *The Six Sigma Revolution: How General Electric and Others Turned Process Into Profits.* New York: John Wiley & Sons.

B. Leadership

1. ENTERPRISE LEADERSHIP

Leadership Roles

One of the innovations of Six Sigma over previous quality initiatives is the organizational structure: It is designed to specifically define roles and support the expeditious achievement of results. In some companies, the dollar value of projects at each level is spelled out in the form of strategic and project goals.

Deployment of Six Sigma

The entire Six Sigma team is responsible for the deployment of a Six Sigma culture; however, it is the Champion who is specifically tasked with the responsibility of planning the deployment of the Six Sigma process. That means the Champion must understand the following:

- Skills required
- Data needed
- Financial requirements (budgeting)
- Specific people tied to the skills
- Locations (meeting rooms, plant floor, and so on)
- Tools or equipment (projectors, computers, ancillary tools, and so on)

Six Sigma Resources

The Executive level of the enterprise provides resources in the form of funding and staffing. Human resources may be asked to provide lists of staff members with the correct qualifications or to develop training programs to teach staff members those skills.

13

Six Sigma Organizational Structure

Figure I.6 shows a representative Executive and belt hierarchy. This tree is not the only way to structure a Six Sigma organization, but it is very common. Some companies choose to use full-time Black Belts; others use part-time Black Belts with a high emphasis on the project. Some companies pursue the "belt" metaphor with other colors, such as yellow.

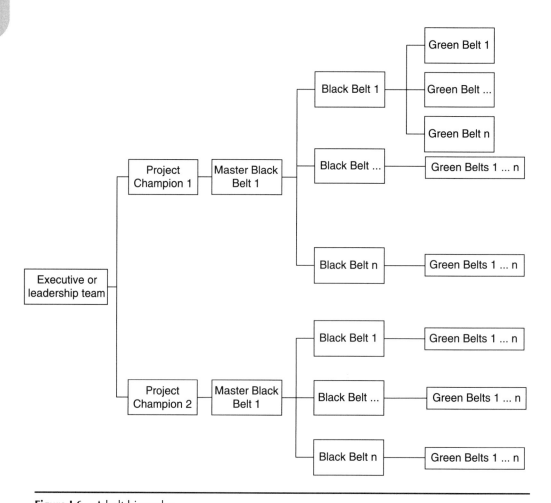

Figure I.6 A belt hierarchy.

The Executive or leadership team functions as a steering committee and controls the overall enterprise budget. The Champion generally facilitates the function of the Black Belt by representing resource needs to the steering committee.

2. SIX SIGMA ROLES AND RESPONSIBILITIES

Executive Roles and Responsibilities

The Executive and/or the steering committee has the responsibility of stating the charter (or mission) of the Six Sigma organization, providing the initial vision and mission statements, and providing overall oversight of Six Sigma activity. Additionally, and perhaps most important, the Executive provides resources for Six Sigma in the form of people and money.

Champion Roles and Responsibilities

The principal function of Champions is developing and implementing the Six Sigma deployment plan or plans. They also perform direct management of the Six Sigma infrastructure.

Master Black Belt Roles and Responsibilities

The Master Black Belt is a technical resource for the Six Sigma team. The Master Black Belt is:

- Statistically proficient
- A trainer of black belts
- A master of large-scale projects (in terms of money)

Black Belt Roles and Responsibilities

Black belts are most frequently full-time technical specialists responsible for delivering on the bottom-line promise of the Six Sigma program and projects.

Green Belt Roles and Responsibilities

Green Belts are typically part-time workers on particular Six Sigma projects—gathering data, performing tests, analyzing results, and so on—under the direction of the appropriate Black Belt.

Other Belt Colors

We have already noted that some companies choose to add other belt colors, particularly if they deploy Six Sigma to the operator levels of the company. This technique can help by making the front-line workers aware of the ideas and significance of the Six Sigma program—they will know when to seek assistance. The operators are at the area that Imai called the *gemba,* the place where the manufacturing actually occurs.[2]

Process Owners Roles and Responsibilities

Process owners are frequently functional managers in charge of specific functions or processes—for example, a line supervisor in a manufacturing facility. The Black Belts and Green Belts cannot accomplish their objectives without the support of process owners.

Table I.1 shows typical roles and responsibilities in a Six Sigma deployment. This list is by no means exhaustive; each organization modifies the standard as the exigencies of business require.

Table I.1   Six Sigma roles and responsibilities.

Title	Roles and Responsibilities
Executive	Focus organization Manage setbacks and retreats Hold organization accountable for Six Sigma success Identify strategic improvement opportunities Commit people and money Drive change (top-level change agent)
Champion	Devise deployment plan Coach Master Black Belts, Executives, and other Champions Help remove obstacles to progress Select Black Belts and projects Report results Manage lessons learned
Master Black Belt	Help Black Belts plan their projects Provide more profound statistical support Train Black Belts and sometimes Green Belts Oversee projects as an advisor Report results to Champions
Black Belt	Full-time technical team leaders Train Green Belts Coordinate with functional managers Use Six Sigma tools Report to Champion
Green Belt	Gather data Analyze data Perform elementary statistical analysis Recognize that an issue exists
Process owner	Drive functional processes (may introduce lean techniques) Manage full-time staff Know where the "skeletons" are buried Support Black and Green Belts Influence their employees

FURTHER READING

Juran, Joseph M. 1989. *Juran on Leadership for Quality: An Executive Handbook.* New York: Free Press.

C. Organizational Goals and Objectives

KEY METRICS

Question: What are key metrics for an organization?

Answer: Any measurements that provide critical information applicable to guiding the enterprise toward success.

Typical business metrics include:

- Return on investment (ROI)

- Return on equity (ROE)

- Return on assets (ROA)

- Net present value (NPV)

- Payback time

- Internal rate of return (IRR)

- Economic value-added (EVA)

Each enterprise defines its own key metrics that indicate how well the business is being run. Some metrics are required by the U.S. Securities and Exchange Commission and others may be required by higher levels of the corporation. In many cases business metrics are part of the Generally Accepted Accounting Practice (GAAP); for example, "cost of goods sold" is a standard division of a balance sheet. A metric becomes a key metric when it has a high enough sensitivity to readily reveal information about the business while being robust—that is, relatively immune to noise. If the metric is insensitive, management will not see enough of a change to make a decision; if the metric is not robust, management may be flailing around making jittery decisions. Additionally, a key metric should be concise and clear.

Key metrics are also valuable because they can be used to model some aspects of the enterprise. One approach that uses a variety of key metrics to build models of the enterprise is System Dynamics, a technique pioneered by Dr. Jay Forrester and popularized by Peter Senge in *The Fifth Discipline*.[3] System Dynamics tools model flows using differential equations, probability distributions, integration, and other mathematical techniques in order to build a network of linear and non-linear relationships. This network has sources and sinks, loops, amplification, and attenuation and has output that can be graphed and analyzed.

The following lists represent potential metrics for use in the enterprise. Companies customize their metrics to reflect and inform on the status of the business strategy.

Example of Key Business Metrics

Human Resources
- Turnover
- Employee complaints
- Competitive "piracy" of employees

Finance (Accounting)
- Payroll variances
- Sick days taken
- Attendance

Purchasing (Procurement)
- Purchase price variance (PPV)
- Inventory turns
- Safety stock levels

Operations
- Variance against build plan
- Stockouts
- Scrap

Engineering (R & D)
- New product launches
- Design iterations
- Requirements scope "creep"

Quality
- Machine capability
- Warranty returns
- Product part approval process completions

Information Technology (IT)

- Up time
- Virus intrusions
- Transactions per week

BALANCED SCORECARDS

Robert Kaplan and David Norton popularized the concept of Balanced Scorecards in a book of the same name.[4] The idea is that at each level of the enterprise, the level below collects data from key process indicators and presents them to the next level up summarized in a scorecard, sometimes called a dashboard.

A balanced scorecard for marketing might include information on:

- Customer complaints
- On-time deliveries
- Customer questionnaire feedback
- Competitive assessment
- Forecasting

Scorecards take the key metrics of the business and, frequently, present them in a metaphorical manner:

- Gages (like a speedometer)
- Vertical meters (like a thermometer)
- Traffic lights
- Chernoff faces (different expressions immediately recognizable for meaning)[5]

. . . and others. The only limit is the imagination.

When a balanced scorecard has been well-designed, the manager should be able to discern the general state of that part of the organization very quickly. Additionally, the scorecard is balanced because paired indicators are used to provide perspective to otherwise abstract metrics. For example:

- Lines of software code versus number of defects per line
- Revenue versus profit
- Complexity versus speed of release

Each of these example values balances one piece of information against another.

An Example of a Balanced Scorecard

Here are the essential metrics as spelled out by Kaplan and Norton in *The Balanced Scorecard.*

Core Financial Measures

- Return on investment/economic value-added (ROI/EVA)
- Profitability
- Revenue growth/mix
- Cost reduction productivity

Core Customer Measures

- Market share
- Customer acquisition
- Customer retention
- Customer profitability
- Customer satisfaction

Core Learning and Growth Measures

- Employee satisfaction
- Employee retention
- Employee productivity

1. LINKING PROJECTS TO ORGANIZATIONAL GOALS

Project Selection Process

Use the following criteria:

- Project is tied to business priorities
- Project has the support of Executive and Champions
- Results are quantifiable
- Problem is significant (4–6 months)
- Organization understands importance of project

When to Use Six Sigma Methodology

The appropriate places for the Six Sigma methodology are those where the problem can be defined explicitly, the current and future states are measurable, the results can be achieved within a third to a half of a year, the project is relevant to overall enterprise goals, and a plan for accomplishment of the project exists or is being completed. The primary measurable for the results is the amount of money saved, although other quantifiable values may be used.

When to Use Other Tools

Sometimes the fruit is hanging so low that a Six Sigma project is uncalled for—just fix the problem. In other cases, we may be dealing with an immature manufacturing organization that needs to spend considerable time on the introduction of lean techniques and bringing their process under control. The degree of control can be measured using process capability numerics (for example, Cpk) or tracked with a control chart (for example, an exponential weighted moving average chart). One definition of "stable" uses the Walter Shewhart concept of statistical control: random variation within upper and lower bounds, the bounds being above and below the mean by three standard deviations.

If a product development has not begun, then Design for Six Sigma is in order, with a much longer time line than a typical Black Belt project.

Links to Organizational Goals

An intrinsic part of the Six Sigma philosophy is that Black Belt projects be linked to organizational goals. When in doubt about the choice of projects, the Master Black Belts and Black Belts should consult with the project Champion and possibly even the executive steering committee. If the organization practices policy deployment (or Hoshin planning), then the goals, objectives, and targets should already be documented. Six Sigma practitioners should recognize that the Six Sigma philosophy is a complement to organizational goals and not an end in itself. Solution choice need not be complicated (see Figure I.7).

2. RISK ANALYSIS

Strategic Risk Analysis

Six Sigma is admirably positioned to help with Business Risk Analysis (BRA) by emphasizing the importance of data. The DMAIC process applies directly to strategic risk analysis. Different kinds of risk are significant:

- Strategic
- Operational
- Supply chain continuity
- Regulatory

SWOT

SWOT is an acronym for strengths, weaknesses, opportunities, and threats. Because it represents the "contraries" of each item, it reminds managers to assess each item. Figure I.8 shows how a SWOT analysis could be laid out. The terms of the analysis are frequently, but not necessarily, qualitative. The addition of an introductory situation description documents and clarifies the need for the SWOT analysis. The Goals and Strategy section documents the steps to be taken subsequent to the SWOT analysis. This kind of tool sees use in the marketing component of an enterprise, although any component can use it when appropriate.

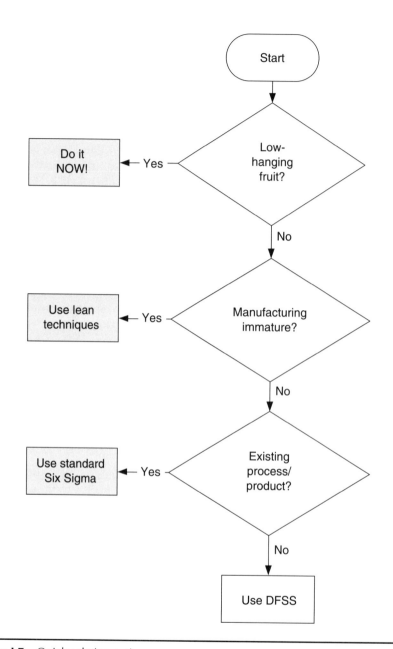

Figure I.7   Quick solution options.

Situation description:
  Where is the situation occurring?
  Who is involved?
  Why is this situation of interest?
  When did this situation begin?
  When is the expected end of the situation?
  What is the situation?

STRENGTHS	WEAKNESSES
Flexible organization Project-oriented Staff well-trained	Staff trained but inexperienced Matrix organization causing problems Too much turnover

OPPORTUNITIES	THREATS
Potential business in China Product already half-designed Price lower than competition	Competition already has project Plant may move to Malaysia Regulatory issue with OSHA Class-action lawsuit

Goals:
  Objectives:
    Target values:

Strategy:
  Tactic 1:
  Tactic 2:
  Tactic 3:

Figure I.8   A format for a SWOT diagram.

Scenario Planning

Scenario planning is a planning technique pioneered by the Royal Dutch/Shell petroleum company and distribution network. When constructing a scenario, the planner looks at current events and then, based on demographic trends and other statistics, puts together a "story" describing a potential sequence of events leading to a specific result.

Typically, scenario planning groups will develop at least four scenarios:

- Pessimistic

- Moderate but pessimistic

- Moderate but optimistic

- Optimistic

The purpose of scenario planning is not so much to predict the future as to open the minds of planners and executive management to options and opportunities in the future.

Local versus Global Optimization

One of the fundamental concepts of the Theory of Constraints is the idea that a local optimization or a collection of local optimizations may not lead to a global optimization. The concept is borne out more quantitatively by Design of Experiments (DOE)—part of the purpose of DOE is separating significant, global optimizations from fruitless local optimizations.

FURTHER READING

Smith, Dick, and Jerry Blakeslee, with Richard Koonce. 2002. *Strategic Six Sigma: Best Practices from the Executive Suite*. New York: John Wiley & Sons.

Snee, Ronald D., and Roger W. Hoerl. 2000. *Leading Six Sigma: A Step-by-Step Guide Based on Experience with GE and Other Six Sigma Companies*. Upper Saddle River, NJ: Prentice Hall Financial Times.

D. History of Organizational Improvement/Foundations of Six Sigma

WALTER SHEWHART

1891: Born in New Canton, Illinois.

1917: Receives doctorate in physics from the University of California at Berkeley.

1918: Joins the Western Electric Company, telephone hardware manufacturer for Bell Telephone.

1924: Suggests that a production process in a state of "statistical control," where only random-cause variation occurs, is necessary to predict output and to run a process cost-effectively; that is, seriously noisy processes are unpredictable—a radical idea in 1924.

1930s: Studies basic scientific topics, such as the speed of light.

1931: Publishes *Economic Control of Quality of Manufactured Product.*

1939: Publishes *Statistical Methods from the Viewpoint of Quality Control.*

1925–1956: Continues his research for Bell Telephone Laboratories and continues publishing.

1956: Retires from Bell Laboratories.

1967: Dies.

Statistical Process Control (SPC) Standards Based on Shewhart's Work (ANSI):

- Z1.1-1941
- Z1.2-1941
- Z1.3-1942

Deming popularized and disseminated Shewhart's concepts of statistical process control and the continuous reduction of variation in processes. Deming also had the honesty to refer to the Plan-Do-Check-Act (PDCA) circle as the "Shewhart circle" and not the "Deming circle," as others called it. Shewhart's work is completely fundamental to the control phases of Six Sigma practice.

Awards

- Holley Medal of the American Society of Mechanical Engineers
- Honorary Fellowship of the Royal Statistical Society
- Honorary Fellowship of the American Society for Quality

Shewhart's Contributions

1. Introduced industrial process control
2. Put industrial process control on a solid statistical basis
3. Developed the classical Shewhart control chart
4. Identified normal random variation
5. Identified variation resulting from assignable causes ("special" causes)
6. Created the Shewhart "ring" or "circle"
7. Mentored W. Edwards Deming, another physicist and perhaps the best known quality guru

The importance of the Shewhart-style control chart cannot be overstated. It is the very heart of statistical process control (SPC) in automotive quality. Although these control charts are relatively insensitive to small changes, they are generally easy to construct and can be kept current by operators on manufacturing lines.

W. EDWARDS DEMING

1900: Born in Sioux City, Iowa.

1928: Awarded doctorate in mathematical physics from Yale.

1928–1950s: Works in the U.S. Government Service, focusing on statistical sampling. Deming used Shewhart's concepts in his work at the National Bureau of the Census. His team brought routine clerical operations statistical process control in preparation for the 1940 population census, providing sixfold productivity improvements in some processes.

1943: Publishes a technical book, *Statistical Adjustment of Data* (still available from Dover Press).

1946: Works as a professor of statistics at New York University's Stern School of Business. Also begins work with the Japanese Union of Scientists and Engineers (JUSE).

1951: Japanese government begins offering annual Deming Prize.

1956: Awarded Shewhart Medal by American Society for Quality Control (now ASQ).

1960: Awarded Second Order of the Sacred Treasure by Japanese emperor.

1970s: Deming's name becomes better known as the Japanese "invade" the United States with high-quality, reliable automobiles, motorcycles, cameras, and other technological devices.

1980: NBC television documentary "If Japan Can, Why Can't We?" makes Deming a quality celebrity.

1986: Works as professor of management at Columbia University and publishes *Out of the Crisis*, which defines Deming's 14 points.

1987: Awarded the National Medal of Technology (U.S.). Creation of British Deming Association.

1993: Dies.

Deming's programs typically led to reductions in scrap and rework, both of which are the essence of non–value added activities. Sadly, he and Shewhart were disregarded in the United States after World War II, when many items were in surplus quantities for years (who cares about quality when you have so much stuff?).

Deming's 14 Points[6]

1. Create constancy of purpose toward improvement of product and service, with the aim to become competitive, to stay in business, and to provide jobs.

2. Adopt the new philosophy. We are in a new economic age. Western management must awaken to the challenge, learn their responsibilities, and take on leadership for change.

3. Cease dependence on inspection to achieve quality. Eliminate the need for inspection on a mass basis by creating quality in the product in the first place.

4. End the practice of awarding business on the basis of price tag. Instead, minimize total cost. Move toward a single supplier for any one item, on a long-term relationship of loyalty and trust.

5. Improve constantly and forever the system of production and service, to improve quality and productivity, and thus constantly decrease costs.

6. Institute training on the job.

7. Institute leadership (see point 12). The aim of leadership should be to help people and machines and gadgets to do a better job. Leadership of management is in need of overhaul, as well as leadership of production workers.

8. Drive out fear so that everyone may work effectively for the company.

9. Break down barriers between departments. People in research, design, sales, and production must work as a team, to foresee problems of production and in use that may be encountered with the product or service.

10. Eliminate slogans, exhortations, and targets for the work force that ask for zero defects and new levels of productivity.

11a. Eliminate work standards (quotas) on the factory floor. Substitute leadership.

11b. Eliminate management by objective. Eliminate management by numbers, numerical goals. Substitute leadership.

12a. Remove barriers that rob the hourly worker of his right to pride of workmanship. The responsibility of supervisors must be changed from sheer numbers to quality.

12b. Remove barriers that rob people in management and in engineering of their right to pride in workmanship. This means *inter alia*, abolishment of the annual or merit rating and of management by objective, management by the numbers.

13. Institute a vigorous program of education and self-improvement.

14. Put everybody in the company to work to accomplish the transformation. The transformation is everybody's job.

Japan

Deming's message to the Japanese reflected his statistical background. He improved Shewhart's manufacturing approach with a qualitative approach linked to non-manufacturing and human variation. He encouraged managers to focus on process variation—a strong precursor to the current Six Sigma movement. The 14 points are largely qualitative and involve concerns particular to management in the enterprise.

The West

Deming attempted to make major changes in the style of Western management—the 14 points are still radical 18 years later. His later work was clearly more management-oriented than statistically based. Much of his most recent management philosophy is contained in his book *Out of the Crisis*. Some readers have felt that the ideas in this book are too idealistic and therefore incapable of implementation. Regardless, these ideas merit consideration and thought, particularly his comments on human relations—which are consistently in favor of the dignity of the worker.

Deming was concerned with delighting, rather than merely satisfying, customers. He produced his 14 Points for management in order to help people understand and implement the necessary transformation. Deming said that adoption of and action on the 14 points is a signal that management intends to stay in business. The 14 Points apply to small or large organizations and to service industries as well as to manufacturing.

The 14 Points are the upside of Deming's philosophy of management. The downside is represented by the Seven Deadly Diseases of management.

Deming's Seven Deadly Diseases[7]

1. Lack of constancy of purpose to plan product and service that will have a market and keep the company in business, and provide jobs.

2. Emphasis on short-term profits: short-term thinking (just the opposite of constancy of purpose to stay in business), fed by fear of unfriendly takeover, and by push from bankers and owners for dividends.

3. Personal review systems, or evaluation of performance, merit rating, annual review, or annual appraisal, by whatever name, for people in management, the effects of which are devastating. Management by objective, on a go, no-go basis, without a method for accomplishment of the objective, is the same thing by another name. Management by fear would still be better.

4. Mobility of management; job hopping.

5. Use of visible figures only for management, with little or no consideration of figures that are unknown or unknowable.

6. Excessive medical costs.

7. Excessive costs of liability.

JOSEPH M. JURAN

1904: Born in the Balkans.

1924: Begins career as engineer.

1951: First version of *Quality Control Handbook* published.

1954: Invited to Japan by Union of Japanese Scientists and Engineers (JUSE); provides seminars to top- and middle-level executives.

1964: *Managerial Breakthrough* published.

1979: Founds Juran Institute.

1980–present: Continues to write books on quality and serve as a consultant to manufacturing companies worldwide.

Major books by Juran are the *Quality Control Handbook, Juran on Quality by Design, Managerial Breakthrough,* and *Juran on Leadership for Quality.* His 12 books have collectively been translated into 13 languages. He has received more than 30 medals, honorary fellowships, and other honors. Like Deming, he received the highest decoration presented to a non-Japanese citizen, the Second Order of the Sacred Treasure.

The *Quality Control Handbook* is now in its fifth edition; if you can only afford one quality book, this is it. The first chapter contains his analogy to the costs of quality: "there is gold in the mine."

Juran has had a varied career in management; his interest has been wider than just quality and he has involved himself in the fundamental principles common to all managerial activity.

Juran's Message

There are many aspects to Juran's message on quality. Intrinsic is the belief that quality must be planned.

His recent book, *Juran on Planning for Quality,* is a gold mine of management concepts completely applicable to the implementation and deployment of Six Sigma. His earlier

Quality Control Handbook is much more technical in nature, generally organized as a one-volume encyclopedia of quality techniques.

Key elements in implementing companywide strategic quality planning are:

- Identifying customers and their needs

- Establishing optimal quality goals (*define*)

- Creating measurements of quality (*measure*)

- Planning processes capable of meeting quality goals under operating conditions (*analyze*, *improve*, and *control*)

- Producing continuing results in improved market share, premium prices (ongoing *control*)

- Reducing error rates in the office and factory (reduction of variation)

Juran's Quality Process[8]

1. Identify the customers.

2. Determine the needs of those customers.

3. Translate those needs into our language.

4. Develop a product that can respond to those needs.

5. Optimize the product features so as to meet our needs as well as customer needs.

6. Develop a process that is able to produce the product.

7. Optimize the process.

8. Prove that the process can produce the product under operating conditions.

9. Transfer the process to Operations.

The Juran Trilogy

Planning—Create a product, service, or process that meets requirements, especially under operating conditions. This thought alone is the foundation for Design for Six Sigma.

Control—Verify that the process runs optimally, reducing process waste. Chronic waste is a cost of poor quality. Control of the process is congruent with lean manufacturing concepts.

Improvement—Improve the process continuously. Quality and process improvement lead to breakthrough.

P–C–I—Planning, Control, Improvement.

Juran concentrates not just on the end customer, but on other external and internal customers as well—a concept that has generally taken hold in forward-thinking manufacturing companies. This idea affects Juran's concept of quality because one must also consider the "fitness of use" of the interim product for the next internal customers.

Joseph Juran's work emphasizes the need for specialist knowledge and tools for successful conduct of the Quality Function. He emphasizes the need for continuous awareness of the customer in all functions.

According to Juran,[9] the mission of his work is:

- Creating an awareness of the quality crisis of the 1980s and going forward

- Establishing a new approach to quality planning and training

- Assisting companies in re-planning existing processes, avoiding quality deficiencies

- Establishing mastery within companies over the quality planning process, thus avoiding the creation of new chronic problems

Juran refers to the widespread move to raise quality awareness in the emerging quality crisis of the early 1980s as failing to change behavior despite company quality awareness campaigns based on slogans and exhortations. Even though quality awareness increased during this period, Juran writes, the general failure to improve was caused by the crusade's lack of planning and substance (an approach congruent with Deming's disdain for "sloganeering"): "The recipe for action should consist of 90 percent substance and 10 percent exhortation, not the reverse."[10]

Juran's Formula for Results

1. Establish specific goals to be reached.

2. Establish plans for reaching the goals.

3. Assign clear responsibility for meeting the goals.

4. Base the rewards on results achieved.

These items are similar to the first portions of DMAIC in Six Sigma. All management by objective (MBO) techniques tie into this simple algorithm as well.

PHILIP CROSBY

1926: Born in Wheeling, West Virginia.

1952–1955: Employed at Crosley.

1955–1957: Employed at Bendix Mishawaka.

1957–1965: Employed at Martin-Marietta.

1965–1979: Employed at ITT, rising to Corporate President of Quality.

1979: *Quality is Free: The Art of Making Quality Certain*, which became a best-seller, published.

1979–1991: Establishes Philip Crosby Associates (PCA). Retires in 1991.

1997–2001: Purchases assets of PCA and starts PCA II.

2001: Dies.

Crosby's Publications

Crosby's Message

Crosby is best known for the concept of *zero defects*. He considered traditional quality control, acceptable quality limits, and waivers of substandard products to represent failure rather than assurance of success. Crosby therefore defined quality as conformance to the requirements that the company itself has established for its products based directly on its customers' needs. He believed that because most companies have organizations and systems that allow (and even encourage) deviation from what is really required, manufacturing companies spend around 20 percent of revenues doing things wrong and doing them over again. According to Crosby, this can comprise 35 percent of operating expenses for service companies. The reduction in non–value added rework and scrap and the improvement in customer relations ultimately lead to improve profitability.

He did not believe workers should take prime responsibility for poor quality; he said management must be set straight—completely compatible with the concepts of Deming and Juran. In the Crosby system, management sets the tone for quality and workers follow their example; while employees are involved in operational difficulties and draw them to management's attention, the initiative comes from the top. All of the great theorists of industrial quality have made it clear that top management must be involved closely with the quality process or it is doomed to failure.

Crosby's Four Absolutes of Quality Management

1. Quality is defined as conformance to requirements, not as "goodness" or "elegance."

2. The system for causing quality is prevention, not appraisal.

3. The performance standard must be zero defects, not "that's close enough."

4. The measurement of quality is the price of nonconformance, not indices.

The 14 Steps to Quality Improvement are the way in which the Quality Improvement Process is implemented in an organization. They are a management tool that evolved out of a conviction that the absolutes should be defined, understood, and communicated in a practical manner to every member of the organization:

1. Make it clear that management is committed to quality.

2. Form quality improvement teams with senior representatives from each department.

3. Measure processes to determine where current and potential quality problems lie.

4. Evaluate the cost of quality and explain its use as a management tool.

5. Raise the quality awareness and personal concern of all employees.

6. Take actions to correct problems identified through previous steps.

7. Establish progress monitoring for the improvement process.

8. Train supervisors to actively carry out their part of the quality improvement program.

9. Hold a Zero Defects Day to let everyone realize that there has been a change and to reaffirm management commitment.

10. Encourage individuals to establish improvement goals for themselves and their groups.

11. Encourage employees to communicate to management the obstacles they face in attaining their improvement goals.

12. Recognize and appreciate those who participate.

13. Establish quality councils to communicate on a regular basis.

14. Do it all over again to emphasize that the quality improvement program never ends.

KAORU ISHIKAWA

1915: Born.

1939: Graduates from the Engineering Department of Tokyo University, having majored in applied chemistry.

1947: Hired as an assistant professor at the university.

1960: Earns his Doctorate of Engineering and promoted to professor.

1989: Dies.

Prizes: the Deming Prize, the Nihon Keizai Press Prize, the Industrial Standardization Prize for his writings on Quality Control, and the Grant Award in 1971 from ASQ for his education program on Quality Control.

Ishikawa is best known as a pioneer of the Quality Circle movement in Japan in the early 1960s. The book *Guide to Quality Control* was translated into English in 1971.

Ishikawa's Message and Techniques

Ishikawa paid particular attention to making technical statistical techniques used in quality attainment accessible to those in industry. At the simplest technical level, his work emphasized good data collection and presentation, the use of Pareto diagrams to prioritize quality improvements, and cause-and-effect (or Ishikawa or fishbone) diagrams.

Ishikawa used the cause-and-effect diagram, like other tools, as a device to assist groups or quality circles in quality improvement. Ishikawa diagrams are useful as systematic tools for finding, sorting out, and documenting the causes of variation in quality in production and organizing mutual relationships between them.

Other techniques Ishikawa emphasized include control charts, scatter diagrams, binomial probability paper, and sampling inspection.

Companywide Quality

Ishikawa, along with Juran, is associated with the companywide quality control movement that started in Japan in 1955 following the visits of Deming and Juran. Using this approach, quality control is characterized by companywide participation from top management to lower-ranking employees. Everybody studies statistical methods. All functional departments are involved. Quality control concepts and methods are used for problem solving in the production process; for incoming material control and new product design control; and for analysis to help top management decide policy, verify policy is being carried out, and solve problems in sales, personnel, labor management, and clerical departments. Quality control audits, internal as well as external, are part of this activity.

As noted, Ishikawa pioneered the concept of quality circles. In some venues, the quality circle is an informal, regular gathering of employees trying to solve work problems using quality tools. In other venues, quality circles are more formal but apply basically the same ideas to solve issues. Although the idea fell into some disfavor during the late 1980s, this author has seen the technique used to save $1 million at a southwestern U.S. wire manufacturer.

Ishikawa's Contributions

1. Product quality is improved and becomes uniform. Defects are reduced.

2. Reliability of goods is improved.

3. Cost is reduced.

4. Quantity of production is increased, and it becomes possible to make rational production schedules.

5. Wasteful work and rework are reduced.

6. Technique is established and improved.

7. Expenses for inspection and testing are reduced.

8. Contracts between vendor and vendee are rationalized.

9. The sales market is enlarged.

10. Better relationships are established between departments.

11. False data and reports are reduced.

12. Discussions are carried out more freely and democratically.

13. Meetings are operated more smoothly.

14. Repairs and installation of equipment and facilities are done more rationally.

15. Human relations are improved.

GENICHI TAGUCHI[11]

1924: Born.

1942–45: Serves in the Astronomical Department of the Navigation Institute of the Imperial Japanese Navy. Also works in the Ministry of Public Health and Welfare and the Institute of Statistical Mathematics, Ministry of Education.

1950–1962: Joins the newly founded Electrical Communications Laboratory of the Nippon Telephone and Telegraph Company with the purpose of increasing the productivity of its R & D activities by training engineers in effective techniques.

1951 and 1953: Wins Deming awards for literature on quality.

1954–1955: Is visiting professor at the Indian Statistical Institute. During this visit, he meets the famous statisticians R. A. Fisher and Walter A. Shewhart.

1957–1958: First version of his two-volume book on Design of Experiments published.

1960: Wins the Deming application prize.

1962: Pays first visit to the United States, as visiting research associate at Princeton University. Visits the AT & T Bell Laboratories. Is awarded his PhD by Kyushu University.

1964–1982: Becomes a professor at Aoyama Gakuin University in Tokyo.

1966: Writes, with several coauthors, *Management by Total Results*, which is translated into Chinese by Yuin Wu.

1970s: Develops the concept of the Quality Loss Function. Publishes two other books in the 1970s and the third (current) edition on Design of Experiments.

1980: Serves as director of the Japanese Academy of Quality.

1982: Becomes an advisor at the Japanese Standards Association.

1984: Again wins the Deming award for literature on quality.

1986: Awarded the Willard F. Rockwell Medal by the International Technology Institute.

1982–present: Works for the American Supplier Institute.

Taguchi's Contributions

Taguchi uses quality loss rather than quality. The loss includes not only the loss to the company through costs of reworking or scrapping, maintenance costs, and downtime due to equipment failure and warranty claims, but also costs to the customer through poor product performance and reliability, leading to further losses to the manufacturer as market share declines.

In his quadratic model of loss, a loss will occur even when the product is within the specifications but is optimal when the product is on target. (If the quality characteristic or response is required to be maximized or minimized, then the loss function becomes a half-parabola.)

Taguchi breaks off-line quality control into three stages:

- Concept design

- Parameter design

- Tolerance design

Concept design is the process of creating a design concept or "up and limping" prototype.

In parameter design, the nominal design features or process factor levels selected are tested and the combination of product parameter levels or process operating levels least sensitive to changes in environmental conditions and other uncontrollable (noise) factors is determined.

Tolerance design is employed to reduce variation further if required, by tightening the tolerance on those factors shown to have a large impact on variation. This is the stage at which, by using the loss function, more money is spent (if necessary) buying better materials or equipment, emphasizing the Japanese philosophy of investing last, not first.

- On-line improvement: made on the production line

- Off-line improvement: made during the design and development life cycle

SHIGEO SHINGO

1909: Born in Saga City, Japan.

1930: Graduates with a degree in mechanical engineering from Yamanashi Technical College.

1930: Employed by the Taipei Railway Factory in Taiwan. There he introduces scientific management.

1945: Becomes a professional management consultant with the Japan Management Association.

1955: Takes charge of industrial engineering and factory improvement training at the Toyota Motor Company for both its employees and its parts suppliers (100 companies).

1956–1958: At Mitsubishi Heavy Industries in Nagasaki, reduces the time for hull assembly of a 65,000-ton supertanker from four months to two months, a new world record in shipbuilding.

1961–1964: Extends the ideas of quality control to develop the poka-yoke, mistake-proofing, or Defects = 0 concept.

1968: Originates the pre-automation system at Sata Ironworks, which later spreads throughout Japan.

1969: Originates the single-minute exchange of die (SMED) system at Toyota (part of Just in Time manufacturing, now called lean manufacturing). As a note, later variations on SMED are known as one-touch exchange of die (OTED).

1990: Dies.

European Influence

- Shingo consulted for die casting Associations in West Germany and Switzerland.

- He consulted for Daimler Benz and Thurner in West Germany and H-Weidman, Bucher-Guyer AG, and Gebr Buhler in Switzerland.

- His first consultancy for an overseas firm was for Citroen in France in 1981.

U.S. Influence

- From 1975 to 1979, he conducted training for the American Company Federal Mogul on SMED and Non-stock Production.

Other companies where Shingo advised include many parts of Daihatsu, Yamaha, Mazda, Sharp, Fuji, Nippon, Hitachi, Sony, and Olympus in Japan, and Peugeot in France. His methods at the U.S. company Omark Industries led to such increased productivity and defect and stock reductions that the company started giving an annual Shingo award to the facility that, out of the 17 worldwide, demonstrated the best overall improvement. Shingo wrote more than 14 major books, most of which are fun to read and amazing in the elegant simplicity of the solutions they propose.

Shingo's concept of mistake-proofing (poka-yoke) was designed to eliminate quality problems rather than using the more statistical approach of monitoring them using control charts. Both methods can be complementary and mistake-proofing should be implemented when feasible. Either way, the action is a containment; that is, no irreversible corrective action has occurred to eliminate the quality issue. Even mistake-proofing occasionally leads to containment, particularly in cases where "limit switches" are used to detect erroneously sized products.

Shingo's Contributions

Shingo predominantly influenced concepts of quality and inventory.

Poka-Yoke or Mistake-Proofing

Shingo moved beyond statistical quality control after observing how the Shizuoko plant of Matsushita's Washing Machine Division had succeeded continuously for one month with zero defects on a drain pipe assembly line involving 23 workers. This was achieved through the installation of 1100 poka-yoke devices. Together, these techniques constitute Zero Quality Control, which can achieve what may be impossible using statistical quality control methods. This concept puts Shingo in alignment with Philip Crosby; however, we need to remember that defect statistics are fundamental to Six Sigma. In other words, we can aim at the ideal but that does not mean that we should drop the measurement and study of defect arrival rates.

Source Inspection (Quality at the Source) to Eliminate Inspectors

Shingo refined his work by introducing source inspections and improved poka-yoke systems that prevented the worker from making errors. Statistical sampling could be eliminated and workers were liberated to concentrate on more valuable activities such as identifying potential error sources.

Shingo argued that posting defect statistics is misguided and that the defectives should be hunted down and eliminated instead.

Single-Minute Exchange of Die (SMED)

This system was developed to cut setup times, enabling smaller batches to be produced. The setup procedures were simplified by using common or similar setup elements whenever possible:

- External setup is what can be done while the machine runs.

- Internal setup is what you must do after stopping the machine.

For example, at Toyota, a die punch setup time in a cold-forging process was reduced over a three-month period from one hour and 40 minutes to three minutes.

TAIICHI OHNO[12]

1912: Born in Port Arthur, Manchuria.

1932: Joins Toyoda Spinning and Weaving.

1943: Joins Toyota Motor Company.

1949: Promoted to machine shop manager at Toyota.

1954: Promoted to director at Toyota.

1964: Promoted to managing director at Toyota.

1970: Promoted to senior managing director at Toyota.

1975: Promoted to executive vice-president at Toyota.

1978: Retires from Toyota, remaining chairman of Toyoda Spinning and Weaving.

1990: Dies.

Supposedly, Ohno discovered the manufacturing pull system by watching purchasing and restocking activity at an American supermarket. He is also responsible for providing the motivation for such lean concepts as:

- Quick change of dies

- Just-in-time manufacturing

- Kanban systems

- Zero or near-zero inventory

- Autonomation (automated line stoppage on error)

What Womack and Jones called "lean manufacturing" is simply the deployment of Ohno's ideas for running a manufacturing organization—particularly the reduction of waste.

Ohno was extremely aggressive in pursuing the reduction of waste as well as the reduction of cycle time. In fact, he felt so strongly about managers keeping in touch with the *gemba*—the shop floor action—that he would draw a circle on the shop floor and expect a clueless manager to spend a day in the circle observing the *gemba*. This action is known as the Ohno Circle.

Ohno's Contributions

1. The "five whys" problem-solving method

2. Identification of the seven wastes (with Shingo)

   – Overproduction
   – Waiting
   – Transportation or movement
   – Time spent in actual processing
   – Stock on hand (inventory)
   – Defective products
   – Rework

3. Andon or visual light warning system

4. Kanban

   – Pickup/transport information
   – Production information
   – Prevention of overproduction and transport
   – Work attached to goods
   – Identifies process when defectives occur
   – Maintains inventory control

5. Balanced production

FURTHER READING

Deming, W. Edwards. 1986. *Out of the Crisis.* Cambridge, MA: MIT Press.
———. 1994. *The New Economics.* 2nd ed. Cambridge, MA: MIT Press.
Juran, Joseph M. 1989. *Juran on Leadership for Quality: An Executive Handbook.* New York: Free Press.
———. 1992. *Juran on Quality by Design.* New York: Free Press.
———. 1995. *Managerial Breakthrough: The Classic Book on Improving Management Performance.* 2nd ed. New York: McGraw-Hill.

Section II

Business Process Management
(9 Questions)

Contents

A. Process vs. Functional View

1. PROCESS ELEMENTS

Process Components

Any given process may be decomposed into subprocesses. Each process and subprocess has inputs and outputs, a transform that occurs during the process, constraints that define and regulate the process, and some means by which the process is accomplished.

We should note that the current version of ISO 9000 has moved away from the predominantly product-based orientation of early versions into a process orientation. In fact, the ISO 9000 definition of a process is similar to the previous paragraph. We should also note that a *procedure* is a specific way to perform a process or subprocess; a procedure is *not* a process.

Process Boundaries

When we completely decompose a process into its constituent subprocesses, we can discover the process boundaries by looking for the movement of outputs into inputs of the next process. In other words, an atomic subprocess is completely defined by its inputs, outputs, constraints, methods, and transforms.

A common way of representing processes in software development is through the use of data flow diagrams. Many other process mapping techniques exist, including military standards like IDEF0 and IDEF3.[13]

Figure II.1 is an example of a process flow; it shows a very simple process of making surface mount and through-hole electronic printed circuit boards.

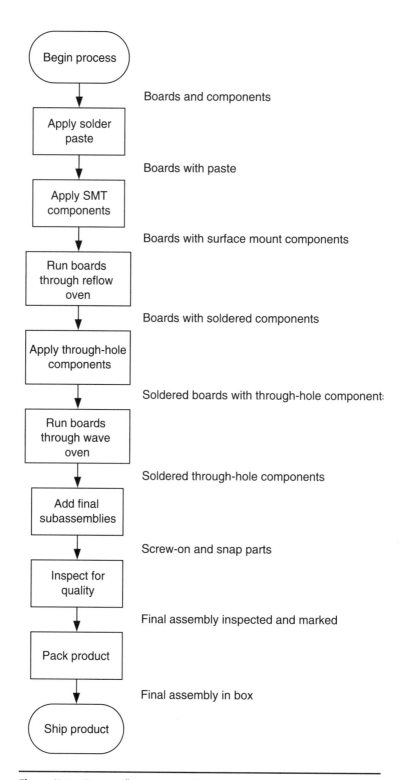

Figure II.1   Process flow using ANSI symbols.

2. OWNERS AND STAKEHOLDERS

Process Owners

Process owners are the persons responsible for process design and performance. The process owner is responsible for sustaining the process returns and identifying improvement opportunities for the process.

Internal Customers

Any downstream recipient of a process output within the enterprise is an internal customer. Similarly, an internal supplier provides the input to an internal process.

External Customers

Any downstream recipient of a process output outside the enterprise is an external customer. These are the people we customarily think of as "customers." External customers are not always the end or final customer, especially for subassembly manufacturers.

Stakeholders

A stakeholder is anybody with a direct interest in a process. Stakeholders generally include, but are not limited to:

- Employees
- Managers
- Customers
- Shareholders
- Regulators
- Suppliers
- Outsources

Stakeholders should not be confused with shareholders, who own stock in the enterprise. Some people view stakeholders as people not directly involved in the process but with an interest in the process.

See Figure II.2 for a high-level view of the relationships.

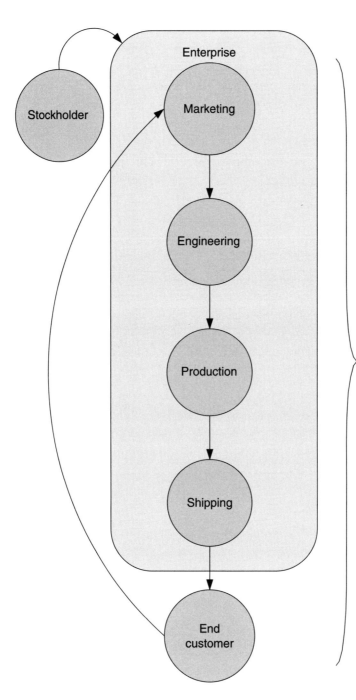

Each bubble is the supplier to the next "customer" bubble. Ultimately, the process loops as the end customer seeks more business with the supplier.

Figure II.2 Some stakeholder relationships.

3. PROJECT MANAGEMENT AND BENEFITS

Managing Projects

The Project Management Institute (PMI) defines five fundamental processes in a project:[14]

- Origination or initiation
- Planning
- Executing
- Controlling
- Closing

See Table II.1 for a mapping of how the PMI model fits with the Six Sigma approach.

Table II.1 Relation of PMI processes with problem-solving techniques.

PMI	Six Sigma	Scientific Method	Shewhart Circle
Initiation	Recognize		
Planning	Define	Formulate problem	Plan
Execution	Measure Analyze Improve	Devise hypotheses	Do Check
Control	Control Standardize Integrate	Collect data from observations and experiments	Act
Closing	[Implicit in Six Sigma]	Test and confirm/ reject hypothesis	

Maximizing Benefits of Projects

The key concept in project maximization is that of planning (define). The old saw that "failing to plan is planning to fail" is exactly the case in Six Sigma projects. A nascent Black Belt should remember the nine process management areas of the PMI model:[15]

- Integration: coordinating all elements
- Scope: control and meet requirements while avoiding "gold plating"
- Time: phasing activities into realistic schedules
- Cost: making certain that project stays within budget *and* meets project financial expectations
- Quality: ensuring the project meets business *needs*
- Human resources: effective use of Champions, Master Black Belts, Black Belts, and Green Belts

- Communications: all activities dealing with input and output of project information

- Risk: identifying, analyzing, and managing threats to project success

- Procurement: purchasing materials and services as well as the logistics of delivering these items in the appropriate quantities at the proper time

4. PROJECT MEASURES

Key Performance Metrics

Any project must have metrics in order to assure intelligible reporting of performance. Typical metrics might include:

- Budget performance

- Schedule variance

- Resource issues

- Risk status

The purpose of these metrics is to provide enough information that a higher level manager, facilitator, or Champion can discern whether or not the project is on track.

Appropriate Project Documentation

The following are examples of appropriate project documentation:

- Project charter (or statement of work) summarizing the purpose, constraints, and goals of the project

- A project plan in the form of a networked schedule

- Reports of the results of each phase of DMAIC

- Economic analysis

Other possibilities include:

- Observations

- Lessons learned

- Red-flagging imminent failure

Figure II.3 is a graphical representation of a project work breakdown structure (WBS). The WBS is a functional decomposition of tasks down to some atomic level, at which a task may not be decomposed any further. Work breakdown structures are commonly decomposed into one of the following structures:

- Deliverables-oriented

- Resources-oriented

- Process-oriented

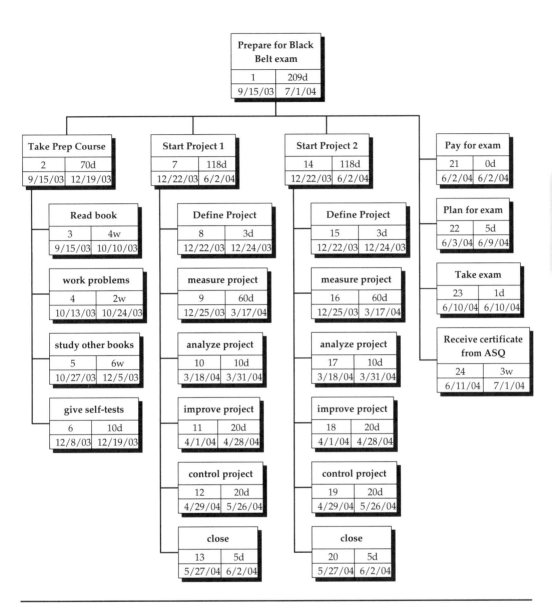

Figure II.3   Black Belt project WBS. Chart produced by WBS Chart Pro from Critical Tools, http://www.criticaltools.com.

In U.S. Department of Defense usage, the WBS top-level items typically become cost centers and are tracked by a variety of techniques, including regular reports to the contract office. These methods may be top-heavy for the Black Belt project; nonetheless, the WBS structure can be extremely useful in providing a checklist that allows the entire project team to know what they need to do and how far they have come during the project.

FURTHER READING

Gupta, Praveen. 2004. *Six Sigma Business Scorecard: Ensuring Performance for Profit.* New York: McGraw-Hill.

B. Voice of the Customer

1. IDENTIFY CUSTOMER

Segmenting Customers to Projects

Customers can be segmented into studiable groups in several ways:

- By market type (for example, automotive)
- By product type (for example, electrical power converters)
- By geographic region (for example, cold climate or warm climate)
- By volume (for example, low volume/high mix)
- By quality demands

. . . and an infinite number of other segments. The goal is to provide the maximum benefit from a given project. Furthermore, the enterprise may be able to apply concepts of mass customization and put the exact product the customer wants into their hands.

Project Impact on Customers within Segments

The prospective Black Belt should analyze the impact on the customer within the segment of interest and assess the financial benefits from the project. In some cases, customers may have their own reasons for *not* changing a product, even when it produces a higher quality product.

Project Impact on Internal/External Customers

The Black Belt project can have an impact on both internal and external customers. The internal customer may have to change a process or a procedure to achieve the optimization discovered during the course of the project. The external customer may have to accept modifications and the resultant updates to part numbers, receipt of quality documentation (for example, Product Part Approval Process documents in automotive quality systems), and other effects of product or process change.

Financial Impact of Customer Loyalty

The Black Belt needs to ask such questions as:

- Is this a customer we want to keep?
- Will this benefit the external customer? Or only reduce cost internally?
- Will the modifications to the product or process improve customer relations?
- How will I communicate change to the customer?

The Black Belt cannot demand a change from the customer, so negotiation skills may be necessary to proceed with modifications. The next section describes a customer evangelist, a very good ally to have, indeed.

What Is a Customer Evangelist?

In years past, Apple Computer Corporation maintained an official job position known as "product evangelist." This person was normally someone with a tremendous amount of enthusiasm for the product—somebody who would proselytize about the product without much prodding. Perhaps the best-known example of a former product evangelist is Guy Kawasaki, who eventually left Apple Computer to start his own company.

A customer evangelist is a customer who is so convinced of the benefits of the product and so entranced by their relationship with the supplier that the customer performs some of the functions of an official spokesperson without being asked. An evangelist:

- Works with their supplier to solve issues.
- Doesn't believe the supplier was negligent when problems occur.
- Defends the supplier to the customer's own corporate staff.
- Sells the product by word of mouth.

Guy Kawasaki gives the following advice on utilizing evangelists:[16]

- Keep in mind that an evangelist is not necessarily the individual with the greatest technical experience.
- Always go to the customers and get involved.
- Let the evangelists figure out how to sell the product—avoid overdirecting them.
- Provide significant amounts of information and promotional material.
- Make them work.
- Listen to their expressed desires.
- Give them "goodies."

2. COLLECT CUSTOMER DATA

Any ethical technique for collecting customer data is fair game when trying to determine the voice of the customer (VOC). Business strategies and goals should be tied directly to knowledge gained from assessing the VOC.

Surveys

Surveys are usually given in the form of a questionnaire. Frequently answers can be given in the form of a Likert scale, which helps improve the accuracy of answers. A Likert scale (named after Rensis Likert) is an ordinal (ordered) scale, frequently using values from 1 to 5, that allows conversion of qualitative responses into quantitative values. Alternatives to the Likert scale are:

1. The Guttman scale: scaling from less extreme to more extreme responses.

2. The Thurstone scale: values are assigned based on whether they are favorable or unfavorable; this scale can be very subjective.

Of course, because we are presenting these surveys to specific customers, the results cannot be considered the product of a random sampling. We want to know what the customer thinks, so why not ask them? As with any questionnaire technique, the choice of questions is critical to the accuracy of the results. Table II.2 shows a snippet of a survey with a Likert scale.

Table II.2 Short portion of a customer satisfaction survey.

Customer satisfaction	Circle your evaluation:				
Item	**Bad**			**Good**	
Arrival condition?	1	2	3	4	5
Installation ease?	1	2	3	4	5
User manual?	1	2	3	4	5
Dealer attitude?	1	2	3	4	5

The creation of surveys is a nontrivial exercise. Many issues must be considered, including:

- Are we after a random sample?

- If we want a random sample, how do we achieve it?

- How do we manage surveys that remain unanswered?

- What scale do we use?

- How do we eliminate potential bias?

- Are we in a multilevel or hierarchical linear situation, where we expect to see sample differences based on natural groupings (for example, different schools in different neighborhoods)?

- How do we analyze the results? What are the best nonparametric tools for looking at the raw data?

- How do we avoid the New Coke phenomenon? New Coke was a product introduced by the Coca-Cola corporation to replace the familiar Coca-Cola in the famous red can. Coca-Cola did substantial market research but still failed to realistically assess the market—a populist uprising effectively forced the reintroduction of the original product under the name of Coca-Cola Classic.

Focus Groups

A focus group is typically a small group of people (fewer than 15) gathered to discuss topics and answer questions; that is, they behave like a panel. They may speak with one another and they are frequently co-located—that is, seated in the same room and allowed to discuss a product or service of interest to an enterprise. The results of focus group work are *qualitative*. The Internet has led to the advent of online focus groups that discuss topics by way of chat room technology. Other focus group techniques can involve switching moderators, electing a group member as moderator, dueling moderators, and mini-focus groups (five to six people).

Interviews

Face-to-face interviews have the advantage of presenting more cues than any other method: facial expressions, body language, skin color (blushing, for example), and verbal expressions. On the other hand, interviews can be extremely labor-intensive and the quality of the results is dependent on the quality of the interviewer and the cooperation of the interviewee.

Observations

Observations can be the product of a second-party supplier audit by a customer. A second-party audit occurs when a customer formally audits a supplier. These observations are normally made in a written audit report.

Observations can also be collected from complaint cards/sheets or casual conversation (for example, in the truck business, riding with a regular driver for some non-business reason).

When tabulated, all methods of customer data gathering should identify the type of source and the probable accuracy of the intelligence and present a distribution when feasible.

3. ANALYZE CUSTOMER DATA

Graphical Tools

Typical graphical tools are:

- Run charts
- Pareto charts
- Control charts
- Scatter plots
- Histograms
- Multi-vari charts
- Factorial and interaction plots (for Designed Experiments)

Statistical Tools

Among other methods of analysis:

- Descriptive statistics

  - Mean, mode, and median
  - Variance and standard deviation
  - Maximum and minimum values

- Analysis of means
- Hypothesis testing

Qualitative Tools

Some qualitative tools are:

- Radar charts, sometimes called spider charts (see Figure II.4 for an example)
- Quality function deployment (QFD), which can also be a quantitative program driver if used in its full flower
- Process decision program charts (PDPCs)
- Failure mode and effects analyses (FMEAs)
- Fault tree analyses (FTAs)

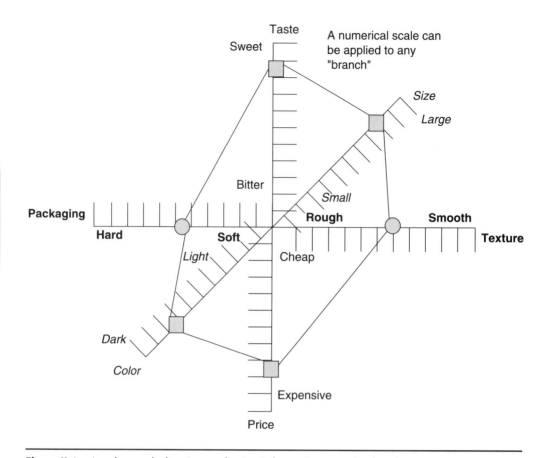

Figure II.4   A radar graph showing qualitative information on ordinal scales.

The kind of graphic shown in Figure II.4 has been used by the executive committee of a company to explain the core business of a division to the middle managers. When used judiciously, a tool like this can display a great deal of information in a small space. The use of color can make the graphic less complex.

4. DETERMINE CRITICAL CUSTOMER REQUIREMENTS

Strategic Product Focus Areas

The top-level focus areas can be seen in Figure II.5. Will the Six Sigma project:

- Improve the quality?
- Speed up launch of the final product?
- Lower the price?
- Any combination of the above?

Figure II.5   Focus area triangle.

Furthermore, an enterprise may focus on a specific technology, like surface-mounted electronic components that will simultaneously lower price and improve quality.

QFD

QFD is a quality function deployment, a direct translation of the original Japanese term for the technique. The first-pass QFD is normally an expression of the VOC and is designed to reveal customer needs and desires. It is a combination of quantitative specification and qualitative decision-making.

Key Project Metrics/Voice of Customer

The VOC may show up in a QFD, in market studies, or in a decision to move to a competitive supplier. The marketing and engineering arms of an enterprise may analyze the apparent critical needs of the customer using a critical-to-quality (CTQ) tree (Figure II.6), decomposing the top-level needs into a finer granularity. The marketing portion of the enterprise may choose to measure the success rates of proposals, quotes, and unsolicited proposals. The quantity of "no bids" may be a meaningful metric.

In the example shown in Figure II.6, a customer may desire a fast automobile. The CTQ tree is a way of analyzing customer desires and breaking these desires into meaningful features.

Process Insights

Customers frequently care a great deal about the quality and level of control of their supplier's processes. A customer can request a second-party audit and either send in their own auditors or bring in another organization to help with the audit.

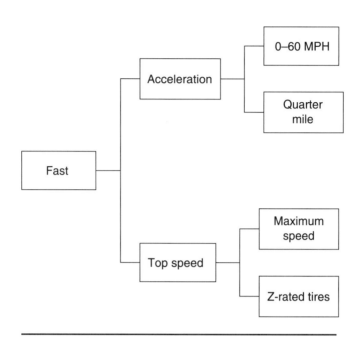

Figure II.6   A simple critical-to-quality tree.

It is to the benefit of the supplier to map out their own processes in detail. In fact, this process mapping has become a derived requirement for organizations pursuing ISO 9001:2000 certification.

FURTHER READING

Zaltman, Gerald. 2003. *How Customers Think: Essential Insights into the Mind of the Market.* Boston: Harvard Business School Publishing.

C. Business Results

1. PROCESS PERFORMANCE METRICS[17]

Calculating DPU

DPU is defects per unit. Defects are nonconforming items; that is, they do not conform to an accepted standard, either industry-wide (for example, IPC for soldering) or customer. Unit" can also be defined as unit area. The key idea is that we are normalizing the data.

The "u" control chart used in statistical process control uses the same concept of defects per unit. Remain aware that defects per unit is an *attribute* value; that is, we do not measure on a continuum.

Calculating RTY

The RTY is the rolling throughput yield. Why RTY instead of prime pass yield (PPY) or first pass yield (FPY)? PPY and FPY tend to conceal hidden factories where rework is done because only the effect at the end of the line is measured. The RTY is an attempt to quantify the effect of these hidden factories on actual yield by capturing the rework and scrap that occur during manufacture.

Calculating DPMO

DPMO is defects per million opportunities. Each product has possible defect locations, which are called opportunities. The value is normalized for a million opportunities so that we can compare apples to apples. The concept of opportunities should be approached with some caution. It is possible to make the Six Sigma calculation very small by increasing the number of opportunities. Since each enterprise may interpret opportunities differently, it is probably best the use DPMO as an *intra*-enterprise measure.

Calculating Sigma Values

The Black Belt can look up sigma values in a table, make a direct calculation, or use a magic formula. Equation (II.1) contains a formula that does exactly this—it calculates the sigma value from the parts per million (PPM).

$$Y_{RT} = RTY = \sum_{i=1}^{n} Y_i, \tag{II.1}$$

where Y_i represents each subprocess yield

$$D = \text{defects}$$

$$U = \text{units}$$

$$O = \text{opportunities for a defect}$$

$$Y = \text{yield}$$

$$TOP = \text{total opportunities} = U \times O$$

$$DPU = -1nY, \text{ where } Y \text{ is the first pass yield}$$

$$DPO = \text{defects per opportunity} = \frac{D}{U \times O} = \frac{D}{TOP}$$

$$DPMO = DPO \times 10^6$$

$$Y_{norm} = \text{normalized yield} = \sqrt[n]{RTY}, \text{ where } n \text{ is the number of steps.}$$

$$\underline{DPMO} = (1 - Y_{norm}) \times 1,000,000$$

$$total\ defects\ per\ unit = -1n(Y_{RT})$$

$$6 \text{ Sigma level with } 1.5\sigma \text{ shift} = 0.8406 + \sqrt{29.37 - 2.221 \times 1n(ppm)}$$

$$Z_{short\ term} = Z_{long\ term} + 1.5\sigma \text{ shift}$$

The Black Belt needs to be wary of simple attribute sampling—that is, straight defect counting with little consideration for the probability of finding defective material. In surface mount soldering, sampling is typically not an issue because all the printed circuit boards are screened with an in-circuit testing devicethat reports any and all failures. From this report, the ppm calculation is straightforward. DPU and DPMO become more complicated if the sample size is insufficient to accurately reflect the defect rate in the material. For example, if in reality we have 30 defects per 1000 units, then we have a probability of observing a defect of exactly 0.03. As we will see later, this situation can be reasonably calculated using a Poisson process, where the mean and variance are equal to the sample size times the probability. If we take a sample of 10 units, our mean value is equal to 0.3. Our calculation of the probability of finding exactly zero failures is 0.74 and the probability of finding exactly one failure is approximately 0.222. That means roughly 74 percent of the time, we will see no failures at all! Clearly, the size of the sample is critical if sampling is going to be used.

Metric Propagate Upward/Allocate Downward

Yield values along the production line propagate through the RTY calculation, causing dramatically small values. RTY is a product, not a sum. If we multiply out a mere three subprocesses, each of which has a 90 percent yield, the rolling throughput yield is roughly 75 percent!

Capability, Complexity, Control

Capability can be translated into Six Sigma metrics—the two are not incompatible. Capability indices are a tool for relating the specification values for a part or a process to the Six Sigma values of the normal distribution. The DPMO number ostensibly allows for apples-to-apples comparisons. Unfortunately, each enterprise defines DPMO in their own way—which means apples-to-apples only works *within* the enterprise itself.

When capability is expressed as parts per million (ppm), we are using a nonparametric index; that is, ppm is not dependent on the underlying distribution of the defect values. The measure is robust, although it provides us with less information than we get from values like Cpk, where centering of the distribution is a consideration.

Manage Use of Performance Measures to Drive Decisions

Because all of these metrics can be translated into other values that may be more familiar to customer and supplier alike (Cpk, ppm, and so on), it is possible to discern a poorly functioning processes and institute corrective action.

Equation II.1 shows the formulae for calculating these values.

2. BENCHMARKING

Benefits of Benchmarking

Benchmarking is about setting a standard of performance for your organization by comparing it to known best practices or other levels of performance. A benchmark becomes a point of reference for excellence and improvement.

Benchmarking probably began as a side effect of surveying. Benchmarks typically represented a known altitude or location—hence the idea of the point of reference.

Downside of Benchmarking

It is possible that your competition or even a different industry is using suboptimal methods. Thus, the choice of organization against whom you benchmark is critical. Additionally, it can be very difficult to do performance benchmarking because your competition is normally eager to keep their trade secrets away from you.

Types of Benchmarking

Benchmarking can be performed against any point of reference:

- Process: Compare your processes against those companies that perform analogous or similar functions; these companies need not be competitors.

- Competitive: Compare your processes directly against those of a competitor. This form of benchmarking is sometimes called *performance* benchmarking, although the work "performance" may appear in any variant of benchmarking.

- Project: Compare processes that are common among many different types of organizations, not necessarily the same as your own company.

- Strategic: Multi-industry technique; for example, your manufacturing company might compare its customer service to that of Disney, Nordstrom, and ASQ (they always answer on the first ring!).

- Performance: Check yourself against your competition.

- Intra-organization: Measure yourself against similar standards in other departments.

- Self: Measure yourself against yourself.

- Collaborative: A group of companies in an industry benchmarks their practices against non-industry practice.

Following is a high-level plan for implementing benchmarked information.

A Benchmarking Plan

1. Look in the mirror and assess your current standards, procedures, and practices.

2. Baseline your current activities so you have a basis for comparison.

3. Choose activities that clearly need improvement (*define*).

4. Choose other organization for comparison.

5. Use whatever ethical methods are available for comparing your activities to those of the other organization—for example:
   –Trade journals
   –Visits
   –Courses offered by the other company (Disney does this)
   –Scholarly analyses (*measure*)

6. Analyze the best practices of the organization or organizations (*analyze*).

7. Clearly articulate the gaps between your performance and theirs and select candidate behaviors for improvement (*improve*).

8. Implement the new behaviors (*improve*).

9. Check results and iterate.

3. FINANCIAL BENEFITS

Project Financial Measures

The Black Belt can use:

- Payback period (simple to calculate)
- Net present value (more involved)
- Internal rate of return (still more involved)
- Return on investment (very difficult)

See Equation (II.2) and Figure II.7 for more detail on the financial formulas.

Payback period = time to pay off invested monies

$$NPV = \sum_{t=0}^{n} \frac{CF_t}{(1+r)^t}$$

n = number of periods

t = time period

r = per-period capital cost

CF = cash flow in time t

$IRR = NPV = 0$, solve for r at $NPV = 0$

(II.2)

Cost of Quality Concepts

Quality costs decompose into the following:

- Appraisal—measuring, assessing, auditing products/services for conformance to standards
- Prevention—training, manuals, work instructions, plans, FMEAs, fault trees, poka-yoke, reviews
- Failure
  - Internal: scrap, nonconforming product
  - External: failure after shipping, frequently at the customer site

Quality Loss Function[18]

The Taguchi quality loss function is a quadratic equation—a parabola—showing increasing cost as a quality characteristic deviates from the target value. Contrast it with the old-fashioned tolerance concept, where *any* value within tolerance is okay. In short,

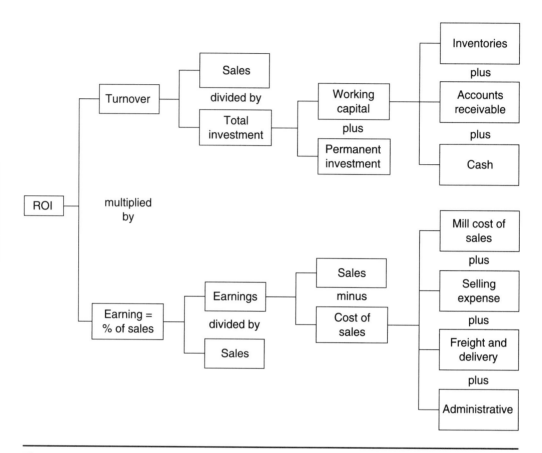

Figure II.7   A way to calculate return on investment.

we are looking at inside tolerance being okay versus not on target being exponentially and increasingly worse. The quality loss function, shown in Equation (II.3), exacts a high penalty for deviations from target.

$$m = \text{target value}$$

$$y = \text{quality characteristic}$$

$$\text{Loss function} = L(y) = k(y - m)^2 \tag{II.3}$$

$$k = (\text{cost of defective product}) / (\text{deviation from target})^2$$

The Quality Loss Function is more significant than its simplicity suggests. The function indicates that we lose quality with *any* deviation from the target value. In a sense, this idea makes a rude counterpoint to Shewhart control charts, where the mean value of a rational subgroup roams between two control limits.

Additionally, the function is a counterpoint to the mentality associated with specification limits—the so-called goalpost mentality. With specification limits, the product is considered acceptable if it lies just within the specification limit and the product is unacceptable if it lies just outside the specification limit. In some cases, the difference between "good" and "bad" can be measured in fractions of a millimeter. Specification limits are not necessarily based on control limits derived from the concept of random variation in process and measurement; in fact, control limits are not dependent at all on the value of the specification limits—hence the concept of quality indices such as Cpk, which incorporate the dispersion of the measurement with that of centering (which is not necessarily the target value).

In some cases, specification limits may be the result of a company policy. In other cases, specification limits may be derived from expected values for random variation. In addition to all this, the concept of worst-case tolerance stackup may enter the discussion if the part is a mechanical piece. In a stackup analysis, the relation of multiple parts can be considered simultaneously to determine if the parts will fit together under worst-case conditions. A variety of methods exist to accomplish the objective of verifying fit, with root square stackup being perhaps the most sophisticated approach to the problem.

However, the Quality Loss Function effectively says we pay a penalty for any deviation from the target (or nominal) value. It is easy to see this in a plot of the loss function as the deviation increases from the target value. Figure II.8 shows the appearance of the Quality Loss Function when potential deviations are taken into account.

Specs for a product
25 +/–0.25 mm
K = 64

Nominal	Deviation	L
25	0.3	5.76
25	0.25	4
25	0.2	2.56
25	0.15	1.44
25	0.1	0.64
25	0.05	0.16
25	0	0
25	−0.05	0.16
25	−0.10	0.64
25	−0.15	1.43
25	−0.2	2.55
25	−0.25	4
25	−0.3	5.76
25	−0.35	7.84
25	−0.4	10.24
25	−0.45	12.96
25	−0.5	16
25	−0.55	19.36
25	−0.6	23.04
25	−0.65	27.04
25	−0.7	31.36
25	−0.75	36

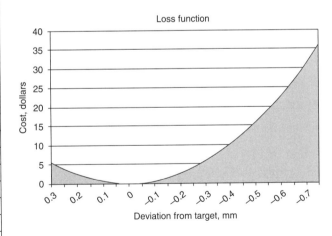

Figure II.8   Quality Loss Function plot.

Section II.3.C

Section II.3.C

FURTHER READING

Camp, Robert. 1989. *Benchmarking: The Search for Industry Best Practices That Lead to Superior Performance.* Milwaukee, WI: ASQC Quality Press.

Section III

Project Management (15 Questions)

Contents

A. Project Charter and Plan

1. CHARTER/PLAN ELEMENTS

Project Charter

The project charter is a document that defines the project for all interested parties: the project manager, project participants, management, customers, and sales force. The document should address the business need driving the project as well as provide a product description. A charter authorizes the project, provides names for the authorization, and provides a top-level description (often one page) of the work to be done. The individual authorizing the project is frequently called the *sponsor*.

A statement of work (SOW), a detailed extension of the charter, defines the work to be done; that is, it helps in controlling the scope of the activities to be performed under the project (or contract). The SOW in this format is crucial when a contractor is doing work on a cost plus firm fixed fee contract (where the risk is on the contracting agency).

Charters are commonly concise; SOWs can be very detailed.

Project Plan

The project plan incorporates all aspects of the PMI model: integration, scope, time, cost, quality, human resources, communications, risk, and procurement. The schedule that many people think of as a project plan is actually only part of the plan.

Electronic tools are available to help manage the project plan—for example:

- Microsoft Project

- Kidasa Software Milestones

- Sciforma PS8

- Primavera Project Planner (P3)

A few of these tools will also support critical chain planning with either a plug-in or intrinsic capability. Critical chain planning accounts for finite capacity that exists in reality and will attempt to find a good solution for balancing resources (but not necessarily the *best* solution because the capacity algorithm may take too long to converge on the optimal solution).

A program manager uses the plan much as an accountant uses a budget or a quality improvement engineer uses benchmarking—as a means for assessing deviations from expected values of time, money, quality, and other factors. Here again, a good electronic tool can help the program manager with a great deal of the calculations regarding costing, earned value, over/under budget, time allocation, critical path calculations, and so on.

The critical path is the longest cumulative, slackless lead time through the network diagram. The network diagram is a directed graph.

The following sample shows how detailed a statement of work can be. This outline can be used as a template to help prevent forgetting or dropping an item.

Statement of Work Sample Outline

Introduction
- Organization
- Identification and address
- Purpose

Project background and objectives

Technical services required
- Task description
- Scope of work

Statement of work
- Description

Deliverables
- Itemized list and due dates

Acceptance criteria

Delivery instructions

Customer-furnished resources
- Facilities, supplies, and services
- Information sources

Documentation

Contractor-furnished resources
- Facilities, supplies, and services

Administrative considerations
- Customer contacts
- Acquisition
- Technical
- Place of performance/work location

    −Hours of work
    −Period of performance

Other direct costs
    −Incidental supplies, equipment, and materials
    −Travel requirements
    −Travel and per diem
    −Other unique costs

Security and privacy

Personal services

Customer review

Reports

Special instructions
    −General and miscellaneous
    −Unique reporting requirements
    −Place of performance/work location

Standards and references

Evaluation criteria

2. PLANNING TOOLS

Gantt Charts

Gantt charts use task lists with adjoining bars to represent time allotted and to schedule days of work. The technique has been around since World War I. It is attractive because of its simplicity. However, it does not show dependencies, nor does it help calculate the critical path. Dependencies occur when the start of one task depends on the completion of another task, a concept that can be extended to multiples in either direction; for example, a collection of tasks may be dependent on one task. The Gantt chart is useful for explaining to team members the timing and sequence of events in a project.

PERT Charts

Program Evaluation and Review Technique (PERT) charts were developed during the Nautilus submarine program in the 1950s. A PERT chart resembles a network diagram in that it shows task dependencies, but true PERT also calculates the following:

- Best expected completion time

- Average expected completion time

- Worst expected completion time

A PERT algorithm then calculates a probabilistic assessment of best- and worst-case scenarios. The PERT technique is complicated and is not used much anymore. A more sophisticated model would look at the distribution of time-to-completion for each task and use Monte Carlo simulation to probabilistically model the potential actions during the project. For example, a given task may exhibit a normal distribution. It is possible to emit random values that also exhibit a normal distribution and that are constrained by the original mean and standard deviation. These values provide data for the model.

Network Diagram

The network diagram (sometimes called an activity network diagram) links tasks with direct arrows showing the path through the task list. Tasks are linked when a task is dependent on a preceding task. Because the network diagram is a graphical representation of a directed graph, the critical path can be calculated. The graphical project management program will usually show the critical path in a contrasting color, like red. The network diagram is a very powerful tool for predicting project success.

Planning Trees

Planning trees are graphical representations of work breakdown structures.

Work Breakdown Structures

Work breakdown structures represent one of the three following ideas:

- Breakdown of deliverables
- Breakdown of resources
- Breakdown of tasks

Currently the first and the third methods are the most common. The WBS lies at the very heart of planning. It should be decomposed to as much detail as is feasible. At each level of the structure, a task may be broken down into smaller tasks. The project manager breaks the project down into some rational set of discrete and manageable pieces. In some very formal cases, the deliverables type of structure is used as a tool for costing the project and each deliverable becomes a cost center for purposes of accounting.

Table III.1 shows a spreadsheet-style Gantt chart.

3. PROJECT DOCUMENTATION

Data/Fact-Driven Project Documentation

Black Belt projects are *always* data-driven. This is the hallmark of Six Sigma projects. A project can only be in a certain number of states or conditions. The section titled "Allowable Project States" enumerates these states and explains them.

Project Spreadsheets

Project spreadsheets can be used to maintain project finances not accounted for by the project software or in place of the project management software. It is important to

Table III.1   Using a spreadsheet to represent a project Gantt chart.

Phase									
Specification	**1**	**2**	**3**	**4**	**5**	**6**	**7**	**8**	**9**
Analyze	*****								
Create WBS		***							
Submit for approval		**	*						
Release to doc control			*						
Design									
Write design doc			****						
Produce drawings			**						
Produce schematics			**						
Design review			*						
Evaluation									
Write test plan				***					
Submit for review				**					
Execute tests					*****				
Write test report									
Release product									
Production									
Buy test equipment				***					
Set up line equipment				***					
Verify bill of materials				*					
Update control plan					***				
Update PFMEA					***				
Maintenance									
Create service part BOM				**					
Create packaging					***				
Track returns						*****	*****	*****	*****

remember that a spreadsheet is *not* a database, nor is it really a project management assistant in the fullest sense.

Project Storyboards

Storyboarding is a technique of combining narrative text and explanatory panels in much the same way that this book has been written. The technique has been used in Hollywood to plan films since the 1930s. It can be very useful for picturing a sequence of events or explaining the process to someone not technically apt.

Phased Reviews (Gates)

Each project normally has five to nine milestone reviews. Because of the DMAIC technique, five reviews makes a lot of sense for Six Sigma projects. A review is an opportunity to ask:

- Did we meet our goals to date?
- What did we not meet?
- Do we need to recalibrate?

These reviews are typically formal, although they need not be.

Management Reviews

In some cases, Black Belt projects are overseen by management, hence the term "management reviews." These reviews are a good way for management to show support for Black Belt projects as well as keep tabs on the financial progress of these activities.

Presentations to the Executive Team

The Black Belt can use storyboards as a stepping stone for creating a presentation for the executive team (steering committee) for the Six Sigma deployment. These presentations are an opportunity to point out successes, solicit support for problems, and collect one's thoughts.

Allowable Project States

Only nine schedule states exist for a project. They are:

1. *Ahead of schedule.* Tasks have been overbuffered (safety lead time) or the team is more efficient than expected.

2. *On schedule.* The plan is being met.

3. *Behind schedule.* Based on the author's experience, "behind schedule" is the most common state.

4. *Suspended (may return).* A project may be suspended when the customer has not been forthcoming with a purchase order. Under suspension, it is clear that the project will most likely return. The team may remain available during this state.

5. *Stopped (may not return).* The project has been stopped after an apparently insurmountable problem has occurred.

6. *Unstarted.* The project is planned, but the resources may not have been assigned.

7. *Completed.* The project has been brought to closure.

8. *Unknown.* The project is out of control. The measurement system has broken down.

9. *Aborted (will never return).* In some cases, executive management will terminate or abort a project permanently.

Analogous states exist for financial condition:

1. Below budget

2. On budget

3. Over budget

4. Budget delayed

5. Out of money temporarily

6. Awaiting expected financing

7. Account closed

8. Unknown

9. Account closed forever

4. CHARTER NEGOTIATION

Creating the Charter

According to the PMI, the project charter is a document created by senior management to authorize the existence of a project. However, typically a project charter is much more than that—it is a controlling document for the entire project.

Negotiating the Charter

Because the charter defines the product and the level of effort required to complete the project, the charter itself is a byproduct of negotiations between project managers and functional managers.

Objectives

- Why are we doing this project?
- What will we accomplish?

Scope

- What is this project about?
- Who is involved (suppliers, customers)?

Boundaries

- What lies within the project?
- What lies outside the project?

The establishment of clear boundaries simplifies the management of scope during the project life. Boundaries also clarify the project definition for the project team.

Resources

- Who will contribute to the project?
- Where will they work?
- How much funding do we have?
- What tools do we have (equipment, software)?
- Are any special skills necessary?

Project Transition

When the project nears completion, it is time for a transition phase that may include the following:

- Lessons learned review
- Recommendations for future projects
- Handoff, if necessary, to the process owners

Project Closure

At project closure, the following should occur:

- Black Belt support draws to a close
- Success is reviewed
- Financial benefits are tallied

What a Project Charter Does . . . Qualitatively

1. Establishes funding and authorization for funding.
2. Sets constraints on the subcontractor relationship (if one exists).
3. Positions support organizations and defines their work.
4. Establishes top-level responsibilities, accountabilities, and flow-down of authority.
5. Defines the significance of the project to participants and the rest of organization and, in some cases, to the customer.
6. Recognizes the project team.
7. Appoints the relevant staff to the project, thereby authorizing their presence.
8. Communicates significant information about the project to the enterprise.
9. Recognizes senior management's role.

The structure of a project charter can be very simple:

Project Overview

- Project purpose
- Project scope
- Project goals, objectives, and targets
- Major issues
- Approvals (the warrant from management to proceed)

Project Plan of Attack

- Project deliverables
- Project quality objectives
- Organization
- Responsibilities matrix
- Support activities plan
- Project facilities
- Project resources
- Risk management approach
- Major milestones/stages
- Overview schedule
- Quality control activities
- Project schedule

Section III.A.4

FURTHER READING

Eckes, George. 2003. *Six Sigma Team Dynamics: The Elusive Key to Project Success.* Hoboken, NJ: John Wiley & Sons.

B. Team Leadership

1. INITIATING TEAMS

Elements of Launching a Team

Launching a team is a process that can follow the Six Sigma problem-solving "algorithm."

Define: Why does the team exist? Who is on the team?

Measure: How does the team know if they have met their goals?

Analyze: Is the team on track? Where are we in the team life cycle?

Improve: Reduce conflict, facilitate, regain focus.

Control: Solicit feedback during the life of the team.

Team Purpose

Create a team mission statement. A mission statement identifies the purpose of the team as well as defining the constituencies to which the team applies, both members and stakeholders. A mission statement defines purpose; a vision statement defines the future.

Team Goals

Establish top-level goals. Goals may be derived from a combination of the mission statement and the vision statement and they can be broken down further into concrete objectives and targets.

Team Commitment

How long will the team last? What are the required skills and traits? Are team members stakeholders in the purpose of the team? Remember that teams are usually fleeting collections of individuals tied for a time by a common bond (the mission).

79

Team Ground Rules

The following list describes some significant ground rules for improving team performance.

Potential Team Ground Rules[19]

1. *Test assumptions and inferences (include testing constraints for validity).* The testing can be done as a group. This concept alone will help prevent "groupthink," where members become afraid to speak out and silence is assumed to be acquiescence.

2. *Share all relevant information (should agree on criteria for relevance).* A team without shared information is probably not much of a team at all. Withholding information is tantamount to playing power games and defeats the purpose of the team.

3. *Use specific examples and agree on what important words mean (specificity reduces pontificating).* The team can formalize the definitions of important words by building a team glossary or dictionary that explicitly defines the terms as well as their relationship to each other.

4. *Explain your reasoning and intent (your reasoning may not be obvious and your intent certainly is not!).* Explaining the rationale is one technique for achieving subsequent buy-in from the team members. Assuming the other team members are rational individuals, an understanding of the logic behind a decision or avowal can become a potent tool for persuasion.

5. *Focus on interests, not positions (this is not a run for political office).* Defending a position can become counterproductive, just as ad hominem attacks are counterproductive because they miss the point.

6. *Combine advocacy and inquiry (stand for something but also be able to question your own position).* This technique enables the practitioner to walk in another's shoes for a while. The idea is to achieve a less egocentric perspective and open the mind to a more global view of the situation.

7. *Jointly design next steps and ways to test disagreements (where do we go from here, and how do we make a decision when there is disagreement?).* The team is really functioning when disagreement management become a joint process.

8. *Discuss indiscussible issues (the assumption buster!).* This tool also helps prevent groupthink, eliminating the tacit agreement of the collective.

9. *Use a decision-making rule that generates the level of commitment needed (could be voting, could be a logic tree—whatever works).* Verify that the tool works by testing it. If not, choose another tool, then stick with it.

Team Roles

Establish a leader, a scribe, and member roles. In some cases, roles can be assumed by different people at different times.

Team Responsibilities

Each role has deliverables. Deliverable items are attached to an individual, defined explicitly, and given a due date. Members cannot deliver abstractions, only items that are defined concretely.

Team Schedules

Deliverables should arrive on schedule. The team should have a mutually agreed upon schedule that drives responsibility and accountability.

Management Support

Create a team charter. The team charter is a short document that defines the team, the mission, the vision and any relevant factor—major deliverables, significant milestones, special resources, and the identity of the team/process Champion.

Team Empowerment

Give the team the authority to do the job for which it was formed. Without empowerment, the team will not achieve its mission. Empowerment is an often-overlooked resource. For Black Belt teams, the project Champion becomes a significant resource for accomplishing the mission.

2. SELECTING TEAM MEMBERS

Skill Sets

The required skill sets can be derived from the definition of the need for the team. In some cases, special skill sets may require an outside adviser (this is sometimes the function of a Master Black Belt). Skills and traits are some of the considerations during resource analysis. An example of the need for a special skill is if the team knows they will need to analyze data using nonparametric (distribution-independent) statistics as opposed to the much more common parametric (distribution-dependent) statistics.

Additional considerations may arise if a team member has a very special skill set that would be missed from their regular job. The team and team leader need to consider the impact of the teaming activity on the normal day-to-day performance of the enterprise. Not all companies have the depth to assign full-time Master Black Belts and Black Belts to projects. Although Six Sigma philosophy and implementation provides significant benefits, some risk is entailed by the need for staffing projects with superior performers.

Team Size

Typical team sizes are in the vicinity of five to seven members. At five members, we are already looking at more than 120 possibilities of arranging members. As the number increases, the complexity of relationships increases as a gamma function (factorially = n!).

This fact also explains why managers typically work best with a span of control of no more than seven direct reports (5040 possibilities!).

Team Representations

Team members may represent different constituencies within the enterprise, but this is less important than assuring the correct body of skills, the correct attitude, the commitment, and the empowerment necessary to complete the project. A set of failed projects is not likely to endear the Six Sigma implementation to upper management. The company must invest in training time, training cost, tool set acquisition, test sample preparation, testing facilities, and any other resource that the team believes they will need.

Figure III.1 shows a team resource matrix, a tool often used to explain the roles of team members in project management scenarios.

	Tasks								
Team	Set times	Call meeting	Take minutes	Acquire data	Analyze data	Recommend improvements	Followup control	Adjourn	Set up rewards
Team leader	◉	◉						◉	
Team scribe			○						
Team cheerleader				○	○	○	○		
Team member				○	○	○	○		
Team member				○	○	○	○		
Champion	△								◉

◉ Primary responsibility   ○ Team members   △ Provide resources

Figure III.1 Team resource matrix used to clarify roles.

3. TEAM STAGES

Forming

A team does not occur simply because a manager has appointed people to a team. Teams require some level of evolution before they really function as a team.

Questions asked during this phase include:

- What is my purpose here?

- Who are these other people?

Storming

Sometimes team evolution can be painful, particularly if the team has been staffed with some mediocre performers. Additionally, some members may have strong biases that conflict with those of other members, leading to the need for conflict prevention, conflict resolution, or some level of facilitation in order to keep making progress.

Questions asked during this phase include:

- What are my expectations? What are their expectations?

- Why aren't my expectation being met?

- What's my role in this?

Norming

The team has evolved into a negotiated peace, but members are not performing at their potential as yet.

Questions asked during this phase include:

- How do I resolve these conflicts? How are we going to move forward?

- How do we get this done as a group "thing"?

Performing

At this point, the team is cross-supporting, with each member providing assistance and motivation for every other member.

Question asked during this phase include:

- What are the criteria for success? (Gosh, we're good!)

Adjourning

All things come to an end and teams are no exception. The adjournment phase can be a period of letdown for members.

Questions asked during this phase include:

- Alas, it is over . . . what a great team and what a great experience . . . !

- Why do I have regrets?

Recognition

Questions asked during this phase include:

- Will they notice our work?

- Will they recognize us as a group? Or individually?

See Figure III.2 for a pictorial representation of this model of teaming.[20] (This is a slightly expanded version of the explanation in *Managers as Facilitators*).

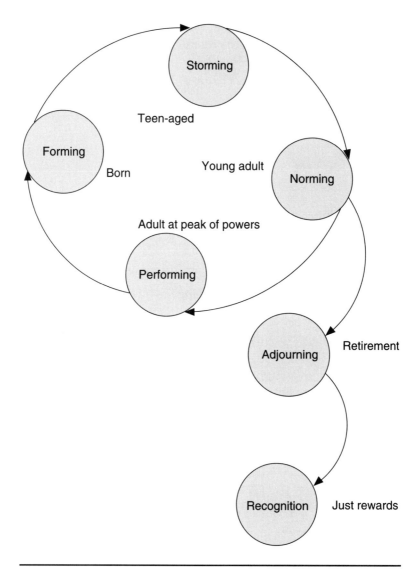

Figure III.2   The 'Orming model of teams with the addition of team retirement.

FURTHER READING

Pande, Peter S., Robert P. Neuman, and Roland R. Cavanagh. 2002. *The Six Sigma Way Team Fieldbook: An Implementation Guide for Project Improvement Teams.* New York: McGraw-Hill.

C. Team Dynamics and Performance

1. TEAM-BUILDING TECHNIQUES

How to Set Goals

The participant should ask:

- What is this meeting about? (Ultimate goal question)
- What are we supposed to accomplish? (Ultimate results questions)
- Why did they ask me? What is my contribution to be?
- How will the group work? What are the ground rules?

How to Designate Roles

Individuals may volunteer for roles, which can then be approved by the group. Roles can rotate from meeting to meeting if the team agrees to this method of assuring equity. A role does not grant any special authority to a participant; rather, it offers specific obligations and responsibilities. Obligations of a role are available for any participant to exercise, but responsibilities may be exercised only by the team member in that role.

How to Apply Responsibilities

The leader or facilitator can make clear what the responsibilities of each role are to be. The responsibility is wedded to the role. Alternatively, the team can arrive at the responsibility matrix through consensus.

Agendas, Hidden and Stated

Agendas guide meetings and help keep them on track; hidden agendas interfere with meetings. A good written agenda can help counteract hidden agendas. The well-crafted agenda should include (1) the agenda topics, if appropriate, (2) a brief explanation of each item and its importance, (3) the individual responsible for each item, (4) the duration of each discussion, and (5) the action needed for each item that requires action.

Coaching

When coaching, a team member is in an instructional mode. The team member can gently use some expert knowledge to instruct (with dignity) another team member in how to perform a specific function more optimally.

Mentoring

A mentor is not necessarily a team member and their role is more advisory than instructive. Frequently, a mentor is a more senior individual who has been around the block a few times.

Facilitation

The facilitator stands outside the team and helps them decide how to decide (consensus, majority rules, multivoting, leadership). They also see to it that all issues that have been raised have addressed, using a "parking lot" board as a temporary holding area. A facilitator can help the team decide on the next step. Moreover, they can summarize results, agreements, and next steps. See Table III.2 for some items that increase the chance of success.

2. TEAM FACILITATION TECHNIQUES

Dealing with Overbearing or Dominant Participants

An overbearing or dominant team member (1) wields a disproportionate amount of influence, (2) consumes a disproportionate amount of "air time," (3) sees silence as an invitation to talk, (4) inhibits the group from building a functioning team, and (5) discourages participation by other members, who then find excuses for missing meetings.

Ways to deal with dominating participants include having the leader engage others, refocusing the discussion, and using a timekeeper, who can keep dominators in check by asking, Who has the floor?

Dealing with Reluctant Participants

In the case where one or two members rarely speak, problems may develop if the quiet ones are not encouraged to participate, and this behavior invites dominators to dominate.

Solutions to reluctance can include deliberately checking around the group, creating activities that rely on participation (trainer-games), recording ideas, and testing whether the team is satisfied with the procedures.

Opinions versus Facts

Some team members may express personal beliefs and assumptions with such confidence that other team members assume they are hearing facts (or groupthink rears its ugly head).

Table III.2   Requisites for team success.

Element	Ideals
Clarity of team goals	Accord on mission and vision
Clearly defined roles	Team members understand what to do and when
Clear communication	• Make clear and direct statements or questions • Be succinct (concise) • Listen actively • Explore rather than debate others' ideas
Beneficial team behavior	• Seek information and opinions • Suggest procedures for reaching a goal • Clarify or elaborate on ideas • Summarize • Test for consensus • Keep the discussion from digressing • Compromise and be creative in resolving differences • Work to ease tension and resolve difficulties • Express provisional group "sense" and check for consensus before proceeding • Work for standards for decision making
Well-defined decision procedures	• Discuss and agree on how decisions will be made • Explore important issues by polling • Decide important issues by consensus • Openly (overtly) test for consensus
Balanced participation	All members contribute equally, in their natural style
Established ground rules	Ground rules for the team are discussed early and agreed on

Section III.C.2

Solutions to opinions include testing comprehension, bringing in the experience of others (asking for suggestions), and deliberately asking for more information.

Groupthink

Groupthink is the nasty tendency of group members to go along with the crowd. In many cases, members will not speak against the majority even when they harbor serious misgivings about decisions. Silence can become a deadly form of acquiescence. However, silence does not obviate responsibility. For example, witnessing the creation of a concentration camp while feigning ignorance of its purpose does not eliminate one's responsibility for its existence—an extreme example, but illustrative of the depths of perniciousness involved with groupthink.

See Table III.3 for a list of some of the negatives associated with groupthink.

Table III.3   Dealing with groupthink.[21]

Conditions	Groupthink occurs when a group is highly cohesive and under a great deal of pressure to make a quality decision. The team members know dissension will delay the process.
Negative outcomes	Examining too few alternatives Failure to critique each other's ideas Disposing of early alternatives Failure to seek expert opinion when it would be helpful Selectivity in gathering information ("only what supports my theory!") No contingency plans
Symptoms	Illusions of invulnerability (a form of paranoia) Explaining away inept decisions Belief in the group's morality (like national socialism) Sharing stereotypes without questioning them Exercising direct pressure Failure to express one's feelings Maintaining the illusion of unanimity (sometimes even "harmony")
Solutions	Use a steering committee that reports to the larger group Support impartial leadership Use different policy groups for different tasks Divide into groups and then discuss differences (breakdown of false unanimity) Discuss within subgroups and then report back Use outside experts Use a devil's advocate to question all the group's ideas Hold an "oops!" meeting to give a final opportunity to opt for an alternate decision

Feuding

Feuders see a meeting as a field of combat—frequently, the issue is not the subject they are arguing about but rather the contest itself, like a sporting match in which other team members, fearing involvement, can become spectators rather than participants.

Some ideas for counteracting feuding are keeping adversaries on different teams, attempting reconciliation (in or out of the meeting), quiet removal of passive-aggressive people (they have hidden agendas), and offering compromise.

Floundering

Floundering occurs when there is:

- An unclear or overwhelming task

- A pattern of false starts and directionless discussions

- No consensus

Solutions to floundering include:

- Clarifying the team's task or goals and time frames

- Pulling together related ideas

- Asking if the group is nearing a decision

- Offering a conclusion for the group to accept or reject

Rush to Accomplishment

When a rush to accomplishment occurs, it is usually because the team has a "do-something" member who is impatient or sensitive to pressure, who urges the team toward hasty decisions, and who discourages efforts to analyze or discuss the decision.

Solutions include reminding the team that quality takes patience; reviewing tasks, time lines, and accomplishments; and making sure that decisions are data-driven (always a good Black Belt practice).

Attribution

Attribution is name dropping, which can be challenged directly. It is also known as a logical fallacy called the appeal to authority.

Discounts and Plops[22]

A Peter Scholtes term, "discounts and plops" occur when important values or perspectives are ignored or ridiculed, making members feel discounted, or when a team member makes a statement that "plops" (the proverbial lead balloon).

Solutions to discounts and plops include helping discounted members identify and openly state what is important, pointing out implicit or explicit norms, and admitting errors.

Digressions/Tangents

Digressions are a trap for members. Relevant anecdotes ("war stories") can lead to digressions, and at meeting's end people wonder how the time slipped away.

To deal with digressions, deliberately focus discussion, agree to change the content of the meeting, use a timekeeper, or use a parking lot, a convenient board at the back of the room for storing digressions for later reference.

Some Common Team Problems

1. *Unilateralism/Authoritarianism.* One person makes the decision and imposes it on the team. Frequently, team members have little input and buy-in is low.

2. *Handclasp.* Two team members decide and inflict their decision on the team. This pattern gives the illusion of being participatory, but still provokes little participation from the other members, who have little buy-in.

Section III.C.2

3. *Minority.* Several members make a decision and impose it upon the majority, who have been marginalized. This technique can look like participatory decision making, but it is only a handclasp among an oligarchy. Decision quality suffers because of the lack of input from the majority, and acceptance is reduced among the majority.

4. *Majority.* The democratic method. When a team is unable to resolve a conflict, there is almost always a suggestion to take a vote—"majority wins." Majority rule has the illusion of equity, but it terminates discussion and reduces decision quality and discussion diversity. It also elicits no acceptance from the minority.

5. *Unanimity.* Solves the problem of commitment. This method may reflect groupthink more than anything else, because it represents tacit agreement.

6. *Consensus.* Difficult to achieve, consensus results in the best decision quality and the highest level of allegiance (buy-in) to the team decision. Alternatives are discussed and honed until a consensus occurs. Beware of groupthink! All methods have some problems, but this one seems to have the fewest downsides.

3. TEAM PERFORMANCE EVALUATION

Evaluation against Goals

Goals are supported by derived objectives, which, in turn, are supported by derived targets. If the objectives have been all been met, then it is very likely that the goals have also been met. Frequently, goals will be expressed in terms of abstractions; for example, "I want a good, quality product." It is up to the team to define what the abstract terms mean, particularly terms such as "quality." Objectives arise as the team examines the more nebulous terminology of the goal and converts the goal into a less qualitative, more quantitative result.

Evaluation against Objectives

If the objectives have been broken down into targets and the targets have been met, then the objectives have been met (the goals have also been met). The functional decomposition from the mission and vision statements to the goals, objectives, and targets leads to a plan.

A plan can be expressed as simply as a checklist or in as complicated a format as a network diagram of all dependencies. The beauty of the checklist is that it makes it very easy for the team leader and team members to assess progress. The only significant feature that a checklist lacks is the expression of task dependencies.

Evaluation against Metrics

Every good Black Belt will use metrics because data lies at the heart of the Six Sigma revolution. Metrics may be used as soon as they are defined. The team may set most of the metrics at the very beginning of their teamwork. Eliminate the metrics that result in senseless measuring and add those metrics that will add value. Evaluation of the change occasioned by a successful (or unsuccessful) team cannot occur without measuring a baseline and the subsequent modification of project status.

Here are some team performance evaluation metrics questions:

1. Did we meet all of our targets?

2. Did we meet all of our objectives?

3. Did we meet all of our goals?

4. What was the variance from the plan and where did it occur?

5. Did we meet our target dates?

6. Did we supply the expected deliverables?

7. Did we improve the problem for which we created the team in the first place?

8. Is the item of concern under control?

9. Did we capture lessons learned? (Not necessarily a goal, but frequently useful to subsequent team efforts.)

10. Did we call for help when needed?

11. Did we stay on budget?

12. Is the quality and reliability of the product equal to or greater than what was expected?

4. TEAM TOOLS[23]

Nominal Group Technique

This technique helps build consensus and buy-in. Here are the steps:

1. Select items of concern from a brainstorming exercise (or other source).

2. Write all items on a flip chart, white board, adhesive notes, or 3×5 cards.

3. Eliminate duplicates.

4. "Publish" final list of items.

5. Have each member rank the items on a piece of paper or a 3×5 card.

6. Combine the rankings and score.

7. You have a democratically chosen a list of priorities!

Force Field Analysis

See Figure III.3 for a graphical representation of force field analysis. The arrows could be set to different lengths to indicate the level of perceived strength for each item of interest.

New House Force Field Analysis			
+ Driving forces			Restraining forces −
More room	▶	◀	BIG, BIG loan
Newer plumbing	▶	◀	Fixing old is not that expensive
Better cooling	▶	◀	Refrigerated costs more than evap.
Better insulation	▶	◀	New insulation costs more than heating bill
Bigger yard	▶	◀	More mowing
New materials	▶	◀	Old house has wood, not pressboard
New location	▶	◀	People know our old address
Shorter drive to work	▶	◀	More traffic in new area
New carpet	▶	◀	Makes old furniture look shabby
Double-pane windows	▶	◀	Old house well sealed over the years
New kitchen	▶	◀	Don't use most appliances anyway
New bathroom	▶	◀	Old bathrooms don't have carpet on floor

Figure III.3   Force field analysis for buying a new house.

Why list items in the force field diagram? For one thing, it brings "collisions" to the surface, so they can become a topic for dialogue. Additionally and more formally, the team can deliberately take steps to reduce or eliminate the restraining forces and enhance or strengthen the driving forces.

Multivoting

Multivoting is a participative technique that, although democratic, puts people on the spot by moving them gently toward a decision. One form goes as follows:

1. Select items of concern from a brainstorming exercise or other source.

2. Identify voting criteria to eliminate crossed purposes and misunderstandings.

3. Give each member a stock of points to distribute as they see fit.

4. Do not allow more than 50 percent of any stock to be placed on any one item.

5. Allow voting with points to occur.

6. Tally the results.

7. You have a democratically chosen a list of priorities!

Conversion/Diversions

Conversion occurs when we proselytize our position so heavily that members capitulate and become advocates. Conversion can also be symptomatic of groupthink.

Diversion occurs when a team member with a hidden agenda keeps distracting the team from the assigned task. Sometimes a bored individual will become the court jester during meetings and entertain the team with witty, but counterproductive, comments. This problem may take a facilitator to correct.

FURTHER READING

Scholtes, Peter, Brian L. Joiner, and Barbara J. Streibel. 1996. *The TEAM Handbook.* Madison, WI: Oriel Incorporated.

D. Change Agent

1. MANAGING CHANGE

Facilitating Change

The rules for the facilitation are straightforward:

- Remove or decrease elements of resistance; that is, make it easy for an individual or group to change (also called barrier removal).
- Treat the involved individuals with great care and respect.
- Show the affected individuals that they are part of a greater whole.
- Inspire them with the magnificence of the obsession (this is not as silly as it sounds; in short form, "paint a picture of the coming glory").

Inspiration will occur naturally if the situation is reinforcing for the individual. A situation is reinforcing if it encourages a repeated behavior.

Managing Changes

See the following list for some ideas on managing change. Productive change can be a good thing for the enterprise and the individuals within it. Regressive change can represent a fallback to a more dictatorial organization, as management tries to control change by edict rather than persuasion and trust.

Tips for Managing Change

1. Instruct the leaders of change.
2. Use a systems approach to organizational behavior.
3. Use a team approach to involve stakeholders in the change process and secure buy-in.
4. Empower others to encourage the implementation of the change efforts.

5. Make plans, but keep them flexible.

6. Realize that there is tension between building readiness for change and the implementation.

7. Provide considerable amounts of training for those involved. Change management may involve coaching or mentoring.

8. Recognize that change happens only through people. Many change processes fail right here, as they demand change rather than reinforcing change. Understand resistance.

9. Prepare for "implementation dip"—a decline in behavior. This is also called an "extinction burst" and is typical of behaviors that suddenly lose their reinforcement.

10. Provide explanations that satisfy the reasoning faculties as well as those involving feelings.

11. Seek out Champions who are interested in change and who have the influence to gently secure it.

12. Realize that change takes time. Changing the corporate culture involves behavior modification at both the group and the individual level.

Simple enterprise reorganization is not necessarily productive change, unless the reorganization leads to improved performance. It is important to have baseline data for the previous organizational structure before the reorganization occurs so that levels of improvement or deterioration can be measured.

Change Agent Techniques

The change agent can:

- Elevate awareness by providing information and eliciting responses.

- Empower teams.

- Inspire participation.

- Provide reinforcement (through recognition, acknowledgment, rewards, and so on).

- Demonstrate that management is participating, too.

2. ORGANIZATIONAL ROADBLOCKS

Organizational Structure

Organizational structures can be vertical (tall) or horizontal (flat). In either case, they will always resemble a pyramid with appendages—the appendages being shareholders who do not play a part in the day-to-day execution of management directives.

Organization Culture

Juran called consideration of the organization culture the second basic rule of change: ". . . discover just what will be the social effects of your proposed technical changes."[24]

He also noted that at the GE Hawthorne plant, the internal social rules were more important to the employees than the official plant rules.

Organizational Constructs

See Figure III.4 for an illustration of some organizational constructs. These are by the no means all of the possible constructs, just some of the major ones.

The strong matrix becomes a weak matrix when no projects department exists and the project manager position may be more of an ad hoc responsibility.

Barriers to Improvement

Organizational structure and constructs, culture, and informal (or hidden) social groups can all be barriers to change.

Overcoming Barriers

In *Managerial Breakthrough*, Juran made several key points about overcoming barriers and influencing change:[25]

- Those who propose change are products of their own history and may not be espousing universal truths.

- The existing culture already has policies and procedures that provide a high level of predictability, often allowing the current participants to wing it.

- The change agent must look at the proposed change from the point of view of the line supervisor, since this will happen anyhow.

- Sweeping master plans pose the risk of sweeping rejections, particularly when they deal with local issues inadequately or incorrectly.

- The change will only be temporary if the "victim" is not wholly and genuinely convinced of the change.

Note that Juran wrote the original version of this book in 1965! Most Six Sigma concepts were espoused by Juran 20 to 30 years before they took hold at Motorola in the 1980s.

3. NEGOTIATION AND CONFLICT RESOLUTION TECHNIQUES

Consensus Techniques

Any kind of voting technique can be used here. It is important for the change agent/leader to beware the tyranny of the majority. This leader might consider a larger version of the interest-based bargaining idea (discussed a few sections later).

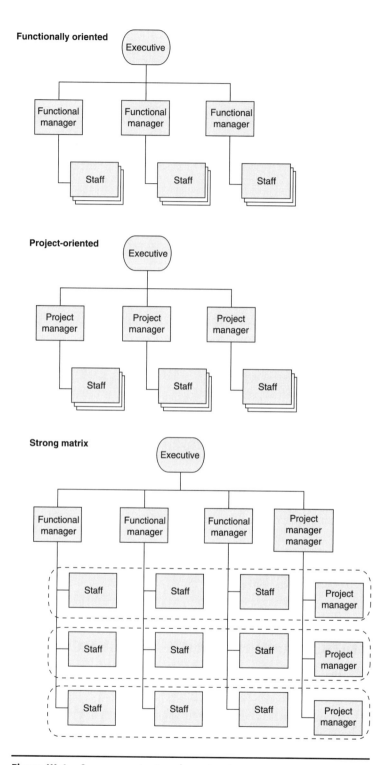

Figure III.4 Some organizational constructs.

Effort/Impact

This concept is very similar to Covey's four quadrants.[26] See Figure III.5 for a Johari window representation.

Small effort, small impact	Great effort, little impact
Do it now, or maybe don't do it. Sometimes this can be put off.	Why do this?
Small effort, great impact	**Great effort, great impact**
Hallelujah! What are we waiting for? We have increased leverage on whatever we are doing.	Okay, sometimes we need to build the great pyramids. These are big vision projects.

Figure III.5 Johari window example.

The Johari window is not a Persian creation; it is named after Joseph Luft and Harry Ingham (Joe-Harry) and first used in mathematical game theory to represent a 2×2 game.

Interest-Based Bargaining (Conflict Resolution)

This kind of bargaining is espoused by Fisher, Patton, and Ury[27] and is frequently called win-win negotiation. It is actually a pragmatic byproduct of game theory, where the best choice in a zero- or fixed-sum game is that which gives the greatest result to both parties. Otherwise:

1. I win, you lose = less than optimal

2. You win, I lose = less than optimal

3. I lose, you lose = way less than optimal

4. I win, you win = optimal

In the prisoner's dilemma version of this "game," neither party can communicate with the other from separate cells or interrogation rooms. The authorities play on this; however, in the conflict resolution version, communication among or between parties is key to resolving the conflict.

We need to remember Fisher, Patton, and Ury's concept of BATNA, which stands for best alternative to a negotiated agreement. Sometimes the best solution is just walking away.

4. MOTIVATION TECHNIQUES

Supporting Participation/Commitment

The key concept here is that the individuals affected by the change, small or sweeping, must be involved actively in its planning and implementation. In this way, they become the true change agents, effecting a cultural shift and owning the change. Imposed change never lasts, and companies that carry out these atrocities soon move on to the latest business buzzwords.

Sustaining Participation/Commitment

If we again consider business as a social system, then the key to sustaining participation and commitment is creating a self-reinforcing social climate, where it is punishing to return to the old way and gratifying to participate in the new.

Herzberg's Two Factor Theory

Herzberg posited two positions to explain motivation:[28]

1. Motivators (or non-hygienic): items that have intrinsic motivation (reinforcers). These items *increase* motivation when present; absence leads to no motivation or runs the gamut from satisfaction to no satisfaction.

2. Hygienic: items that provide extrinsic motivation (weak reinforcers). These run the scale from no dissatisfaction to dissatisfaction. Hygienic items are not as powerful as non-hygienic items.

When combined, Herzberg's two factors provide a continuum; see Figure III.6 for an abbreviated picture of the continuum.

Maslow's Pyramid of Needs

Maslow's pyramid of needs[29] represents a progression from "animal" requirements to a higher, humanistic level. A higher need only becomes significant when a lower need is satisfied (see Figure III.7).

1. *Physiological needs.* Needs for oxygen, water, reasonable temperature, and nutrients. Furthermore, needs for activity, rest, sleep, and waste elimination.

2. *Safety and security needs.* Does not become significant until the needs of level one are met.

3. *Belonging needs.* Becomes significant when needs at levels one and two have been met. These could be considered social or "love" needs.

4. *Esteem needs.* We have the needs of levels one, two, and three. Esteem needs break down into other-directed respect/admiration needs and self-respect needs.

5. *Self-actualization* occurs as individuals begin to realize their individual potential.

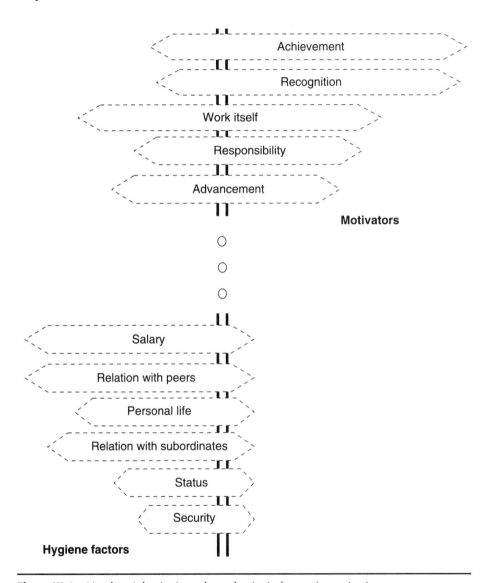

Figure III.6 Herzberg's hygienic and non-hygienic factors in motivation.

Section III.D.4

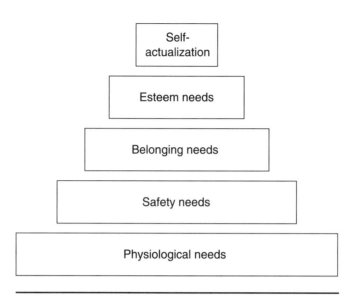

Figure III.7   Maslow's pyramid of needs.

5. COMMUNICATION

Communication Techniques

Communication techniques other than conflict resolution basically fall into two areas: listening and assertion (stating). See Figure III.8 for a simple information theory model of communication.

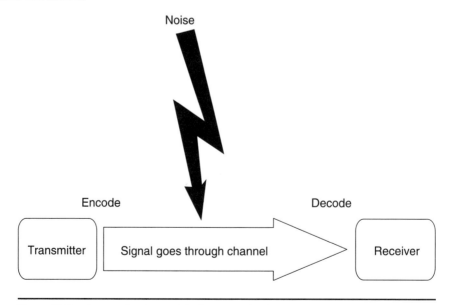

Figure III.8   A very simple model of communication.

Communication is what the receiver decodes, not what the transmitter encoded. Encoding and decoding are transmuted by the reinforcement history of the transmitter and receiver, respectively. When these histories are wildly different, communication becomes difficult due to improper decoding.

Listening

Active listening requires participation. The following list represents major techniques used when listening:

- Reflection of feelings: mirroring to the speaker the emotions apparent in his communication; that is, making sure you are on the same page in terms of feelings. Example: "You feel < > ."

- Reflection of meanings: not only mirroring the feelings but adding facts. Example: "You feel < > because < >."

- Summative reflection: briefly restating the main themes (motifs) and feelings (emotions) exposed over the duration of a conversation, certainly over a longer period than a single statement. This technique is most useful when problem solving.

Asserting

Assertion is not hostility. In fact, aggression is not hostility. The word "aggression" comes from the Latin for "to move toward" and is a characteristic that should be cherished. Alas, another misused word. The alternative to assertion is submission, which is generally considered to be a negative characteristic.

One form of assertive phrase is stated as "When you <do this thing>, I feel very <some sensation> because it <creates this feeling> for me." Another model[30] suggests:

- Describing the behavior

- Explaining the situation (feelings)

- Specifying the facts

- Describing the consequences (this might become hostile)

FURTHER READING

Colenso, Michael. 2000. *Kaizen Strategies for Successful Organizational Change: Enabling Evolution and Revolution within the Organization.* London: Prentice Hall Financial Times.

E. Management and Planning Tools

Section III.E

AFFINITY DIAGRAMS[31]

Affinity diagrams are used to cluster thoughts or ideas that are the output of brainstorming, mindstorming, or other idea-generating activities. Because traditional affinity diagram work is a team effort, it can encourage participation and buy-in from team members.

A typical procedure to develop an affinity diagram might go as follows:

1. Define the topic of interest.

2. Brainstorm ideas. Remember, there should be no criticizing during this phase. The idea is to generate as many adhesive notes or 3×5 cards as possible. These can be affixed to a white board or bulletin board in any kind of order.

3. Sort all the ideas into related clusters. Do not give the clusters titles yet.

4. If the team activity has settled down, open a discussion of heading cards or adhesive notes for the various clusters.

5. The team might choose to migrate the affinity diagram to a tree diagram if this makes sense.

6. Record the results.

An older variant of this kind of activity is the Japanese KJ method, named after Jiro Kawakita (Japanese use the surname first). In the KJ method, the card technique is used to partition hard data into groups, rather than using ideas.

See Figure III.9 for an example of an actual affinity diagram used for laboratory improvement using SmartDraw.

Improving the Laboratory

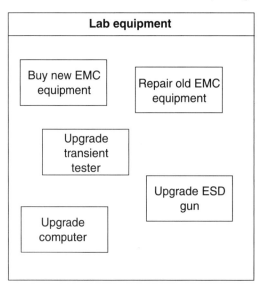
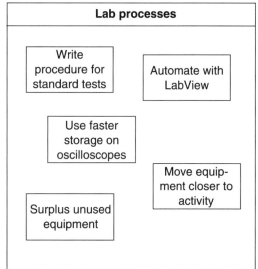
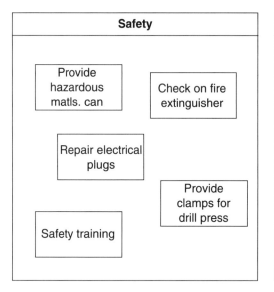
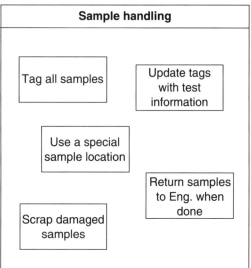

Figure III.9   An affinity diagram collected and put together for laboratory improvement.

INTERRELATIONSHIP DIGRAPHS

The interrelationship digraph (direct graph means arrows, not lines, connect the nodes) is another potential successor to the affinity diagram. As the name suggests, the purpose of the diagram is to illuminate relationships among issues. It may be a very appropriate choice when the issues do not nicely fit into a hierarchical arrangement like a tree diagram.

A typical procedure for creating an interrelationship digraph might be:

1. Define the purpose of the diagram (of course . . . you are a Black Belt, right?).

2. Gather people who have expertise in the area(s) of interest. These diagrams require more in-depth knowledge than some other approaches.

3. Take the results of the brainstorming session or the affinity diagram session and spread them out on a board or a large table.

4. Draw arrows between cards that have some kind of relationship. You can even use yarn or string if that helps, although that makes it difficult to show directionality.

5. Iterate until the team accepts the diagram.

6. Each card is a node. Nodes with more ingoing and outgoing arrows than other nodes have a rank. A higher rank may indicate a function or issue that is driving the others.

7. Record the results of the whole exercise.

Figure III.10 shows an example of a laboratory situation expressed as a digraph using SmartDraw.

TREE DIAGRAMS

Tree diagrams are a convenient way to represent data that falls into hierarchical classifications or categories. They are the major alternative to using a table to represent information. Many other diagrams are derived from the basic tree:

- Fault trees

- Why-why

- How-how

- Organization charts

- Management Oversight and Risk Tree Analysis (Department of Energy)

- Taxonomy of living beings

- Ontologies

- Bills of materials

- Work breakdown structures

- Any kind of outline

- Indices (for example, a book index can be represented as a tree

Similarly to the affinity diagram, a team can put 3×5 cards or adhesive notes on a wall, a board, or a table and begin to establish the hierarchy of information. Lower levels should represent more detailed information than higher levels.

Section III.E

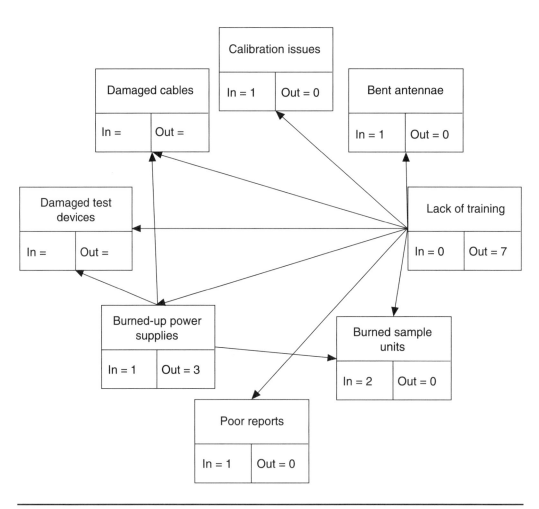

Figure III.10 Interrelationship digraph depicting the relationship of problems in an electromagnetic compatibility laboratory.

See Figure III.11 for an example of a hierarchical breakdown in a laboratory.

PRIORITIZATION MATRICES

The purpose of a prioritization matrix is to narrow down choices. These matrices can be used to compare components, design features, strategies, costs, and so on. In some cases, a more involved version of these matrices can become a pairwise comparison method.

A typical process might look like:

1. Define the purpose of the analysis.

2. Gather a team.

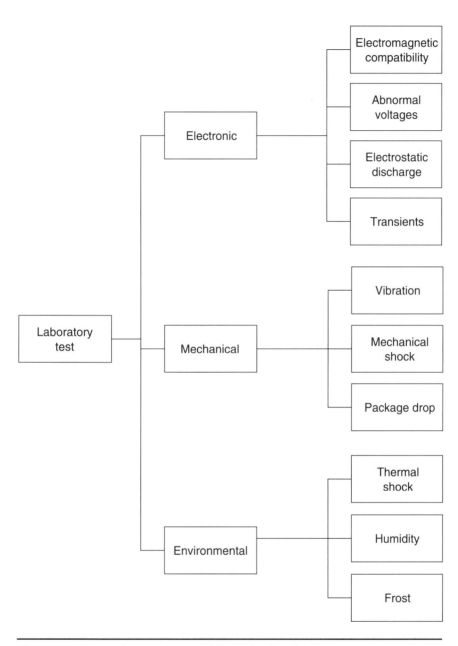

Figure III.11   Tree diagram showing different kinds of laboratory tests.

3. List criteria significant to evaluation.

4. Weigh criterion against criterion with an L-matrix.

5. Weight option versus criterion with another L-matrix.

6. Compare each option on all criteria with a summary L-matrix

Figure III.12 shows the layout for a prioritization matrix, generated by SmartDraw.

Step 1—Criterion vs. criterion

Criteria	Criterion 1	Criterion 2	Criterion 3	Criterion 4	Row total	Relative decimal value
Criterion 1						
Criterion 2						
Criterion 3						
Criterion 4						
					Grand total:	

1 = Equally important
5 = More important
10 = Much more important   Relative decimal value = Row total / Grand total
1/5 = Less important
1/10 = Much less important

Step 2—One criterion vs. all options (can have many of these)

Criterion 2	Option 1	Option 2	Option 3	Option 4	Option 5	Row total	Relative decimal value
Option 1							
Option 2							
Option 3							
Option 4							
Option 5							
						Grand total:	

Step 3—Summary matrix

Summary	Criterion 1	Criterion 2	Criterion 3	Criterion 4	Row total	Relative decimal value
Option 1						
Option 2						
Option 3						
Option 4						
Option 5						
					Grand total:	

Figure III.12   Prioritization matrix layout.

MATRIX DIAGRAMS

The following sections show examples of matrix diagrams. The numbers in the unshaded cells indicate the power of the relationship at the cross-section of the headings. Matrix diagrams provide a way to represent a large quantity of information compactly. On the downside, if the matrix diagram becomes too complex, comprehension will most likely suffer.

At least five formats exist for matrix diagrams:

L-shaped Matrix

The L-shaped matrix (Table III.4) is the most common of these tools. It compares two variables, using target symbols, triangles, and circles (or numbers) to qualitatively identify the relationship between the variables. If you are already familiar with quality function deployment, you will recognize the structure.

Table III.4   The "L" diagram.

	R1	R2	R3	R4
L1	1	2	3	4
L2	1	2	3	4
L3	1	2	3	4
L4	1	2	3	4

T-shaped Matrix

The T-shaped matrix compares three variables, two along the bar and one along the stem, using target symbols, triangles, and circles (or numbers) to qualitatively identify the relationship between the variables.

Table III.5   The "T" diagram.

M4	1	2	3	4
M3	1	2	3	4
M2	1	2	3	4
M1	1	2	3	4
	R1	R2	R3	R4
L1	1	2	3	4
L2	1	2	3	4
L3	1	2	3	4
L4	1	2	3	4

Y-shaped Matrix

The Y-shaped matrix compares three variables, but two at a time, so you end up with a three-dimensional representation of three L-shaped matrices.

X-shaped Matrix

The X-shaped matrix is similar to the T-shaped matrix. but it relates four values. It compares four variables, using target symbols, triangles, and circles to qualitatively identify the relationship between the variables. The row and column headers form an "X" when tipped 45°.

Table III.6   The "X" diagram.

1	2	3	4	M4	1	2	3	4
1	2	3	4	**M3**	1	2	3	4
1	2	3	4	**M2**	1	2	3	4
1	2	3	4	**M1**	1	2	3	4
S1	**S2**	**S3**	**S4**		**R1**	**R2**	**R3**	**R4**
1	2	3	4	**L1**	1	2	3	4
1	2	3	4	**L2**	1	2	3	4
1	2	3	4	**L3**	1	2	3	4
1	2	3	4	**L4**	1	2	3	4

C-shaped Matrix

The C-shaped matrix is similar to the Y-shaped matrix, but it can compare all three variables at once by positioning the item of interest in three-dimensional space. Because of its complexity, it is not used very often. It is also difficult to interpret visually.

PROCESS DECISION PROGRAM CHARTS

A process decision program chart (PDPC) is a variant of the tree diagram. It can be used as a simple alternative to FMEA or FTA. In the automotive supplier environment, it is probably not an acceptable tool for anticipating failures.

A typical way to build a PDPC is:

1. Define the goal.

2. Gather a team.

3. List steps (if looking at a process) or components/subsystems (if looking at a product) and begin to decompose problems in a tree structure from the initial set of steps or subsystems.

4. Show responses to the problems using a graphical cloud.

5. Record the results.

Figure III.13 presents a simple example of a PDPC. The "O" means selected; the "X" means difficult or impossible. The PDPC presents a superficial resemblance to a fault tree. Fault trees, however, can be converted directly into networks of Boolean logic. Fault trees are effectively a grammar for representing the causes and effects related to problems.

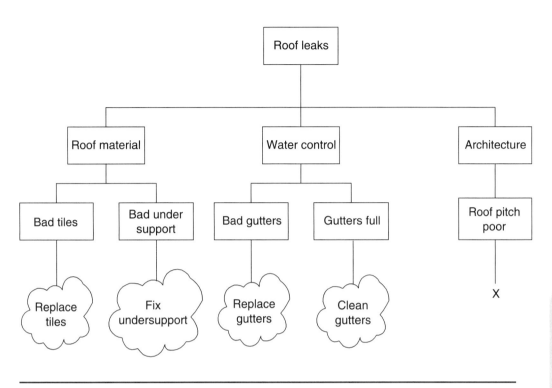

Figure III.13   PDPC for a problem with a house.

The Department of Energy has taken the fault tree concept to a high level—it is called Management Oversight and Risk Tree, or MORT, analysis. Normally, a MORT analysis happens after an accident occurs. A small task team will run through approximately 1500 questions to sort out all the issues involved in the accident. The MORT tree is already spelled out; the team works through the tree and decides which items are not relevant to the investigation.

The FMEA is primarily an automotive industry technique for listing potential problems and dealing with them before they happen. Users will assign occurrence (frequency), severity, and detection values to each item on a scale of 1 to 10. They then multiply the occurrence times the severity times the detection to get a risk priority number (RPN). A comparison of all RPNs for a given product or system should elicit those that are the most problematic.

ACTIVITY NETWORK DIAGRAMS

An activity network diagram is one of the most significant tools used by the project manager. It shows the dependencies of every task in a directed graph and, with special software, it can also show the critical path in a contrasting color. Different kinds of software support different levels of information in each task box of the network diagram. Most current project management software can convert these diagrams to a hybrid Gantt chart/network diagram that shows time bars *and* dependencies. If the dependencies are incomplete—if we have "hangers" that appear out of nowhere—then we cannot mathematically compute a true critical path. Thus, it is essential that every task be tied to another task. Only the kickoff task and the terminal tasks are not connected on both sides.

A typical procedure is:

1. Define the goals, objectives, mission, vision, and so on.

2. Gather a team.

3. Create a WBS from the items in #1.

4. Tie the dependencies together with arrows showing the correct flow.

5. Check for hangers.

6. Record the results.

Figure III.14 shows a snip from a larger plan for testing a product in a laboratory.

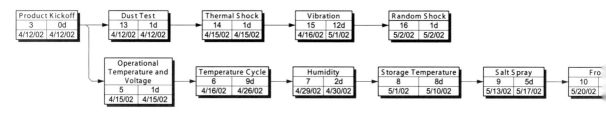

Figure III.14   A network diagram for some tests using Microsoft Project and Chart produced by PERT Chart Expert from Critical Tools.

FURTHER READING

Brassard, Michael. 1996. *The Memory Jogger Plus.* Rev. ed. Methuen, MA: QOAL/QPC.

Section IV

Six Sigma Improvement Methodology and Tools—*Define* (9 Questions)

Contents

A. Project Scope

PROJECT DEFINITION/SCOPE

Constraints

Constraints can be viewed as limitations or as defining boundaries. Typical constraints to consider when defining project scope are the following:

- Resources—Resources are a very real constraint issue. Without finite loading algorithms/policies, organizations may overload their employees, which distorts the plan.

- Target dates—also known as "drop-dead" dates.

- Dependency constraints—These frequently upset the best-laid plans. Events that are dependent on something else happening are always at risk. When the primary event occurs late or not at all, the dependency deviation cascades through the plan.

- Duration constraints—Material lead times are a typical example of this constraint. The team may have to adjust its plan if the material cannot be on-site at the desired time.

- Financial constraints—Once spending has been authorized in the project charter, the project has a budget. Unexpected contingencies may cause serious constraint issues.

Assumptions

Assumptions might just as well be called expectations. They can also be considered constraints. If assumptions are not taken into consideration at the beginning of a project, the team may be led into a situation of false expectations with the corresponding failure to execute.

Using a Top-Down Approach

One of the most potent tools in scope definition and control is the WBS. The project manager should make every effort to break the workload down into atomic tasks and then get sign-off on the plan. When this level of breakdown exists, it is much more difficult for an internal or external customer to slip changes in.

Product Description

Products are *deliverable* items, also known as deliverables. As with the WBS, the more complete the definition of the deliverable, the easier it is to control the scope.

Scope Management Plan

The team may choose to create a formal scope management plan that details *how* the scope is managed, how change is introduced, and the cost of change. So-called scope creep can lead to the downfall of a project—people keep adding new ideas, fleeting enthusiasms, demands, and features until a focused project becomes a diffuse mess. Planning for scope control from the very beginning of a project can help retain the focus that led to the approval of the project in the first place.

Here are some scope questions to ask at the start of and during a project:

1. *Why* are we defining the scope this way?
2. Why are we changing the scope?
3. What are the benefits of this product?
4. Is the product missing significant features?
5. Have we defined the product with QFD?
6. Where is the value in the project/product?
7. Are there any other valid solutions?
8. Have we used as much detail as we can now?
9. What does the customer want?
10. What does the customer need?
11. Do we have sign-off on this product description?
12. Do we have sign-off on these deliverable items?
13. Do we know how we can accommodate change?
14. How do we justify change?

15. Have we designed the product taking potential recall issues into consideration?

16. Even though we have specified the scope of the program in detail, do we have the flexibility to expand the scope if authorized by executive authority?

HOW TO USE A PARETO CHART

What It Is

The basic Pareto chart is an *ordered* histogram, usually of frequency of item, with the highest count leftmost and the lowest count rightmost. Additionally, many Pareto charts will show cumulative values with an overlaid line chart, normally representing the percentage of the total supplied by each given category.

Because the abscissa (x-axis) represents categories, we are looking at a nominal scale. However, because the ordinal (y-axis) supplies frequency information and because we sort the histogram by frequency, we are really looking at an ordinal scale.

The so-called Pareto principle says that 80 percent of failures are caused by 20 percent of the parts, or 80 percent of property is owned by 20 percent of the people, and so on. The point is to discern what is significant and what is not.

How to Construct a Pareto Chart

1. Define the problem of interest.

2. Consider whether you are looking at a time series.

3. Measure the values of interest.

4. Analyze the results into rank order.

5. Improve on the situation by taking action on the significant few items.

6. Repeat for control.

Interpretation

In some cases, the count should be converted into monetary units (for example, dollars) to get an idea of the financial impact of the problem. Furthermore, the Black Belt should examine the categories to ensure that a small but critical category (for example, safety issues) is not ignored.

See Figure IV.1 for a sample Pareto chart. We would certainly want to check on the first three items. Note how the first three or four items have a cumulative value of 72.6 percent and 82.2 percent, respectively. These three to four problems are causing 70 to 80 percent of the problem.

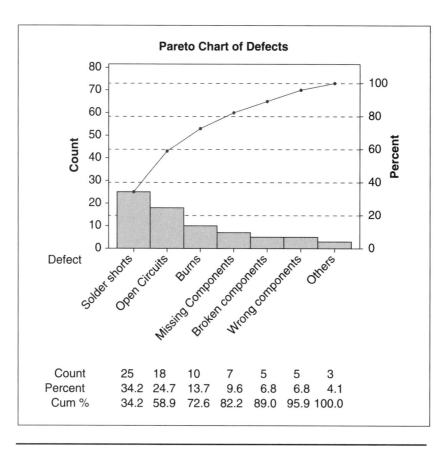

Count	25	18	10	7	5	5	3
Percent	34.2	24.7	13.7	9.6	6.8	6.8	4.1
Cum %	34.2	58.9	72.6	82.2	89.0	95.9	100.0

Figure IV.1   Example of Pareto chart showing count and percentage.

HOW TO BUILD A MACRO MAP

As the name suggests, a macro map (Figure IV.2) is a very high-level representation of an object or a process. In lean manufacturing, the macro map can be used to clarify large-scale handoffs, multiple storage points, and wasted time. The macro map need only be as complex as is necessary to determine the workflow. It is not always an easy job to resolve a process into essential tasks while identifying those tasks that are not essential. In transactional Six Sigma—the Six Sigma methods of interrelationships and workflow—mapping is a powerful tool. If we can create the map *and* simulate the workflow, we are in a position to study the effects of various changes. An example of this technique is creating a system dynamics model with a tool like Vensim by Ventana Systems, or (for Macintosh) Stella or Ithink from ISEE Systems.

The Seven Wastes

The following are the seven wastes of production:

1. Overproduction—piles of finished goods or work in progress (WIP)

2. Transportation—large-distance movement using vehicles

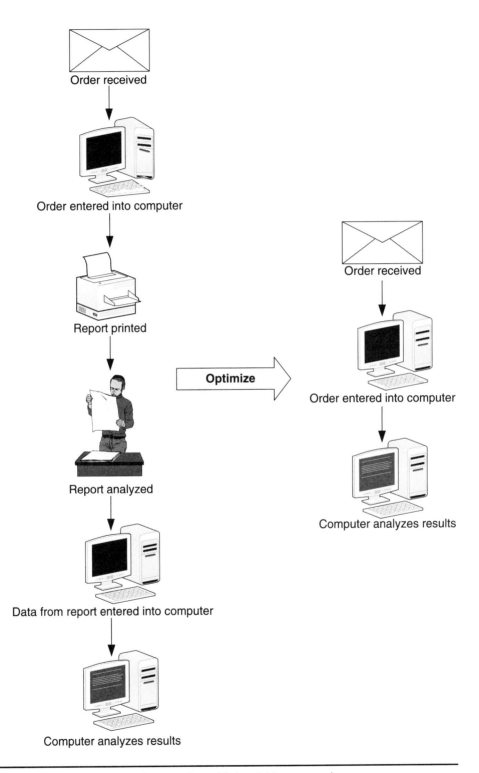

Figure IV.2   Macro map with non-value-added activities removed.

3. Waiting—unsynchronized manufacturing lines

4. Motion—machines not located closely enough

5. Processing—unnecessary processing; even more common in the front office

6. Inventory—heaps of safety stock and "what if" material

7. Defects—scrap and nonconformance

Additionally, we might consider the inappropriate use of people—using the wrong skill sets, eliminating training, abusing and overworking the staff—as "people waste."

Value-added versus Non-value-added

Mapping can help identify value-added tasks versus non-value-added tasks. The work is not trivial and addition of value may not be obvious.

Refer back to Figure IV.2, which shows a very simple macro map. Here are issues seen in the macro map:

- Five handoffs

- Three non-value-added steps (can you find them?)

- Time wasted unknown, but certainly more than the seconds it would take for the computer to analyze the data

FURTHER READING

Womack, James P., and Daniel T. Jones. 2003. *Lean Thinking: Banish Waste and Create Wealth in Your Corporation.* Rev. ed. New York: Free Press.

B. Metrics

PRIMARY METRICS—QUALITY, CYCLE TIME, AND COST

The old joke in software engineering was: "fast, good, cheap—pick any two." The statement can be applied with some justice today.

Measuring Quality

Actually, the key measurement in Six Sigma is the cost of *poor* quality. The Black Belt can gather up the costs of preventive and appraisal activities. To this can be added the cost of internal failure, which may show up directly as scrap or be hidden in the master production schedule as a scrap percentage. External failure typically shows up as return merchandise authorization (warranty) and field failures (warranty) and, in the worst case, as a major lawsuit or recall.

An additional method for measuring cost is the Quality Loss Function developed by Taguchi. This is a quadratic equation (parabola) that shows how not only the enterprise, but also society, loses as the manufactured part deviates from the target specification.

Measuring Cycle Time

In many cases, cycle time is associated with so-called takt time, which is defined as

(available daily production time) / (required daily quantity of output)

However, the enterprise has many cycle times in all locations, including accounting, purchasing, engineering, operations, human resources, and custodial. The reduction of cycle time alone can produce significant improvements in profitability.

An alternative to the cycle time calculation is Little's Law[32], one variant of which can be stated as

cycle time = (work in process inventory)/(throughput),

123

which says we must reduce work in process (WIP), increase throughput, or both if we wish to reduce cycle time. Throughput measures the output of a work center or of a manufacturing line; that is, the concept of cycle time is scalable.

Another frequent measure of cycle time is inventory turns, which divides the throughput by all WIP and finished goods inventory to yield the number of turns per unit time, which is commonly expressed in the form of turns per year.

In *Quick Response Manufacturing*, Rajan Suri points out that more time may be wasted in the front office than in the manufacturing/operations area of the house.[33]

Measuring Cost

Just as one can find hidden quality issues in hidden factories (scrap heaps and rework centers), an enterprise can have significant amounts of hidden cost issues. If the accountants do not understand the true cost of developing and then manufacturing a product, it is extremely difficult to develop a pricing model for proposals that makes any sense. Standard cost accounting models use terms like overhead, direct labor, and indirect labor, often without justifying the source of their numbers. See Table IV.1 for a look at how monies are normally represented in the enterprise using a balance sheet. Other measures of cost might include:

- The scrap rate

- Value-added to non-value-added ratio

- The rework rate

- Return merchandise authorizations (RMAs)

- Field failure returns and warranty cost

These are all in addition to the normal cash flow and balance sheet type metrics used by accounting and finance departments.

An operating statement, on the other hand, provides detail to the formula:

$$revenues - expenses = net\ income$$

CONSEQUENTIAL METRICS

Consequential metrics are all founded on primary metrics.

Enterprise Metrics

At the enterprise level, the metrics are as large-scale as the enterprise itself. Clearly, the balance sheet and the operating statement provide fundamental values regarding the health of the business. Shareholders usually want to know about:

- Profit versus loss

- Return on investment

- Return on assets
- Debt-to-equity ratio
- Major stock movement

Operational Metrics

These can be day-to-day metrics related to the within-enterprise measurement of activities. These can be measures like:

- Schedule attainment
- Percentages of scrap and rework
- Inventory shortages and negative inventory
- Obsolete inventory
- Parts for return to vendor
- Pilfering rate
- Spoilage rate if raw material and/or finished goods are non-durable

. . . and many others.

Table IV.1   Standard format for a simple balance sheet.

Assets			Liabilities		
Current			**Current**		
Cash	80,000		Accts. payable	10,000	
Inventory	20,000		Note payable	2000	
Prepaid ins.	8000		Total current		12,000
Total current		**108,000**			
Plant			Long-Term		
Vehicles	70,000		Mortgage	88,000	
Machines	95,000		Total long-term		88,000
Total Plant		165,000	Capital		
			Owner equity	173,000	
	Total	273,000		Total	273,000

Assets = Equities
Assets = Liabilities + capital
Assets = Creditors' equity + Owners' equity

The following lists outline some performance metrics.

Inventory-Related Metrics

- Inventory on hand
- Inventory in transit
- Obsolete inventory
- Supplier on-time order shipping percentage
- Consigned inventory/ATP (available to promise)

Transportation-Based Metrics

- On-time delivery
- On-time pickup
- Claims ratio
- Rating and billing accuracy percentage

Warehousing Metrics

- Orders processed
- Order accuracy
- On-time receiving
- On-time departure
- Inventory accuracy
- Cycle counts
- Quantity picked/handled per man-hour
- Rush shipments handled

Employee or Personal Metrics

At the employee level, the metrics are indeed personal. From the human resources point of view, we look at such items as:

- Turnover
- Employee complaint levels
- Harassment issues
- Accident rates

FURTHER READING

Hopp, Wallace J., and Mark L. Spearman. 2000. *Factory Physics: Foundations of Manufacturing Management*. 2nd ed. New York: McGraw-Hill.

Maskell, Brian H. 1991. *Performance Measurement for World Class Manufacturing: A Model for American Companies*. New York: Productivity Press.

Section IV.B

C. Problem Statement

PROBLEM DECLARATION

Define the Problem

The quickest place to start is to use Kipling's six friends: who, what, when, where, why, and how:[34]

- Around whom does the problem occur? (This is not for purposes of blame—sometimes a training issue is the cause.)

- What occurs when the problem happens?

- When does the problem occur? What happens before the problem? What happens after the problem? Does the system recover from the problem?

- Where does the problem occur? Are we having trouble with a specific subsystem located in the same spot or with the entire system? In other words, how localized is the problem? How general is it?

- Why does the problem occur? See Figure IV.3 for more on this. The diagram is a graphical way to structure the 5 Whys.[35]

- How does the problem occur? (Describe the apparent steps as explicitly as possible.) Does there seem to be a precipitating event?

- How and why is this problem significant? This question is important if management support will be necessary in order to resolve the issue or release resources (money, people, equipment) in order to solve it.

All of the preceding considerations should be included in a situation statement that describes the problem completely.

Other Considerations

Kepner and Tregoe pointed out that it is frequently just as important to know the "is not" as it is to know the "is."[36] Sometimes, knowing where something doesn't happen gives us a real clue as to the cause of the event.

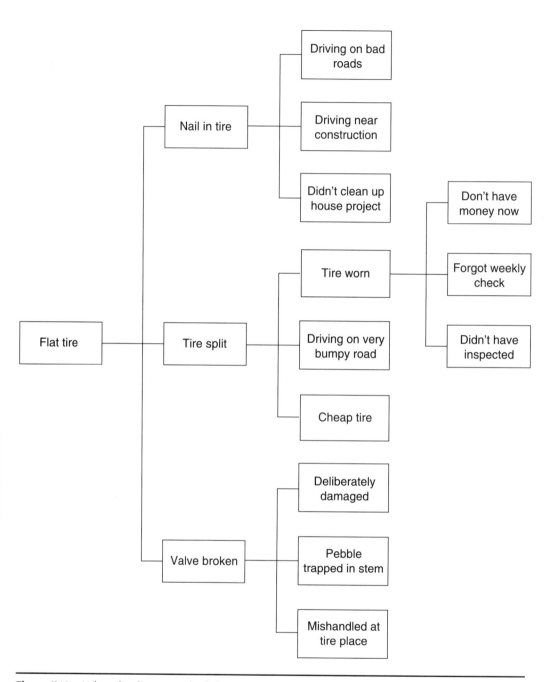

Figure IV.3 Why-why diagram to look for a root cause.

The Black Belt analyzing a problem should know as much as possible about the inputs and outputs of the system and the alleged transform between the inputs and outputs. Keep in mind that a problem is always misbehavior that can be observed. Causes, on the other hand, are frequently unobservable and must be inferred from circumstances.

HOW TO BASELINE

Baselining is a significant concept in Black Belt projects. The concept is so important that it is encapsulated in the "M" of DMAIC ("measure").

Baselining accomplishes several objectives:

- We understand the current level of performance of the item of study.

- We provide ourselves with data for analysis.

- We may learn enough to provide us with clues for the improve ("I") phase of the project.

If we have performed the Define phase properly, we should already understand the inputs, outputs, and transform portions of the process. In essence, we have a preliminary black-box model of the process or product under study. As we proceed through the phases of the project, we should be able to elaborate on this model until we have a more or less complete description. See Figure IV.4 for a capability study of laboratory test durations. It would be difficult to discern improvement if we didn't already know the current behavior of the laboratory. Additionally, one of the questions we might ask ourselves during problem solving is, "what would this behavior be like if the problem were not there?"

Capability studies can be applied to *anything* so long as we know the specification limits and gather data that relate the actual behavior to those limits. The MINITAB six-pack in Figure IV.4 shows a capability study of the approval time required to make a decision about an engineering change request. Note that the distribution is *not* normal—a goodness-of-fit (Anderson-Darling) test for distribution type suggests that this distribution is exponential. The exponential distribution makes some sense in this case because we might anticipate that approval times have increased frequency early in the process with some items lingering out into the "tail."

How does this capability study provide us with any grist for the problem-solving mill? It supplies us with the *current* state of the system. If the throughput of this department has become a problem, we have a baseline against which to measure improvement. Furthermore, we can use the control chart concept (the I chart and the moving range chart in Figure IV.4) to look for assignable causes when we see unusual deviations from statistically controlled behavior (the behavior that lies between the UCL and LCL lines).

The Black Belt should not forget any historical data that may be available, especially if it is of high quality. If we are dealing with a product, it is sometimes extremely difficult to extract quality historical data from a customer. They may already be unhappy and feel reluctant to expose their warranty management system. If we are dealing with an internal process, the Black Belt can use existing control charts, capability analyses, Gage R&R studies, and process control plans (for automotive processes).

Section IV.C

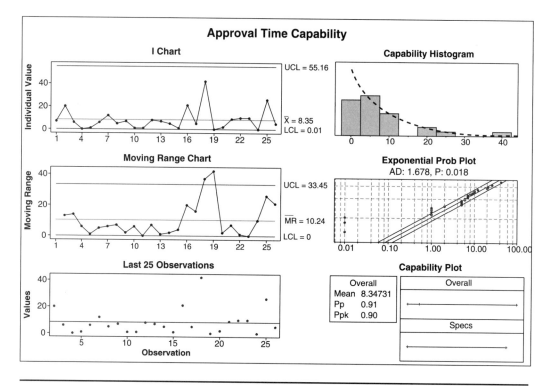

Figure IV.4   Baseline capability study for approval of engineering change requests.

Other Considerations

Black Belts can strengthen their case by including baseline financial information, such as:

- Cost of poor quality
- Quality loss function
- Warranty expenses
- Scrap
- Time wasted
- Use of air freight due to delayed shipping
- Carrying cost in the warehouse
- Stockouts
- Expedite charges

IMPROVEMENT GOALS

ISO 9000 and derivative standards require evidence of continuous improvement without discussing what continuous improvement really means. In Six Sigma, this kind of nebulous statement is unsatisfactory. Six Sigma techniques are all data driven. We need to know how to set goals.

Preliminaries

If we have done our preliminary legwork we should already have a project charter (Define) to guide us through the project. That means we have some kind of mission statement (basic purpose), a vision statement (where we are going with this project), and probably a statement about goals. If the goals have not been set, they can be derived from well written mission statements and vision statements.

Setting Goals

The acronym frequently used for goal-setting is "SMART":

S   Specific

M   Measurable (hey, Six Sigma!)

A   Attainable (4–6 months)

R   Relevant or realistic (relevant by being tied to business goals)

T   Time line (a real plan)

While the acronym may seem simplistic, it helps to focus on what goals have to be in order to be useful. Nebulous phrases like ". . . improve the divisional quality" don't give us enough information as to *how* we can succeed.

Table IV.2 shows a technique for creating mission and vision statements. While this method will not win prizes in literature, it does the following nicely:

- Identifies the constituencies or stakeholders.

- Defines what we are doing right now to serve these constituencies.

- Clarifies what we can do in the future to improve our relations with these constituencies.

Compare this idea with typical mission statements that are full of abstract terms like "quality" and "best." A good set of mission and vision statements should allow for the immediate derivation of a set of goals that represent the gap between the mission and vision statements.

Section IV.C

Table IV.2   A tool to aid in the development of meaningful mission and vision statements.

Whom do we serve?	How do we serve them?	How do we serve them better?
Constituency 1	Run tests Report results	Run tests more quickly Report results with recommendations
Constituency 2	Make warranty recommendations	Make warranty recommendations with financial information
Constituency 3	Perform RMA analysis Report results	Perform analysis more quickly Report results with recommendations
Constituency 4	Perform field failure analysis Report results	Perform analysis more quickly Report results with recommendations

The first column defines those we serve, our constituencies. A mission statement that does not define the stakeholders tends to be too generic to have much meaning. A good mission statement is a collection of statements that employees and customers can use to assess the position of the enterprise.

The second column in Table IV.2 can be modified into sentences together with the constituencies list to provide a straightforward *mission* statement. The third column can be modified into sentences together with the constituencies list to provide a straight-forward *vision* statement.

FURTHER READING

Bothe, Davis. 2002. *Reducing Process Variation: Using the DOTSTAR Problem-Solving Strategy.* Vols. 1 and 2. Cedarburg, WI: Landmark Publishing Company.

Section V

Six Sigma Improvement Methodology and Tools—*Measure* (30 Questions)

Contents

A. Process Analysis and Documentation

1. TOOLS

The Order of Documentation

Policies ::: Procedures :: Work instructions : Records

This is the typical setup for an ISO 9000-style quality management system.

Policies are broad guidance statements. Policies are more like general rules when they are well written. A policy statement might read something like, "under no circumstances will known nonconforming product be shipped to a customer."

Procedures are high-level sequences of events. Procedures provide an execution format for the rules stated in the policies. We should be able to derive every procedure in our system from the policy document and policy statement. A procedure is somewhat like a statement of work in that it tells the reader what must be done, defines the resources, and perhaps even specifies time limits, but it typically does not provide the detailed information necessary to actually execute the task. These are called work instructions.

Work instructions are low-level detailed sequences of events; they may resemble a statement of work in condensed form. One powerful format uses the following headings in a table:
- Actor or doer
- Action
- Comment or information

This format makes for very concise collections of intelligible instructions.

Records provide evidence that activities actually occurred. Records usually exist as forms or checklists.

An organization, especially under ISO 9000:2000, may choose to develop process maps, which can be IDEF0 diagrams, flowcharts, data flow diagrams, or anything else that makes sense. The new *ISO/TS 16949 Implementation Guide* shows numerous examples of process diagrams. A control plan can be a process diagram (like a flowchart) with control points—that is, inspection or check points in the process. In the automotive world, a process control plan is a special—and very large—table that lists a variety of information (key characteristics, stage, contingencies, and so on) about that particular process. Figure V.1 shows activities listed in the ANSI format, with control points indicated by wide arrows. Alternatively, the practitioner could represent this flow using production symbols as defined by ASME, in which case the control points would be indicated by a diamond or a triangle.

A work instruction will typically consist of the following:

- Author name

- Approval name

- A unique number

- Date this version issued

- Revision value for this version

- Purpose of work

- Scope of work (where applicable)

- The steps to accomplish the task (may be called "Procedure" or "List of Instructions")

2. PROCESS INPUTS AND OUTPUTS

SIPOC Diagrams

The most common diagram used to represent processes, inputs, and outputs is the SIPOC diagram (Figure V.2)—that is, Supplier-Input-Process-Output-Customer. The example shown in Figure V.2 details the printed circuit board layout process. Of course, the method can be generalized to any kind of process, including those in the service industry. Figure V.2 shows one method using the SmartDraw format that concisely encapsulates the significant characteristics of the process and associated data.

Alternatively, these relationships can be documented through a variety of diagrams, including Ishikawa (cause and effect), data flow diagrams, swim lane charts, relational matrices, and so on. Many of these were covered in Section III.E.

Let us continue with our description of the SIPOC diagram. The IPO part of the diagram is a descendant of a more than 30-year-old technique used by IBM to document algorithms, especially for the COBOL language.

Figure V.3 shows a generic IPO diagram. How can such a simplistic diagram be important? IPO diagrams are useful when going through the thought process leading up to, for example, a designed experiment. The inputs can be potentially significant factors and the outputs are the responses measured during the experiment. Alternate dia-

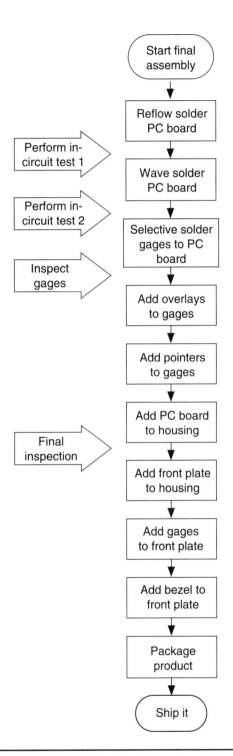

Figure V.1   Flowchart of an instrumentation manufacturing
process with control points.

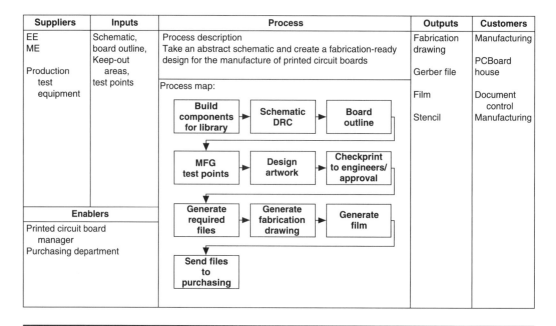

Suppliers	Inputs	Process	Outputs	Customers
EE ME Production test equipment	Schematic, board outline, Keep-out areas, test points	**Process description** Take an abstract schematic and create a fabrication-ready design for the manufacture of printed circuit boards	Fabrication drawing Gerber file Film Stencil	Manufacturing PCBoard house Document control Manufacturing

Figure V.2   Detailed SIPOC diagram.

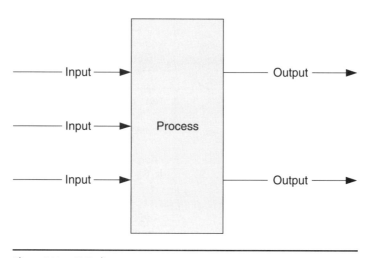

Figure V.3   IPO diagram.

grams are the P-diagram and the noise diagram. The simplicity of the IPO diagram, however, makes it extremely easy to teach to tyro Black Belts.

Comments on Diagrams

Some diagrams—for example, the SIPOC diagram—are more or less specific to the Six Sigma community. However, these diagrams are only standard in the sense that most Six Sigma practitioners understand them. Understanding is the point of diagramming.

As long as team members understand the meaning and purpose of a given diagram, any technique that aids comprehension should be used. Some examples, to name a few:

- Data flow diagrams
- State diagrams
- ITU Z.120 message sequence charts (MSCs)
- ITU Z.100 system definition language (SDL) charts
- Universal Modeling Language (UML) diagrams
- Any member of the IDEF family of flow diagrams
- The ANSI flow chart standard
- System dynamics simulation diagrams
- Hierarchical tree diagrams

FURTHER READING

Jacka, Mike J., and Paulette J. Keller. 2002. *Business Process Mapping: Improving Customer Satisfaction.* New York: John Wiley & Sons.

B. Probability and Statistics

1. DRAWING VALID STATISTICAL CONCLUSIONS

In statistics, we describe two kinds of data groups: the population and the sample.

The Population

A population is the totality of a group. In set theory, we consider every member of the universe of discourse to be the population. An example of a *finite* population is the hairs on your head. An example of an *infinite* population is the set of all coin tosses.

A collection of information about a population is called *descriptive statistics.* A single piece of information about a population is called a *parameter*.

The Sample

A sample is a proper subset of a population. A set, $Sample_2$, is a proper subset of another set, $Population_1$, if every element in $Sample_2$ is in $Population_1$ and $Population_1$ has some elements that are not in $Sample_2$.

If a sample is representative of a population, it is *homoscedastic* (variances are homogeneous).

If a sample is not representative of a population (that is, the variance is not homogeneous), it is *heteroscedastic*.

A test or a set of tests about a sample or a population is called *inferential statistics.* The results of the tests are used for drawing inferences about the data.

A single piece of information about a sample is called a *statistic*.

Kinds of Data

Discrete data represent a set of integers or whole values. The population of your toes is an example of discrete data. In sampling theory, discrete data are often referred to as *attribute* data.

Sometimes we have hybrid information, where discrete data vary across a continuum. We might call this by an oxymoronic name, discrete continuous data. An example

143

would be a dial with discrete detent values or an automobile transmission with six forward gears. It would be difficult to classify these data as attribute data.

Continuous data represent a set of real values; they are continuous in the mathematical sense of being non-denumerable and can be represented on a computer by a floating point number. In sampling theory, continuous data are often referred to as *variable* data.

See Equation V.1 for the basic symbols of statistics with an explanation.

$$Population\ mean = \mu = \frac{\sum_{j=1}^{N} X_j}{N}$$

$$Sample\ mean = \overline{X} = \frac{\sum_{j=1}^{n} x_j}{n}$$

$$Population\ variance = \sigma^2 = \frac{\sum_{j=1}^{N} \left(X_j - \mu\right)^2}{N} \tag{V.1}$$

$$Population\ standard\ deviation = \sqrt{\sigma^2}$$

$$Sample\ variance = s^2 = \frac{\sum_{j=1}^{n} \left(x_j - \overline{X}\right)^2}{n-1}$$

$$Sample\ standard\ deviation = \sqrt{s^2}$$

When discussing populations, we generally use Greek letters; when discussing samples, we generally use Latin letters. The capital "N" refers to the size of the population, the lowercase "n" refers to the size of the sample. The standard deviation is the square root of the variance, which puts the standard deviation in the same units as the mean (it is difficult to discuss the meaning of squared units in the case of the variance). When doing statistical calculations that require a value like the variance, always use the variance and *not* the standard deviation. The variance is a derivable value, while the standard deviation is a convenient value for human understanding.

2. CENTRAL LIMIT THEOREM AND SAMPLING DISTRIBUTION OF THE MEAN

Central Limit Theorem

The distribution of a set of averages tends to be normal, even when the distribution from which the average is computed is decidedly non-normal.

The distribution of an average will tend to be normal as the sample size increases, regardless of the distribution from which the average is taken, *except* when the moments (mean, variance, skewness, kurtosis) of the parent distribution are nonexistent. All practical/useful distributions in statistics have defined moments, thereby not invalidating the central limit theorem.

Because of this counterintuitive theorem (whose proof is non-trivial!), we are able to use the rather convenient normal distribution for a great deal of sampling theory.

Sampling Distribution of the Mean

Let's say we take random samples from a population. We calculate the mean. The mean is random because it comes from a random sample. From the central limit theorem we know the distribution of the sample will tend to normality. This distribution is called the *sampling distribution of the mean*. Now we know why the assumption of normality is generally reasonable when we deal with random means from samples chosen randomly from a population.

Standard Deviation of the Sampling Distribution

The more common name for this value is the standard error. The standard error is typically expressed as the standard deviation divided by the square root of the sample size (remember that while sampling, we are usually in the world of the t distribution and its rules).

Confidence Intervals

We are dealing with a random sample. The sample has a mean that is also random. We can estimate, based on the standard deviation (square root of the variance), that a given value will lie within a region. Because the standard deviation can be expressed in terms of percentage probability, we now have a way of stating our confidence that our value lies within this interval, which is the mean plus or minus the standard deviation (that is, the standard error).

A very common use of sampling theory lies the industrial application of control charts, where samples of a process are taken and sample statistics applied.

Equation V.2 shows the mathematical appearance of some of these ideas.

Here is the standard deviation of the sampling distribution of the mean:

$$\sigma_{\bar{x}} = \frac{\sigma}{\sqrt{n}}, \qquad (V.2)$$

where n is the sample size.

Here is the expression for a confidence interval:

$$\overline{X} \pm Z_{\alpha/2} \frac{\sigma}{\sqrt{n}}$$

Remember that Z tells us we are using standard normal form, where

$$Z = \frac{x - \mu}{\sigma},$$

Section V.B.2

which allows us to speak of the normal distribution in units of standard deviation. Most tables use this format and the units are convenient.

3. BASIC PROBABILITY CONCEPTS

Independence

Any event is independent when it is immune to influence from any other event. Mathematically, we do not have a contingent probability; in short, the event exists as if it is the only event. A typical example is a coin toss. Even though we toss the same coin over and over again, whether it is heads or tails at any given time is completely independent of any value it may have been previously.

Mutually Exclusive

If event A and event B cannot occur simultaneously, then these events are mutually exclusive. The mutually exclusive rule is a variant of the logical statement that we cannot say "A and not-A" without contradiction. If A occurs now, then B cannot occur now—it can occur earlier or later, but not now.

Complementary Probability

If the value "1" indicates certainty (a probability of 100 percent) and we are dealing with P(A), then the complement of P(A) is 1 – P(A). In many probability and statistics books, the complement of the probability p is represented as q. This usage is particularly evident in the formula for binomial probability, where we have the probability of an event occurring times the probability of the event *not* occurring times the number of combinations.

Joint Concurrence of Events

See Equation V.3 and Figure V.4 for these rules. Clearly, a situation involving joint concurrence is a situation in which the idea of mutual exclusion does not apply. Joint probabilities can become complicated very quickly. One of the most famous versions of joint probability is known as Bayes's Theorem, where a posterior probability is contingent upon a prior probability—the distribution of the data shifts as event occur. Bayes's Theorem is not typically part of the body of knowledge of a Black Belt, but it can have important implications in reliability engineering.

We study the probability of event A and event B:

$$0 \leq P(A) \leq 1 \qquad \text{(V.3)}$$

For the complement, we have

$$P(A)^C = 1 - P(A)$$

When B is a proper subset of A (they are not equal), then

$$\text{If } B \subset A, \text{then } P(B) \leq P(A)$$

If the probabilities of A *or* B are independent, then

$$P(A \operatorname{or} B) = P(A \cup B) = P(A) + P(B) - P(A \cap B)$$

When looking at the logic here, you add the odds and subtract the evens! $P(A)$ has one item (odd) and $P(AB)$ has two items (even). If the probabilities of *A and B* are independent, then

$$P(A \operatorname{and} B) = P(A \cap B) = P(A)P(B)$$

Observe the use of "and" instead of "or"! If the probabilities of *A or B* are mutually exclusive, then

$$P(A \cup B) = P(A) + P(B)$$

A conditional probability—that is, the probability of B given that A has occurred—is

$$P(B \mid A) = \frac{P(AB)}{P(A)}$$

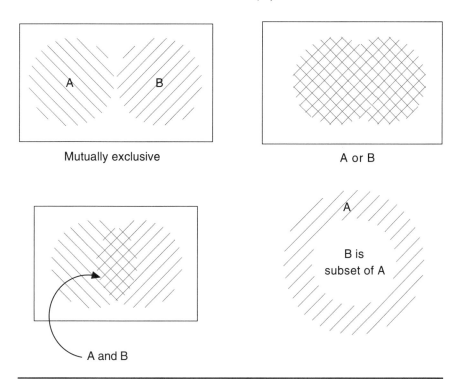

Figure V.4   Venn diagrams representing probability logic.

FURTHER READING

Stamatis, D. H. 2001. *Six Sigma and Beyond: Statistics and Probability.* Vol. 3. Boca Raton, FL: St. Lucie Press.

C. Collecting and Summarizing Data

1. TYPES OF DATA

Continuous Data (Variables)

Continuous data are data that vary without discontinuity across an interval. The values of continuous data are typically represented by floating point numbers. The interval can be assumed to be infinitely divisible. In electronics, analog data are always continuous data; digital data may *represent* continuous data.

Continuous data require instruments capable of measuring the data in the first place. The more sensitive the instrument, the greater the illusion of continuity. Continuous data are desirable because the sample sizes that are required in order to learn anything about the population are much smaller than they are with other kinds of data.

Discrete Data (Attributes)

Discrete data are composed of individual values, typically represented by integers over an interval. Typical discrete data situations are go/no-go, up/down, in/out, 0/1, true/false, and rare/medium/well done/burnt.

Discrete data are normally much easier than continuous data to measure. In binary situations like true/false, you need only make a decision. Although discrete data are typically easier to measure, they most often require *much* larger samples to make any kind of sensible statement about the population.

Figure V.5 shows graphs of the two kinds of data. The first chart has discrete data. It might be argued that money is continuous, but it does have a smallest increment of one penny in the United States. The second chart represents a measured continuous value of water flow.

Converting Attribute Data to Variable Data

Under certain conditions, we may approximate the normal distribution, shown in Equation (V.4) or, alternatively, approximate the discrete distribution. In each case, the formula resembles the standard "Z" formula for calculating the Z value for the standard

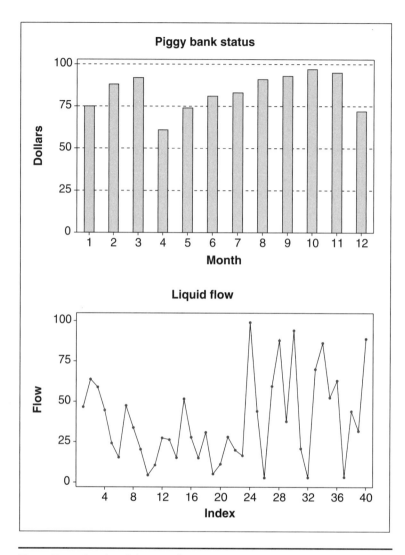

Figure V.5 Graphs of discrete data versus continuous data.

normal distribution: a value minus the mean, all divided by the standard deviation. For the binomial case,

$$Z = \frac{X - \mu}{\sigma} \approx \frac{X - Np}{\sqrt{Npq}},$$

(V.4)

where N is very large and neither p nor q is very close to zero. The higher the sample size, the better. The closer the probability to 0.5, the better. The closer the probability to 0.5, the smaller the sample size it takes to approximate normality. For the Poisson case,

$$Z = \frac{X - \mu}{\sigma} \approx \frac{X - \lambda}{\sqrt{\lambda}}$$

by the standard deviation.

2. MEASUREMENT SCALES

The acronym for the data scales is NOIR, which is the French word for "black."

Nominal

A nominal scale has no zero value and no numerical values whatsoever. The only thing that can be said of a nominal scale mathematically is that a value is either equal or not equal. An example of a nominal scale would be flavors of ice cream at Baskin-Robbins. Nominal scales are useful in qualitative analyses. What is truly amazing about this kind of data is that we can analyze it statistically using statistical tests that compare observed counts to expected counts (counted values).

Ordinal

The ordinal scale refers to rankings and ratings. Values are not necessarily a specific unit apart from each other, but they are ranked in order. Ordinal values are most commonly represented as counts.

You can determine whether two results are equal or whether one result is greater than the other (otherwise the scale would make no sense). In some cases, a median may be calculated and non-parametric statistics used to describe the values on the scale. An example of an ordinal scale is the Pareto chart so often used in quality analyses.

Interval

An interval has no true zero, no "absolute" zero; however, the basic units are equidistant from each other—unlike the ordinal, which has no such requirement—and simple math can be performed using these values.

A typical interval scale is Fahrenheit or Celsius degrees because absolute zero is effectively undefined on these scales, certainly not as zero.

Ratio

With the ratio scale, 40 means twice as much as 20, which is *not* the case with the interval scale. Ratio scales have an absolute zero value, which is why $40/20 = 2/1$; hence the word "ratio."

As we move from nominal to ratio scales, the number of statistical tests available increases significantly. Statistics is a quantitative method, so as the scale becomes more quantitative, the ability to use quantitative tools correspondingly increases.

Table V.1 summarizes the measurement scale information.

Table V.1   Some features of the various data types.

Scale	Math operations	Examples	Allowed transformations	Statistics calculations
Nominal	= [1]	Discrete colors, names of groups under study, sexes, political parties	1 to 1	Frequency, proportions, mode, Chi-square, binomial
Ordinal	= [1] < >	Letter grades, any questionnaire or test system that uses scales	Order-preserving	Median and non-parametric hypothesis tests
Interval	= [1] < > + − x /	Distance from reference point	Linear	Mean, standard deviation and most parametric tests
Ratio	= [1] < > + − x / $x/y = a/b$	Kelvin and Rankine scales of temperature, speedometer	Multiplication by constant	All of the above plus geometric mean and coefficient of variation

3. METHODS FOR COLLECTING DATA

Check Sheets

A check sheet is a simple tally sheet. Hash marks may be used to represent the count. The counts of types can be rearranged later. Check sheets are one of the seven quality tools. Table V.2 shows how simple a check sheet can be. Note that in most cases a check sheet is a very good example of nominal data—we have counts for each category of interest. This data can be readily analyzed using chi-squared methods.

Table V.2   A simple check sheet.

	Paper on floor?	Tools put up?	Antennae hanging up?	Batteries covered?	Chemicals stowed?
8 a.m.	X	X	X	X	X
10 a.m.			X		
12 p.m.		X	X	X	X
2 p.m.	X		X	X	X
4 p.m.	X		X	X	X
Total	3/5	2/5	5/5	4/5	4/5

Coding Data

Data can be coded as a means of providing a short form for classification. Coding can make data entry more succinct and computerized analysis much simpler. A simple way to code data is to simply record the variation from a historical mean. Coding has mathematical advantages when dealing with linear algebra, and the examination of the variation is just as valid as it is with raw data. It is common for the tools used in DOE to code the data for actual calculation. The user normally has the option of reviewing the calculations either coded or uncoded. We have used the variation from the historical mean to create an individual/moving-range control chart for equipment downtime data (after proving the data was normal!). Table V.3 shows an example of using deviation from the mean as the method for coding.

The example represents hours of machine downtime. In this particular case, we probably won't see much benefit from coding to the average. With some Shewhart-style control charts, using coding to some value can make the charts easier to maintain.

Another common use for coding occurs in the creation of arrays of data for DOE. Usually the data will be coded either –1 to 0 to 1 or from 0 to 1 instead of using the original data values. The coding simplifies and improves the calculation of results for analysis of variance and regression methods.

Table V.3   Example of coded control chart data.

Week	Downtime	Coded downtime
1	0.32	–45.57796296
2	13.85	–32.04796296
3	3.35	–42.54796296
4	71.12	25.22203704
5	26.42	–19.47796296
6	35.15	–10.74796296
7	14.12	–31.77796296
8	40.94	–4.957962963
9	20.6	–25.29796296
10	38.14	–7.757962963
...	...	...
50	41.31	–4.587962963
51	22.31	–23.58796296
52	16.27	–29.62796296
53	38.06	–7.837962963
54	24.53	–21.36796296
Total downtime	2478.49	
Mean	45.89796296	

Automatic Gaging

Automatic gaging occurs when we let a machine—effectively a robot—do the gaging work for us. The issue here is whether the machine is capable or not. The capability of the machine needs to be determined by a machine capability study on some preplanned schedule. Gage repeatability and reproducibility will be within-sample and sample-to-sample, so we could say that we have done Gage R&R on the machine. A typical example of a machine like this is a selective solder machine. Automatic gaging should be tested occasionally to verify that the machine gages properly.

4. TECHNIQUES FOR ASSURING DATA ACCURACY AND INTEGRITY

Random Sampling

Random sampling occurs when a proper subset of a given data population is selected in such a way that any given data item has as much a chance of being selected as any other data item. Most random sampling presupposes that the data is randomly distributed and that any errors are independent of any other errors.

It is essential that the Black Belt understand the presuppositions; otherwise, serious errors can be introduced into the data. Some hints follow:

- We have seen engineering change data that showed an underlying exponential distribution.

- Warranty returns should be fitted to a Weibull distribution first.

- The population should be homoscedastic.

- We are usually safe in assuming some kind of normality thanks to the idea of the central limit theorem, which tends to assume a normal distribution regardless of the underlying distribution.

Stratified Sampling

When performing stratified random sampling, we divide our universe of discourse (our population) into divisions and sample randomly within each division. The concept can be as trivial as taking random samples from each file cabinet in an office.

Sample Homogeneity

Sample homogeneity is important because without it, we have great difficulty saying much about the population. We must first assume that the population is homoscedastic—that variances through the population are themselves homogeneous. We can then assume that rational subsamples of the population will also show some level of homoscedasticity.

When heteroscedasticity occurs, investigators can draw dramatically incorrect conclusions. This was the case some years ago when investigators showed that people living near high power lines had higher rates of cancer. It turned out that the particular sample they took *did* have higher rates of cancer, but it was not caused by the high power lines. Nobody proved otherwise until some individuals challenged the study by examining a sample from a population of electrical utility linemen, who are exposed to high power lines as part of their job, and found no correlation between exposure to high power lines and cancer.

The following list briefly covers the types of sampling. More advanced texts cover topics like questionnaires (non-trivial), multi-level modeling, longitudinal studies, and a whole lot more. All of these methods use sampling to save time and money.

Types of Sampling

Attribute-Based

- Single sampling: Take one sample and accept or reject the lot.

- Double sampling: Take a smaller first sample and decide whether to accept the lot or draw another sample.

- Multiple sampling: The same as double sampling, taken to the nth degree.

- Continuous sampling: Sample some numbers of units continuously until a predetermined number of units has been accepted, and switch to an interval sampling plan until a defect is discovered, at which point, switch back to the original sampling technique.

- Dodge-Romig: A special kind of double sampling.

- Skip lot sampling: Similar to continuous sampling, except lots are used instead of individual sample units.

Variables-Based

- Single sampling: Analogous to attribute sampling.

- Mixed sampling: Variable samples and attribute samples.

In general, sampling occurs according to a *sampling plan*. Most sampling plans are in the form of tables, the most common of which are ANSI Z1.4 for attributes and ANSI Z1.9 for variables. Tables exist for Dodge-Romig in their original publication and for continuous sampling in MIL-STD-1235.

5. DESCRIPTIVE STATISTICS

Central Tendency

Central tendency is a characteristic of samples such that they tend toward the average (mean) value regardless of the distribution. Most parametric statistics rely on this characteristic in order to make calculations. Measures of central tendency are the following:

- The mean: the sum of all values in the population or distribution divided by the count (number) of values.

- The median: the midmost individual value in a set of values in a sample or population. If the midmost value is actually two values (that is, if we have an even-numbered set of values), then the average of the two is taken to be the median.

- The mode: the most frequent value in the set of values. In some cases, data sets have two peaks of frequency, called bimodal distributions. Bimodal distributions typically suggest that the data has been collected from two distinct distributions (be aware of this when problem-solving).

Dispersion

Dispersion is a measure of the spread around the mean of a sample or a population—that is, the *lack* of centrality. Normal values for dispersion are expressed as variance and the square root of the variance, which is the standard deviation. The standard deviation is convenient because the root returns the variance value back to the same units as the mean.

Frequency Distributions

All distributions with enough samples demonstrate some difference among the frequencies of the constituent values. Distributions the Black Belt *must* know about are the following:

- Normal distribution

- Standard normal (Z) distribution

- T distribution

- Chi-square distribution

- F distribution

- Binomial distribution

- Poisson distribution

- Hypergeometric distribution

All of these are covered elsewhere in this book.

Cumulative Frequency

The cumulative frequency is another way of representing the distribution. Values increase as we go from left to right, very much like the cumulative line on the Pareto diagram. Figure V.6 shows a single sample of data fit against the log of the cumulative frequency of four distributions.

This diagram shows a test for four distributions. The straight line is the cumulative distribution on a log-log scale. The lower the Anderson-Darling number, the better the fit, so this one could be Weibull, lognormal or normal; however, our eyes tell us it is most likely a lognormal distribution with outliers in the early data. If we choose the normal distribution in spite of the Anderson-Darling number, then we should be prepared

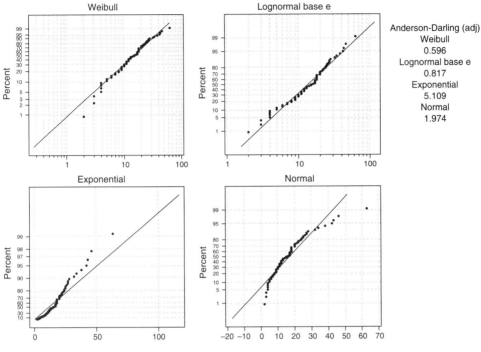

Figure V.6   Choosing a distribution based on the data fit.

to provide a rationale for our choice. We should also be cautious about simply choosing the Weibull distribution—it mimics other distributions. In this particular data set, we know that we are talking about defect arrival rate—typically modeled with a lognormal distribution.

Also note that the Anderson-Darling method is not the only method for checking for goodness of fit. Two other methods are:

- Chi-squared goodness of fit
- Kolmogorov-Smirnov goodness of fit

6. GRAPHICAL METHODS

Stem-and-Leaf Plots

The steam-and-leaf method uses the data itself to create a plot. In most cases, the value to the left of the decimal point is the stem and the values to the right of the decimal point are the leaves.

Section V.C.6

Here is a stem-and-leaf plot for same data in the histogram in Figure V.7:

Count = 30, leaf unit = 0.10 (in this case, all values are integers, so leaves are 0.0).

The first column is cumulative until the presumed median value.

3	20	000	
5	21	00	(Note: We have two "21.0" values—"5" is the cumulative number of values)
7	22	00	
9	23	00	
11	24	00	
15	25	0000	
15	26	00	
13	27	00000	(Note: the median lies here)
8	28	0	
7	29	00000	(Note: We have five "29.0" values—"7" is the cumulative starting at the high end)
2	30	00	

Box-and-Whisker Plots

The box-and-whisker plot shows the maximum and minimum values at the end of the whiskers (refer back to Figure V.7). The box contains all the data between the twenty-fifth percentile and the seventy-fifth percentile. The whiskers represent the rest of the distribution. The horizontal line in the box is usually the median or middle value of the data, although some software allows the user to define this to be the mean. The plot allows the user to visually ascertain the general appearance of the data as well as determine the symmetry.

Run Charts

A run chart shows the data over time; in fact, time series are nearly always represented as run charts. One special kind of run chart is the control chart. Additionally, run chart data can be used for some non-parametric tests for randomness.

Scatter Diagrams

Scatter diagrams simply show the points of data unconnected by lines. In the example in Figure V.7, the data is extremely random.

Scatter plots can give a quick overview of the disposition of the data. Frequently, a scatter plot will reveal patterns in the form of clumps of data. Special kinds of scatter plots will show specific symbols for certain kinds of conditions—for example, demographically interesting phenomena like deaths from certain disease conditions.

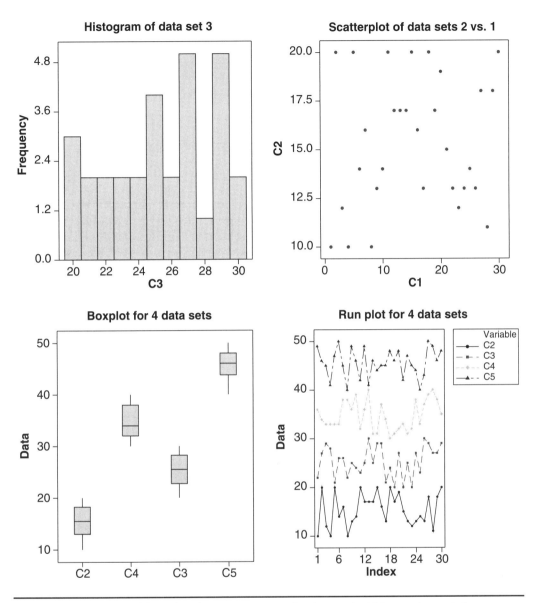

Figure V.7   Four types of data plots (histogram, scatterplot, box-and-whisker, and run plot).

Weibull Plots

A Weibull plot is a plot of the data against the Weibull distribution. Weibull plots are very common in reliability analyses. Typically we plot the values against the cumulative density function on a log scale because it is very easy to fit and to analyze the error. Additionally, the shape factor beta tells us a great deal about the type of failure: <1 = relatively random failure; >1 = increasing wear-out. In reliability, one of the worst distributions is the normal distribution, because this distribution normally reflects a very rapid wear-out scenario.

Note that the Weibull plot can be used to analyze any case where we wish to study some kind of event against a probability that the event has occurred. That is why the Weibull plot also sees use in analyses of maintenance, hospital incidents, accidents, heart attacks, and specific failure modes.

Normal Plots

A Normal plot is a plot of the data against the normal distribution. Normal plots are very common in all analyses. Typically we plot the values against the cumulative density function on a log scale because it is very easy to fit and to analyze the error. Unless we are looking at the means of samples, it is important to prove the normality of the data before assuming this distribution. With the means of samples, of course, the central limit theorem tells us the distribution should be normal regardless of the underlying distribution (another statistical miracle!).

In the particular case of Shewhart control charts, we should always analyze the underlying distribution before using the chart, except in the case where we are looking at the means of samples. Some Shewhart charts (n and np) assume a binomials distribution while others (c and u) assume a Poisson distribution.

Testing for Distribution Type

The plots in Figure V.8 show some results of testing for a distribution. We have used the reliability analysis function of MINITAB to take a look at some ways we can represent failure data. With some statistical software (MINITAB in particular), we can look at as many as 14 distributions simultaneously. It is important that we retain some common sense when looking at distributions—just because our data seems to fit a logistic distribution does not necessarily mean that the logistic distribution is the best explanation. We should understand *why* a particular distribution appears to explain the data.

The PDF is the probability density function; it represents the distribution as a density. The Weibull or lognormal is a fit against a log-log plot; the abscissa represents a value like hours or miles and the ordinal represents the percentage of failure. The hazard function is the failure rate over time (in this case, months) and the survival function represents the fraction remaining over time.

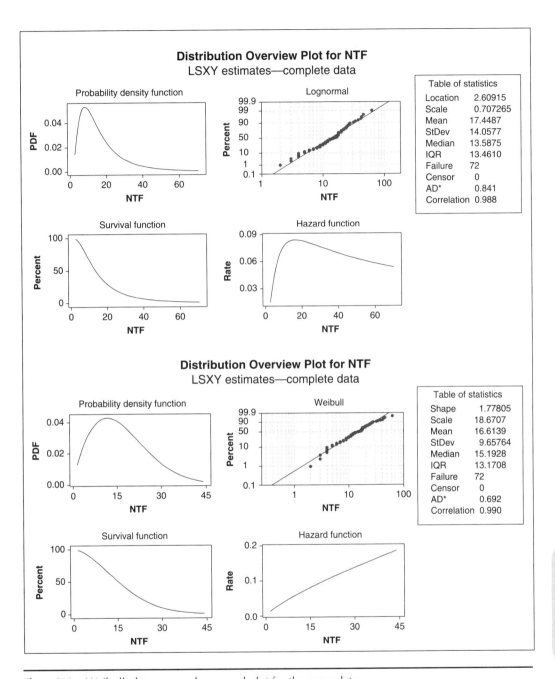

Figure V.8   Weibull plot versus a lognormal plot for the same data.

FURTHER READING

Levine, David M., Patricia P. Ramsey, and Robert K. Smidt. 2001. *Applied Statistics for Engineers and Scientists: Using Microsoft Excel(r) and MINITAB(r).* Upper Saddle River, NJ: Prentice Hall.

D. Properties and Applications of Probability Distributions

1. DISTRIBUTIONS COMMONLY USED BY BLACK BELTS

Binomial

Binomial distribution is used when we are looking at two-way problems, like accept/don't accept.

$$p(A) = \binom{N}{A} p^A (1-p)^{N-A}, \text{ given a sample size of N and A winners. } (1-p) = q.$$

$$\text{mean} = \mu = Np$$

$$\text{variance} = \sigma^2 = Npq$$

$$\text{standard deviation} = \sqrt{Npq}$$

(V.5)

A discrete distribution, the binomial distribution is also known as a Bernoulli process. Note that the binomial distribution can be described as the *combination* of N things taken r at a time × the *probability* of r things occurring × the *complement* of the probability ($q = 1-p$) of the remainder occurring.

Poisson

A discrete distribution, the Poisson is used especially with rates, where lambda (λ) is the rate of failure. The Poisson distribution is frequently used in sampling when the probability of failure is relatively small.

$$p(X) = \frac{\lambda^X e^{-\lambda}}{X!}$$

$$\text{mean} = \mu = \lambda$$

$$\text{variance} = \sigma^2 = \lambda$$

$$\text{standard deviation} = \sigma = \sqrt{\lambda}$$

(V.6)

Hypergeometric

The hypergeometric distribution is different from both the binomial and the Poisson distributions in that it is especially applicable when the population is small enough that sampling alters the probability of an event occurring; for example, when dealing with a deck of cards, the hypergeometric distribution is applicable.

$$p(x, N, n, m) = \frac{\binom{m}{x}\binom{N-m}{n-x}}{\binom{N}{n}},$$

N = population size

n = sample size

m = known quantity of "good"

(V.7)

x = probability of interest

$$\text{mean} = \mu = \frac{nm}{N}$$

$$\text{variance} = \sigma^2 = \left(\frac{nm}{N}\right)\left(1 - \frac{m}{N}\right)\left(\frac{N-n}{N-1}\right)$$

See Figure V.9 for examples of the binomial and Poisson distributions in graphical format. Note that in both distributions, the shape changes with the size of the sample and the probability. Do *not* assume normality. Normality is approximated only under special conditions.

Normal

Used whenever possible, this is a continuous distribution of great power. For over a century, the normal distribution has received the lion's share of scholarly study, which is why so many tools are available for analysis using this distribution.

$$\textit{Probability density function} = Y = \frac{1}{\sigma\sqrt{2\pi}} e^{\frac{(x-\mu)^2}{2\sigma^2}}$$

$$\textit{Mean} = \mu = \frac{\sum x_i}{N}, \text{ for a population}$$

(V.8)

$$\textit{Variance} = \frac{\sum_{j=1}^{N}(X_j - \mu)^2}{N} = \sigma^2, \text{ for a population}$$

$$\textit{standard deviation} = \sqrt{\sigma^2} = \sigma, \text{ for a population}$$

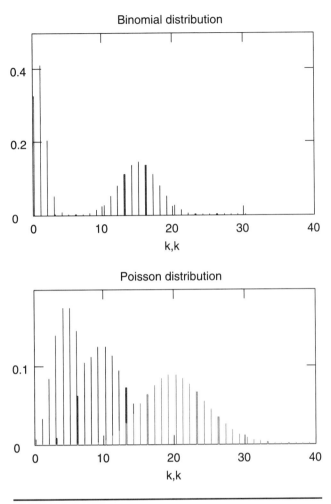

Figure V.9   Binomial and Poisson distributions with different probabilities.

T

$$t = \frac{x - \mu}{s}\sqrt{N-1} = \frac{\overline{X} - \mu}{\hat{s}/\sqrt{N}},$$

(V.9)

which is analogous to the Z statistic derived from the normal distribution

$$= Z = \frac{\overline{X} - \mu}{\sigma/\sqrt{N}}$$

Section V.D.1

The t distribution is given by

$$Y = \frac{Y_0}{\left(1 + \dfrac{t^2}{N-1}\right)^{N/2}} = \frac{Y_0}{\left(1 + \dfrac{t^2}{v}\right)^{(v+1)/2}},$$

where v represents the degrees of freedom.

Chi-squared

The value

$$\chi^2 = \frac{Ns^2}{\sigma^2},$$
(V.10)

that is, the ratio of the sample variance to the population variance when both values are known. The distribution is defined to be

$$Y = Y_0 \left(\chi^2\right)^{v-2/2} e^{-\chi^2/2}$$

See Figure V.10 for some graphical examples of distributions.

Note that even at a relatively small sample size, the t distribution still assumes a relatively normal appearance.

Moments of a Distribution

A distribution has four moments: the mean, the variance, the skewness, and the kurtosis. The mean expresses information about central tendency and the variance expresses information about the dispersion about the mean. The skewness expresses information about asymmetry around the mean and the kurtosis describes the degree of "squashiness" in the distribution.

F

Let X be a χ^2 random variable with degrees of freedom v_1.

Let Y be a χ^2 random variable with degrees of freedom v_2.

We can define an F (after Sir Ronald A. Fisher) such that

(V.11)

$$F = \frac{X/v_1}{Y/v_2}$$

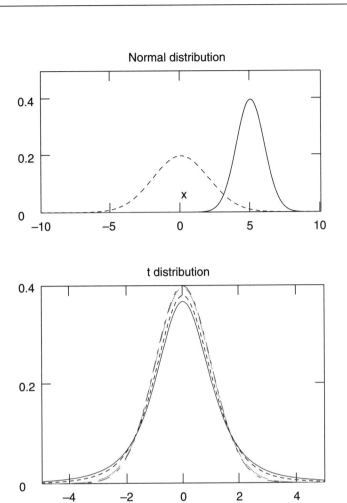

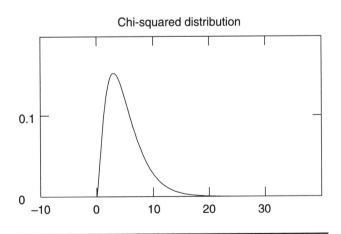

Figure V.10   Two symmetrical distributions (normal and t) and one asymmetrical (chi-squared).

The distribution is defined to be

$$f(x) = \left(\frac{\Gamma\left(\frac{v_1 + v_2}{2}\right)\left(\frac{v}{v_2}\right)}{\Gamma\left(\frac{v_1}{2}\right)\Gamma\left(\frac{v_2}{2}\right)} \right)\left(\frac{x^{(v_1/2)-1}}{\left(1 + \frac{v_1 x}{v_2}\right)^{(v_1+v_2)/2}} \right), x > 0$$

See Figure V.11 for a graph of the F distribution with different degrees of freedom. The F distribution is particularly important in the Analysis of Variance (ANOVA)—a technique frequently used in the Design of Experiments (DOE) to test for significant differences in variance within and between test runs.

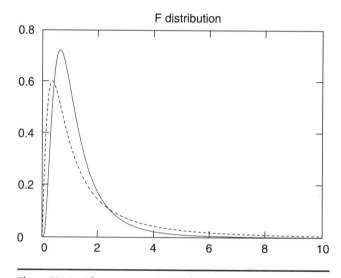

Figure V.11   The asymmetrical F distribution.

2. OTHER DISTRIBUTIONS

Bivariate

$$f(x, y) = \frac{\left[e^{-\frac{1}{2(1-\rho^2)}} \right]\left[\left(\frac{x - \mu_1}{\sigma_1}\right) - 2\rho\left(\frac{x - \mu_1}{\sigma_1}\right)\left(\frac{y - \mu_2}{\sigma_2}\right) + \left(\frac{y - \mu_2}{\sigma_2}\right)^2 \right]}{2\pi\sigma_1\sigma_2\sqrt{1 - \rho^2}} \qquad \text{(V.12)}$$

μ_1 and μ_2 are the two means, respectively.

ρ is the correlation coefficient of the two random variables.

Exponential

$$P(x) = \frac{1}{\mu} e^{-\frac{x}{\mu}} = \lambda e^{-\lambda x}, \text{ the right-hand description being the most common format.}$$

$variance = \sigma^2 = \dfrac{1}{\lambda^2}$, λ being the rate at which the event occurs. $\hspace{2em}$ (V.13)

$standard\ deviation = \sigma = \dfrac{1}{\lambda}$; hence μ is mean time between failures!

Lognormal

Similar to the normal, but the natural log of normal values.

μ is the location parameter (log mean)—that is, the mean of the data set subsequent to the log transformation

σ is the scale parameter (log standard deviation). The scale parameter strongly controls the shape of the distribution.

$$f(x) = \frac{1}{x\sigma\sqrt{2\pi}} e^{-\frac{1}{2}\left(\frac{\ln x - \mu}{\sigma}\right)^2} \hspace{2em} (V.14)$$

Weibull Distributions

The Weibull distribution is the most significant tool used in reliability analyses.

$$f(x) = \frac{\beta}{\eta}\left(\frac{t - \gamma}{\eta}\right)^{\beta - 1} e^{-\left(\frac{t-\gamma}{\eta}\right)^{\beta}}, t > 0$$

$\beta = $ shape parameter

$\eta = $ scale parameter $\hspace{4em}$ (V.15)

$\gamma = $ location parameter

$$\mu = \theta\left(1 + \frac{1}{\beta}\right); \sigma^2 = \theta^2\left[\Gamma\left(1 + \frac{2}{\beta}\right) - \Gamma^2\left(1 + \frac{1}{\beta}\right)\right]$$

See Figure V.12 for illustrations of these distributions.

Section V.D.2

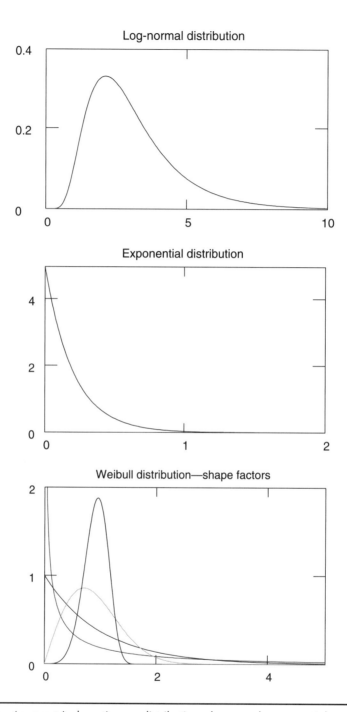

Figure V.12   Asymmetrical continuous distributions: lognormal, exponential, and Weibull.

FURTHER READING

Pitman, Jim. 1993. *Probability*. New York: Springer-Verlag.

E. Measurement Systems

1. MEASUREMENT METHODS

Attribute Screens

All screens are also known as sorts. That means 100 percent inspection of all pieces. In the case of an attribute screen, the disposition of the parts will be on a go/no-go basis. Use when the percentage of nonconforming material is high or not known. Typically, although not always, attribute screens are much quicker than variables-based screens, where a measured value on a continuous scale is used. One example of an attribute screen would occur if a readily observable cosmetic defect were the deciding issue.

Gage Blocks

These are physical blocks or plates of varying dimensions that can be stacked and used as a measuring device. When they are stacked, you "wring" them—move them into relation with each other such that an accurate measurement is achievable. The blocks are calibrated to a standard and the measuring procedure is slow.

Calipers

There are two types of caliper:

Vernier: A Vernier caliper does not have a dial for easy reading. In general, the user should have some training in the use of the Vernier scale before using the caliper.

Dial: Dial calipers have largely replaced the Vernier caliper. They usually have a large round dial that readily displays the measured value in a large, easy-to-read format. See Figure V.13 for a picture of a dial caliper and a micrometer.

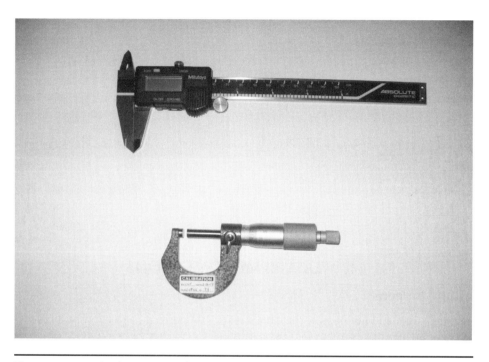

Figure V.13   Dial caliper (top) and micrometer (bottom).

Micrometers

Micrometers are similar to calipers, but they are threaded and measure a much shorter length (travel is always 1 inch at the maximum). Micrometers can take a bit of skill to use well because the flat surface of both portions must set evenly against the item under measure.

Optical Comparators

Optical comparators use a projection method to show the profile of the item of interest magnified on a screen at 10x, 20x, or 50x. This image is compared to a transparent overlay (usually with critical-to-quality parameters marked). The image can be moved slowly with special screw-type controls. See Figure V.14 for a picture of an optical comparator used in an incoming inspection facility.

Tensile Strength

Tensile strength is the maximum strain and stress that a material—for example, steel—can withstand before breaking. On a standard graph, the highest resistance to dimensional change is called the ultimate tensile strength.

Titration

Titration is a method of calculating the concentration (molarity) of a dissolved substance by adding known quantities of a reagent (usually with a pipette) of known concentra-

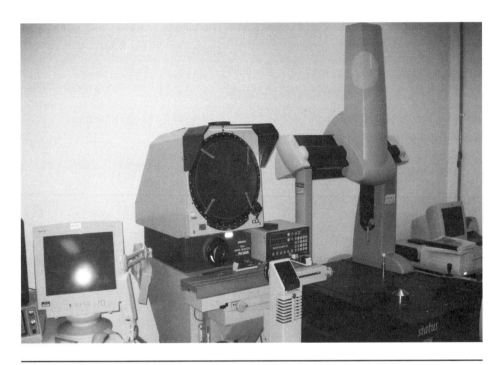

Figure V.14   Mitutoyo Optical Comparator (center).

tion to a known volume of test solution until a reaction is observed. In short, this is a method of using chemicals to determine a threshold.

2. MEASUREMENT SYSTEM ANALYSIS[37]

Repeatability

Repeatability is the measurement variation that occurs on one measurement tool used several times measuring the same characteristic on the same part.

Reproducibility

Reproducibility is the measurement variation of the average of measurements made by different technicians using the same tool, the same characteristic, and the same part.

Measurement Correlation

Measurement correlation is typically the relationship between a measuring instrument and its standard, since the measurement of both involves variation. This can also refer to correlation between different instruments or different kinds of instruments.

Bias

Bias is the difference between observed measurement averages and the reference value and generally indicates a trend—that is, "on average, how much are we always off?"

$$Bias = \frac{\sum_{i=1}^{n} x_i}{n} - T,$$ (V.16)

where n is the sample size and T is the standard or target value.

Percent Agreement

Percent agreement is obtained by taking the goodness-of-fit value from the linear regression, R, and multiplying by 100.

Precision/Tolerance (P/T)

Sometimes a really good precision-to-tolerance ratio will make poor discrimination an acceptable option. Poor discrimination occurs when the measurement system has insufficient resolution to measure anything but a set of apparently discrete values. In the formula, shown in Equation (V.17), the numerator is the standard deviation caused by measurement variability. We also assume that (1) measurement errors are independent, (2) measurement errors are normally distributed, and (3) measurement error is independent of part size. See Figure V.15 for a comparison of precision and accuracy.

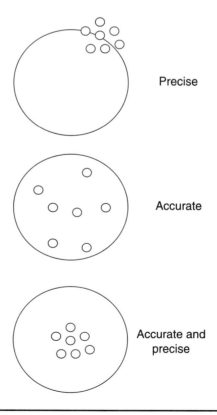

Figure V.15 A target metaphor for accuracy and precision.

$$\frac{\text{Precision}}{\text{Tolerance}} = \frac{6\sigma_E}{\text{total tolerance}} \quad\quad\quad (V.17)$$

Accuracy is related to how the mean of our measurements compares to the desired value. Precision is concerned with the dispersion about the mean.

Precision/Total Variation (P/TV)

P/T calculations compare precision (or dispersion) against the specification limits. The calculation of precision to total variation, shown in Equation (V.18), compares the precision (dispersion) to total variation—that is, precision, repeatability, and reproducibility variation considered together.

$$\frac{\text{Precision}}{\text{Total variation}} = \frac{6\sigma_E}{\text{Total variation}} \quad\quad\quad (V.18)$$

Linearity

Linearity measures the bias across the operating range of a tool or instrument. Plot measured values against the reference to obtain the bias. Fit the data with a linear regression. Convert gage linearity to a percent of process variation by multiplying by 100 and dividing by the process variation.

ANOVA

All calibrations are performed using a "reference." A reference should represent a 4-to-1 or a 10-to-1 improvement in precision. When the reference values are available, use the following equation:

Error = (observed value) – (reference value)

Otherwise, use this equation:

Error = (observed value) – (part average)

Control Chart Methods

Control can also be used to assess the ongoing stability of measuring instruments ("are they drifting?"). Because we measure the values, we can use variable sampling and use the mean and range method for the control chart. See Section VIII.A, "Statistical Process Control," for a fuller discussion of all types of control charts.

Nondestructive

Nondestructive methods include the following:

- Dye penetrant
- Magnetic particle

- Eddy flux
- Ultrasonic

Destructive

Destructive methods include the following:

- Tensile test (see Figure V.16)
- Impact test
- Hardness test
- Vibration to failure (see Figure V.17)
- Accelerated life testing

Figure V.16   Instron pull tester used for destructive testing.

Attribute Systems

Attribute systems are any type of measurement system that is based on go/no-go gaging. An example is the spark plug gage commonly used on automobiles—it either is or isn't a specific size. These gages are sometimes called limit or feeler gages.

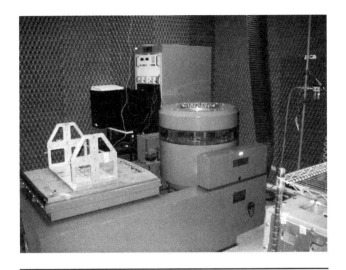

Figure V.17   Unholtz-Dickie vibration table for destructive testing.

3. METROLOGY

Calibration Standards

In the United States, calibration standards are largely maintained by the National Institute for Science and Technology (NIST). Traceability to NIST standards is:

> ". . . the property of the result of a measurement or the value of a standard whereby it can be related to stated references, usually national or international standards, through an unbroken chain of comparisons all having stated uncertainties."[38]

The standards are required to be:

- Invariable
- Accessible
- Usable

Measurement Error

Measurement error is the sum of irreducible random error (natural variation) and error introduced by the measurement itself:

Measurement error = random error + systematic error

Random error = dispersion around the mean
  –Within-operator
  –Between-operator
  –Intrinsic (physical property of material)

Systematic error = sometimes called "bias"

Figure V.18 shows a small taxonomy of sources of error in a measurement system.

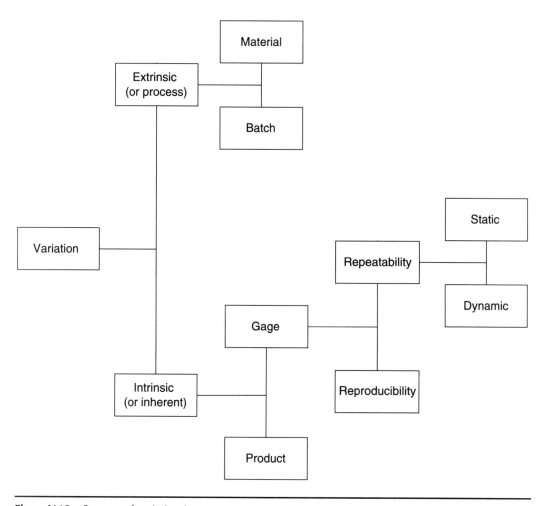

Figure V.18   Sources of variation in a measurement system.

Calibration Systems

At the highest level, a primary reference standard is assigned a value by direct comparison with a reference base. Only mass (kilogram) is defined by an artifact that is maintained by the Bureau International des Poids et Mesures in Sevres, France.

The hierarchy is primary standard → transfer standard → working standard → calibrate gages/instruments.

Control and Integrity of Standards and Measurement Devices

A control chart procedure is used to monitor instrument precision. The procedure is designed to be used in real time after a baseline and control limit for the specific instrument have been ascertained from a database of short-term standard deviations. A separate control chart is required for each instrument.

Assuming small changes, the EWMA control chart is a good candidate for tracking the calibration status of the instrument because the EWMA control chart is sensitive to smaller changes than is the typical Shewhart control chart.

Repeatability standard deviation:

$$s_1 = \sqrt{\left(\frac{1}{\sum_k v_k}\right) \sum_k v_k s_k^2}, \tag{V.19}$$

where v represents the degrees of freedom and the kth s is the variance.

$$v = n - m + 1, n \text{ difference measurements and } m \text{ items.}$$

Standard uncertainty is defined to be

$$u = \sqrt{s_{test}^2 + \left(\frac{nominal\ test}{nominal\ restraint}\right)^2 s_R^2}$$

The expanded uncertainty is $U = ku$, k being the critical value from the t table for v degrees of freedom, or 2.

FURTHER READING

Bucher, Jay, ed. 2004. *The Metrology Handbook*. Milwaukee, WI: ASQ Quality Press.

F. Analyzing Process Capability

1. DESIGNING AND CONDUCTING PROCESS CAPABILITY STUDIES

Designing Process Capability Studies

See "Generic Process Capability Study" for an application of DMAIC to process capability studies. Process capability studies may extend to months; machine capability studies can be as short as a month.

Conducting Process Capability Studies

1. Assess existing stability.

2. Gather data.

3. Estimate standard deviation for population.

4. Perform normality test.

5. Estimate spread ± 3 standard deviations (sample or population).

6. Assess process capability.

7. Interpret process capability (see "Generic Process Capability Study").

Identifying Characteristics

The Black Belt will measure key process output variables and possibly key process input variables if correlation or DOE will be used.

Identifying Specifications/Tolerances

Specification and tolerances may have been determined during QFD. Re-assess and use them. Machine suppliers may provide specifications for the equipment. The most elegant method is to perform the Parameter Design and Tolerance Design techniques recommended by Taguchi.

Developing Sampling Plans

For variables, the sampling plan can be taken from ANSI Z1.9. Typically, sample sizes are in the range of 5 to 10 sample measurements, which are normally averaged for the control chart. For attributes, the sampling can be taken from ANSI Z1.4. Typically, sample sizes range from 25 to 200 assessments. It is a trade-off: variables are harder to measure but have small samples, while attributes are easy to assess but have very large samples.

Verifying Stability and Normality

The Black Belt must do enough analysis to be certain that obvious special causes like setup, tooling, and material have been accounted for. *No prediction can be made regarding a process that is clearly out of control.* A stable process is a process that is *in control*.

The process is said to be in control when special (assignable) causes have been eliminated from the process and only random variation (common cause) remains. When the process is in control, we say the process is "stable."

The degree of normality can be determined by plotting the data against normal probability paper (or, better, using a software package like JMP, Statistica, or MINITAB to generate the plot).

Generic Process Capability Study

1. *Define* the process.
   - Decide on characteristics to be managed (characteristics should be critical to quality—CTQ).
   - Relate to customer needs.
   - PFMEA and process problem areas (also look at process control plan).
   - *Define* the measurement system.

2. *Measure* the process.
   - Run chart used as antecedent to control chart.

3. *Analyze* the process.
   - Evolutionary operations (EVOPS).
   - Statistical testing.
   - Preliminary control chart.
   - Calculate preliminary (short-range) Cp and Cpk.

4. *Improve* the process.
   - Use problem-solving tools.
   - Remove special causes.

5. *Control* the process.
   - Box-Jenkins and Box-Luceño.
   - Feedback to comparator, but *not* tampering!
   - Calculate short-range (Cp and Cpk) and long-range (Pp and Ppk) values on ongoing basis.

2. CALCULATING PROCESS PERFORMANCE VS. SPECIFICATION

Natural Process Limits

If the natural process limits are outside the capability of the process or the machine, it will only appear to work under special causes. Natural process limits are the product of common causes. These limits can be made worse by tampering, which occurs when an operator tries to improve the process without using a real control algorithm such as Box-Jenkins.

Specification Limits

A specification limit is defined by engineers as the acceptable limit of a critical characteristic. It is *not* the same as the control limits. If the natural control limits are outside the specification limits, the process is *not* capable. Interestingly, a process can be in statistical control (that is, within control limits) and still not be capable. Capability relates statistical information to specification limits.

Process Performance Metrics

The fundamental measure of process performance is the total range of the process's variation. Other metrics like percent defective can be represented with a score card similar to the MINITAB "sixpacks" shown in figures V.19 and V.20.

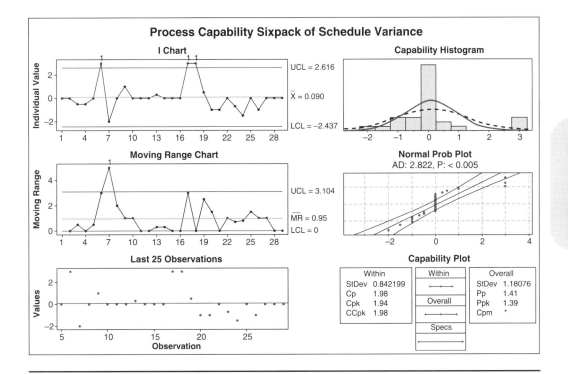

Figure V.19 Capability study of a scheduling analysis.

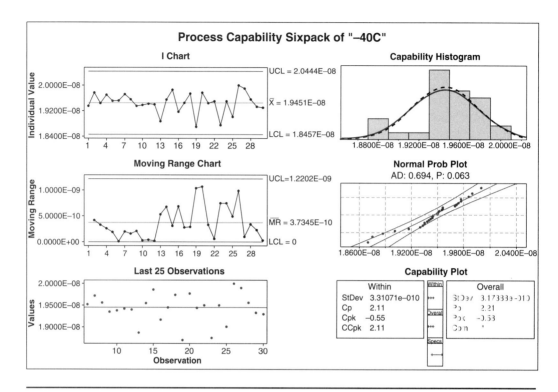

Figure V.20   Capability study of a capacitor at –40°C.

U.S. automotive suppliers are required to perform capability analyses as part of the Production Part Approval Process (PPAP) and the Advanced Product Quality Planning (APQP) system. Capability studies can be performed on any process where specification limits exist and statistical data are available. The Black Belt can assess overall process capability using historical data (Pp and Ppk indices) or the Black Belt can sample from a process under statistical control and use other indices (Cp and Cpk).

3. PROCESS CAPABILITY INDICES (PCIS)

Cp

Cp is a measure of the short-range capability of the process. Its weakness lies in the fact that it does not take into account any target value. It is, however, useful as an indicator of potential process capability. The Six Sigma value of Cp is 2.0.

Cpk

Cpk is similar to Cp but takes into account the centering of the process within the specification limits (*not* the control limits). Cpk is always less than or equal to Cp. Any other statement indicates a miscalculation. Note that both Cp and Cpk calculations use the standard deviation based on an estimation using R/d_2. From this, we know that these values are based on rational subgrouping in a process that is under statistical control.

Cpm

Cpm is used when a target value within the specification limits is more significant than overall centering. It also fits in with the philosophy of the Quality Loss Function. Cpm is a little more complicated to calculate than Cp and Cpk.

Limitations

The difficulty with PCIs lies in trying to summarize an abstraction called "capability" in one number. Additionally, it is wise to present—at least—both Cp and Cpk when using these numbers.

A high Cp but a low Cpk tells you the process is probably sound, but for whatever reason the results are coming out off-center and are probably unacceptable to the customer. I have seen this case when an automotive gage was coded for a linear overlay, but the overlay was actually nonlinear. The high Cp and the low Cpk suggested something was wrong in the design and not out on the line.

Non-parametric Cp and Cpk

Non-parametric values for Cp and Cpk can be calculated by using the same fraction for noncompliance as with the normally distributed version. Non-parametric values are not necessary if the means of rational subgroups are used; otherwise, it is wise to prove normality before assuming it.

Equation (V.20) shows the standard calculations for Cp and Cpk.

Capability index:

$$USL = \text{upper specification limit}$$

$$LSL = \text{lower specification limit}$$

(V.20)

$$C_p = \frac{USL - LSL}{6\hat{\sigma}_{\bar{R}/d_2}}, \hat{\sigma}_{\bar{R}/d_2}$$

is the estimated standard deviation (short term).

Capability index, centered:

$$C_{pk} = \min\left\{ \begin{array}{c} \dfrac{USL - \bar{X}}{3\sigma_{R/d_2}} \\[2ex] \dfrac{\bar{X} - LSL}{3\sigma_{R/d_2}} \end{array} \right\}$$

Long-term capability index:

$$P_p = \frac{USL - LSL}{6\hat{\sigma}_s}, \hat{\sigma}_s$$

is the sample standard deviation (long-term).

Long-term capability index, centered:

$$P_{PK} = \min \left\{ \begin{array}{c} \left| \dfrac{USL - \overline{X}}{3\sigma_S} \right| \\ \dfrac{\overline{X} - LSL}{3\sigma_S} \end{array} \right\}$$

Special "centering":

$$C_{pm} = \frac{(USL - LSL)}{6\sqrt{(\mu - T)^2 + \sigma^2}},$$

where T is the target value.

Note that the Cp and Cpk indices are based on control chart estimators (d_2). The use of a control chart estimator implies that Cp and Cpk are derived from the result of rational subgrouping (the sample group size). No such restriction applies to the Pp and Ppk indices. Cp and Cpk must come from a process that is under statistical control, whereas no such restriction applies to the Pp and Ppk indices.

4. PROCESS PERFORMANCE INDICES

Pp

See the previous section for the defining equation and note the difference from the short-range metric. Many companies do not use the Pp index because it is difficult to explain to operators and the interpretation is more confusing.

Ppk

See the previous section for the defining equation and note the difference from the short-range metric. The Ppk index has the same issues as Pp with regard to interpretation.

Comment about Process Performance Metrics

Performance metrics are an attempt to put a lot of information into one magic number. As long as we remember what we are doing, we can avoid "religious wars" over the meaning of a given Cpk.

Additionally, we would expect to see a difference between Pp/Ppk and Cp/Cpk if the 1.5 sigma shift is meaningful. In the late 1980s and early 1990s, Motorola used the 1.5 sigma shift to allow some slack in the PPM because Shewhart-style control charts had only a 50 percent chance of capturing a 1.5 sigma shift in the data. Additionally, the theory was that it was typical for a process to drift a little bit over a longer period of time without ever really being out of control.

One might consider the Pp and Ppk indices to refer to the historical process performance regardless of whether the process was in control or not; hence, the Pp and Ppk values are nearly always less than their Cp and Cpk counterparts. Do the Cp and Cpk measurements only apply to a given batch of product? Yes. However, if the process remains in statistical control, it would not be illegitimate to refer to Cp and Cpk for the process. Also, keep in mind that Cp and Cpk are calculated based on results that are a byproduct of rational subgrouping; subgrouping is not relevant to Pp or Ppk calculations.

See Figure V.21 for a more complete analysis of a component (a capacitor) using the process capability analysis in MINITAB.

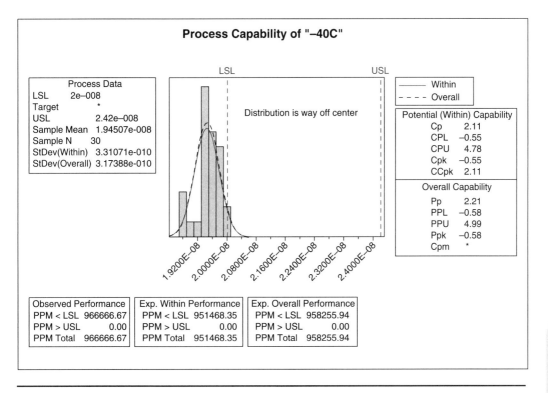

Figure V.21   Capacitor study. Product is potentially capable, but not very close to the center.

5. SHORT-TERM VS. LONG-TERM CAPABILITY

Short-Term Data Are Collected

Cpk is much more common than Ppk. Also, the way many companies take Cpk is very much like the definition of Ppk.

An additional consideration concerns the meaning of Ppk. Do we really care about long-term capability or do we really want to know what this process is doing right now so we can do something about it immediately?

When Only Attributes Data Are Available

The problem here is not that attributes data are so bad, but rather that the attributes give us raw numbers regarding failure rates and don't really tell us anything about measurement drift, wear, and other variable information. We can discern trends and all the other standard control tests but we cannot really say in which direction the process is drifting.

Changes in Relationships That Occur When Long-Term Data Are Used

When we use the standard deviation for the normal variables control chart (xbar-R), we use a standard deviation of that sample [Equation (V.21)], also known as the standard error, which can be calculated from the control chart values,

$$\sigma_R = \frac{\overline{R}}{d_2}, \text{ for samples (short-term)}$$

$$\sigma_i = \sqrt{\frac{\sum\left(X - \overline{X}\right)^2}{(n-1)}}, \text{ or the sample standard deviation, long-term}$$

(V.21)

The calculation for short-term is based on subgrouping; the calculation for the long term doesn't consider subgrouping at all.

Interpret Relationships between Long-Term and Short-Term Capability

Since the impact of outliers tends to diminish over the long term, the Ppk and Pp values can be better than the equivalent Cpk and Cp values. The important consideration is the meaning and purpose of the measurement. We want our measurements to:

- Mean something.

- Tell us something quick enough to do something about it.

If this is so, then the Ppk and Pp are really just nice marketing information. Equation (V.22) shows some typical values used in industry.

$$\text{Capability ratio, } CR = \frac{1}{C_P}$$

$$\text{Long-term capability ratio, } PR = \frac{1}{P_P}$$

Converting from Z to C_{PK}

$$C_{PK} = \frac{Z_{min}}{3}$$

(V.22)

Note that Z_{min} is the unadjusted sigma level!

$Z_{min} = 3, \therefore C_{PK} = 1$

$Z_{min} = 4, \therefore C_{PK} = 1.33$

$Z_{min} = 5, \therefore C_{PK} = 1.67$

$Z_{min} = 6, \therefore C_{PK} = 2$

Note: using high Cpk values implies very good centering of the process between specification limits. Given that a Cp of 2 is equivalent to a Six Sigma process, why use the Cpk value? Good question. We show Equation V.22 because a Cpk can be equal to a Cp when the process is perfectly centered; however, use with caution.

6. NON-NORMAL DATA TRANSFORMATIONS (PROCESS CAPABILITY FOR NON-NORMAL DATA)

We expect to measure normally distributed data when using variables-based control charts. In fact, the central limit theorem suggest that the mean data in a homoscedastic sample will naturally tend toward the mean.

Unfortunately, not all processes are so cooperative. We have seen at least one major process where an exponential distribution was a significantly more accurate representation of the actual data.

Additionally, the normal distribution itself may be so badly skewed (tipped to one side) that the data cannot be analyzed using the typical methods. One method that has been used for heavily skewed distributions is the mirror image technique. The Black Belt can pick a side of the distribution, rotate it around the mean and produce a pseudo-distribution for one side of the real distribution. The Black Belt must build *two* pseudo-distributions in order to make this work, calculating means and standard deviations for both of the pseudo-distributions. The engineer will calculate the capability of the process based on one side or the other, looking at both.

If the data is truly exponential, then the area under the curve must be calculated using a standardized ratio:

$$\text{Standardized ratio} = \frac{X}{\overline{\overline{X}}} \tag{V.23}$$

Calculate a standardized ratio for both limits

$$\frac{USL_{EXP}}{\overline{X}_{EXP}} \text{ and } \frac{LSL_{EXP}}{\overline{X}_{EXP}}$$

Other than this, the charts are analogous to those for the normal distribution.

The Weibull distribution can also be used for analysis of capability. Figure V.22 show an example of a capability study using a Weibull distribution (a sixpack generated with MINITAB). Notice how the apparent distribution very much resembles an exponential distribution. This is another example of using the Weibull to provide us with the real distribution.

Yet another possibility is to transform the data into "normal" data using the Box-Cox transformation. Equation (V.24) shows the formulae used for the Box-Cox transformation. These calculations are non-trivial and most statistical software will add the transformation as desired.

$$For\ \lambda \neq 0, x(\lambda) = \frac{\left(x^2 - 1\right)}{\lambda} \tag{V.24}$$

$$For\ \lambda = 0, x(\lambda) = \ln(x)$$

Section V.F.6

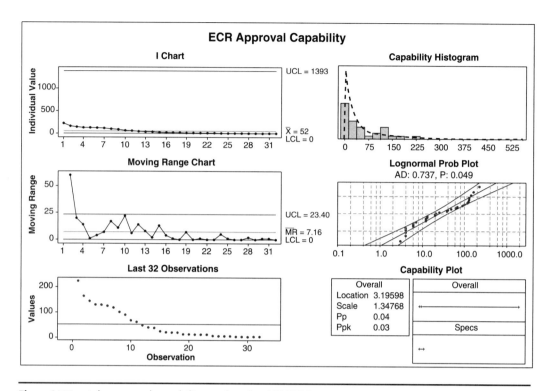

Figure V.22   A log-normal capability study using MINITAB.

Using a likelihood algorithm (non-trivial), maximize the logarithm of this function:

$$f(x) = -\frac{n}{2}\ln\left[\sum_{i=1}^{n}\frac{\left(x_i(\lambda) - \bar{x}(\lambda)\right)^2}{n}\right] + (\lambda - 1)\sum_{i=1}^{n}\ln(x_i),$$

where the arithmetic mean is

$$\bar{x}(\lambda) = \frac{1}{n}\sum_{i=1}^{n}x_i(\lambda).$$

Hint: Do this with software designed to perform the transformation!

7. PROCESS CAPABILITY FOR ATTRIBUTES DATA

Sigma Level

Attribute charts represent an indirect approach to the overall Six Sigma. However, the defect levels from c and u charts, in particular, can be used to calculate Six Sigma values directly (DPMO) or the Sigma value can be calculated from the Cpk/Ppk values (Table V.4).

Table V.4 The interrelationships among Cp, Cpk, Sigma limits, and PPM.

Cp	Sigma level	No 1.5 sigma shift		1.5 sigma shift	
		PPM	Cpk	PPM	Cpk
1.33	4.0	64.0	1.33	6210.0	0.83
1.67	5.0	0.6	1.67	230.0	1.17
1.83	5.5	0.02	1.83	32.0	1.33
2.00	6.0	0.002	2.0	3.4	1.5

Figure V.23 shows the results of an attribute capability study. We are using a p chart, so we are looking at percent or proportion defective. The PPM is terrible, so the sigma level is somewhere in the vicinity of 2.25 sigma (1.5 sigma shift) or a variables-type Cpk of approximately 0.25. Note that the percent defective is approximately 34 percent.

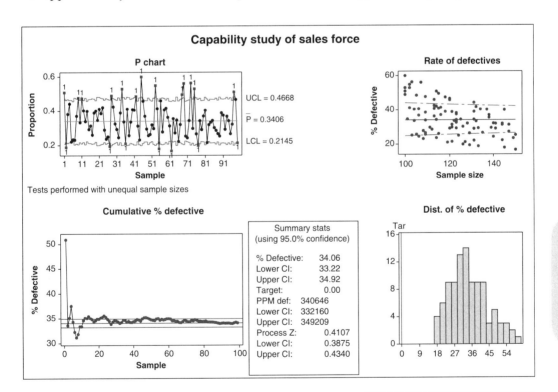

Figure V.23   Attribute capability study of sales failures.

Remember that the sigma level can be determined from the DPMO calculations, and what is DPMO but a measure of attribute information? The Black Belt should be able to switch among the values of Cpk, sigma level, and PPM with ease. Use tables like Table V.4 with caution, because the assumptions for the different measures are not necessarily the same: Cp and Cpk are usually based on the results of sampling subgroups, but the value can be a non-parametric version. The sigma level is distinctly based on an assumption of normality in the data and ppm is a standardized defect count.

FURTHER READING

Montgomery, Douglas C. 2004. *Introduction to Statistical Quality Control*. 5th ed. New York: John Wiley & Sons.

Section VI

Six Sigma Improvement Methodology and Tools—*Analyze* (23 Questions)

Contents

A. Exploratory Data Analysis

1. MULTI-VARI STUDIES[39]

Positional Variation

Positional variation is frequently within-piece variation, but it can include the following:

- Machine-to-machine variation

- Line-to-line or plant-to-plant variation

- Within-batch variation (if members of the batch occupy special positions—for example, different locations in a furnace)

- Test positioning variation

Cyclical Variation

Cyclical variation looks at the piece-to-piece changes in consecutive order. We look for patterns in groups, batches, or lots of units.

Temporal Variation

Temporal variation is the time-to-time or shift-to-shift variation—that is, variation across time.

Sampling Plans for Sources of Variation

A nested plan looks like this:

Day

  Part

    Location within part

Crossed designs look like this:

Shielded				Not shielded			
Electrolytic cap		Ceramic cap		Electrolytic cap		Ceramic cap	
Long wire	Short wire	Long wire	Short wire	Long wire	Short wire	Long wire	Short wire

Crossed designs are the only ones that can show interactions among factors.

Creating and Interpreting Charts

In Figure VI.1, we can see immediately that the largest variation is caused by the boss and not by the shift or the group. Notice how obvious the differences are in this diagram, which was prepared using MINITAB.

Multi-vari charts can be very simple, yet they are a powerful way to analyze data graphically and get similar results to what might be achieved using DOE.

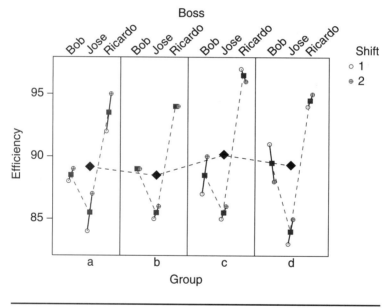

Figure VI.1   Multi-vari chart.

2. MEASURING AND MODELING RELATIONSHIPS BETWEEN VARIABLES

a. Simple and Multiple Least-Squares Linear Regression

Regression is a statistical technique for measuring the variation/relationship between two or more variables. If the relationship is linear and has more than two variables, we called it multiple least-squares linear regression. Linear analysis may not be the best solution. An alternate example is the Quality Loss Function, which is quadratic. Other powers—such as the cubic (third power)—can be found in some systems with curves in two directions. Other regression techniques may fit to a power law, a polynomial, or a logarithmic scenario.

Following is a listing of the relevant regression equations.

A line has the general equation $Y = a_0 + a_1 X$.

We can solve for a_0 and a_1 by simultaneously solving

$$\left\{ \begin{array}{l} \sum Y = a_0 N + a_1 \sum X \\ \sum XY = a_0 + a_1 \sum X^2 \end{array} \right\}, \tag{VI.1}$$

which is the standard equation for the least squares line.

The solution of which is

$$a_0 = \frac{\left(\sum Y\right)\left(\sum X^2\right) - \left(\sum X\right)\left(\sum XY\right)}{N\sum X^2 - \left(\sum X\right)^2}$$

$$a_1 = \frac{N\sum XY - \left(\sum X\right)\left(\sum Y\right)}{N\sum X^2 - \left(\sum Y\right)^2}$$

The measure of the relation of the two variables is the correlation coefficient r:

$$r = \frac{\sum\left(x_i - \bar{x}\right)\left(y_i - \bar{y}\right)}{\sqrt{\sum\left(x_i - \bar{x}\right)^2 \left(y_i - \bar{y}\right)^2}},$$

where $\bar{x}$ and $\bar{y}$ are the mean x and the mean y.

The r value may be plus or minus.

The correlation of determination is r^2 and can only be positive.

$r^2 \times 100$ = percentage variation.

We can use the t distribution to test for the null hypothesis that $r = 0$.

$$t_0 = \frac{r\sqrt{n-2}}{\sqrt{1-r^2}}, if \left|t_0\right| > t_{\alpha/2, n-2} \text{ (using one-side t table)}$$

We can calculate the residuals by $e_i = y_i - \hat{y}_i$, or the difference between predicted and actual values.

b. Simple Linear Correlation

If r approaches 1, we say it is positively correlated; if r approaches –1, we say it is negatively correlated. If the value of r approaches zero from either side, we say it is not well correlated.

The t-test shown in Equation (VI.1) is one method of saying some correlation exists given a confidence level based on the t-table (usually 95 percent confidence, 5 percent significance).

Correlation is *not* the same as causation; however, it can suggest causation. When we correlate smoking with lung cancer we show a mathematical relationship but not necessarily a pathological relationship among the variables. The argument for causation gains increased plausibility when a mechanism can be proven. Additional statistical techniques can be brought into the argument, such as Bayesian analysis and ANOVA. Beware of sloppy hypothesis testing!

Calculate and interpret the correlation coefficient and its confidence interval, apply and interpret a hypothesis test for the correlation coefficient, and understand the difference between correlation and causation.

c. Diagnostics

Residuals can be used to check for autoregression (time series), goodness of fit (by plotting the residuals against the real values), and normality.

Interpreting Regression Results

The R-value varies between –1 and 1. The closer the value is to –1 or 1, the better the fit. Negative R-values represent an inverse relationship: one value goes up as the other goes down. R is also known as the *coefficient of determination*.

R^2 is the percentage of total variation in the response. The higher the R^2 value, the better the model fits your data. R^2 varies between 0 and 1, since it is the square of R.

The p-value relates to the probability of calculating a test statistic equal to or greater than the observed test statistic. We compare the null hypothesis against a rejection threshold of some value—typically 0.05, although other values may be used. A p-value near zero suggests that the null hypothesis is false and that a difference is likely. P-values approaching 1 suggest no detectable difference given the sample size used. In general, if we are looking for meaning, the lower the p-value, the better.

CI is the confidence interval on many graphical outputs. It is normally expressed as "the confidence interval of the < >," where < > may be the mean, the median, or some other measure. If we have 95 percent confidence interval of the mean, then there is a 95 percent probability that the mean lies between the upper and lower confidence limits.

The prediction interval (PI) is the range in which the predicted response for a new observation is expected to fall. The interval has lower and upper limits (like the CI), calculated from the confidence level and the standard error for the prediction. It is always more dispersed than the confidence interval because of the additional uncertainty involved in prediction.

Regression Example

The following data are an example of exploring a relationship between x and y without necessarily implying causation:

X	Y
65	68
63	66
67	68
64	65
68	69
62	66
70	68
66	65
68	71
67	67
69	68
71	70

The complete output from MINITAB follows. The regression equation is $Y = 35.8 + 0.476\,X$. See figures VI.2 and VI.3 for the graphs. We want normality, but it would be better if residuals clustered closer to the 0 value on the histogram.

Predictor	Coef	SE Coef	T	P
Constant	35.82	10.18	3.52	0.006
X	0.4764	0.1525	3.12	0.011

$S = 1.404$ $R\text{-}Sq = 49.4\%$ $R\text{-}Sq(adj) = 44.3\%$

Analysis of variance

Source	DF	SS	MS	F	P
Regression	1	19.214	19.214	9.75	0.011
Residual error	10	19.703	1.970		
Total	11	38.917			

Obs	X	Y	Fit	SE fit	Residual	St resid
1	65.0	68.000	66.789	0.478	1.211	0.92
2	63.0	66.000	65.837	0.691	0.163	0.13
3	67.0	68.000	67.742	0.408	0.258	0.19
4	64.0	65.000	66.313	0.574	−1.313	−1.03
5	68.0	69.000	68.219	0.453	0.781	0.59
6	62.0	66.000	65.360	0.819	0.640	0.56
7	70.0	68.000	69.171	0.650	−1.171	−0.94
8	66.0	65.000	67.266	0.418	−2.266	−1.69
9	68.0	71.000	68.219	0.453	2.781	2.09R
10	67.0	67.000	67.742	0.408	−0.742	−0.55
11	69.0	68.000	68.695	0.539	−0.695	−0.54
12	71.0	70.000	69.648	0.775	0.352	0.30

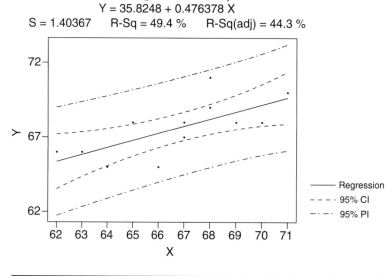

Linear Regression Example
$Y = 35.8248 + 0.476378\ X$
$S = 1.40367 \quad R\text{-}Sq = 49.4\ \% \quad R\text{-}Sq(adj) = 44.3\ \%$

Figure VI.2 Linear regression with confidence interval.

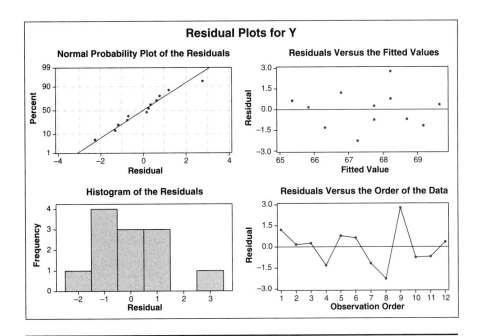

Figure VI.3   Residual analysis of linear fit.

FURTHER READING

Kleinbaum, David, Lawrence L. Kupper, and Keith E. Muller. 1998. *Applied Regression Analysis and Other Multivariable Methods.* 3rd ed. Pacific Grove, CA: Brooks/Cole Publishing Company.

B. Hypothesis Testing

1. FUNDAMENTAL CONCEPTS OF HYPOTHESIS TESTING

a. Statistical vs. Practical Significance

The following list provides a simple step-by-step plan for performing hypothesis testing. Note that a statistically significant difference may not equate to a practically significant difference and, as usual, this issue is most likely tied in with the measurement system and what factors are critical to quality.

Steps in Hypothesis Testing

1. Carefully state the hypothesis. Do not record data until the hypothesis has been clearly stated.

2. Choose an alpha value (or risk rejecting our hypothesis if it is really true).

3. Choose the test statistic.
   - Chi-squared relates population or expected values to sampled values of variance.
   - F-statistic relates the variances of two samples.
   - T-statistic tests the differences in the means of two samples.
   - Z-statistic tests the differences in the means of two populations.

4. Define pass/fail criteria in terms of acceptance of the test. It is usually a good idea to look at the picture of the distribution in the tables.

5. Choose a representative sample randomly from a homoscedastic population and calculate inferential statistics for the sample (mean, standard deviation, and so on). Compute the test statistic and compare the calculated value with the tabular value to accept or reject the hypothesis.

6. Use common sense in coming to a conclusion.

7. Remember to verify or explain the underlying distribution and any assumptions you may have made.

8. If there is some doubt about the underlying distribution, consider testing your measurement using non-parametric methods.

b. Significance Level, Power, and Type I and Type II Errors

Significance is the complement of confidence, so a confidence interval of 95 percent (0.95) yields a significance of 5 percent (0.05).

A type I error occurs when we fallaciously reject good material—that is, we reject the null hypothesis when it is true.

A type II error occurs when we fallaciously accept bad material—that is, we fail to reject the null hypothesis. Please note that this does *not* imply acceptance of the null hypothesis, a common error.

Type I probability is normally expressed as significance or alpha. Type II probability is normally expressed as beta and is usually much more difficult to calculate.

Power is 1 – beta, the complement of beta. This is the probability of rejecting the null hypothesis when it is false. We want our tests to have as much power as possible to increase the likelihood of correct rejection.

The heart of sampling theory lies in selecting a cost-effective sampling such that type I and type II errors are minimized.

c. Sample Size

Let's assume a 95% confidence interval—which calls for the value of 1.96 from the standard normal distribution.

For variable data from a normal population:

$$N \geq \left(\frac{1.96}{\delta}\right)^2 \sigma^2, \tag{VI.2}$$

where

$$\delta = \text{error of estimation}$$

$$\sigma^2 = \text{variance of the population}$$

For binomial data, use proportions:

$$n = \frac{Z^2 \bar{p}(1-\bar{p})}{(\Delta p)^2},$$

using Z to approximate standard deviation.

$$\Delta p = \text{proportion interval}$$

$$\bar{p} = \text{proportion rate}$$

2. POINT AND INTERVAL ESTIMATION

Efficiency/Bias of Estimators

Estimators are values calculated from samples without a confidence interval. For example, Equation VI.3 shows the bias that changes a population variance to a sample variance.
    Population variance is defined to be

$$\sum_{i=1}^{N} \frac{\left(\mu - X_i\right)^2}{N}, \tag{VI.3}$$

where N is the size of the population and μ is the population mean.
    Sample variance is defined to be

$$\sum_{i=1}^{n} \frac{\left(\overline{X} - X_i\right)^2}{n-1},$$

where n is the sample size and $\overline{X}$ is the sample mean.

The bias is $\dfrac{N}{n-1}$. As n approaches N, the bias approaches zero.

Tolerance Intervals

A confidence interval covers a population parameter (for example, from a Z-test) or a sample statistic (for example, from a t-test) with some declared confidence. We can also state the coverage for a fixed proportion of the population with a declared confidence. This kind of an interval is called a tolerance interval. The endpoints of a tolerance interval are generally referred to as tolerance limits. An application of tolerance intervals to manufacturing involves comparing specification limits prescribed by the client with tolerance limits that cover a specified proportion of the population. Do *not* confuse with engineering tolerances.

Confidence Intervals

Here is a generic format for confidence intervals:

CI = Estimator +/− Standard error of the estimator

Following is a comparison of tolerance intervals with confidence intervals:

- Confidence limits are limits within which we expect a given population parameter (for example, the mean) to lie.

- Confidence intervals shrink toward zero with increase in sample size.

- Tolerance limits are limits within which we expect a stated *proportion* of the population to lie.

- Tolerance intervals tend toward a fixed value with increase in sample size.

Prediction Intervals

The appropriate equations follow.

$$\text{Goal: predict value of } x_{n+1}$$

$$\text{Residual of prediction} = \overline{X} - X_{n+1}$$

$$\text{Standard error of mean } = se_{\overline{X}} = \frac{s}{\sqrt{n}} \qquad (VI.4)$$

$$\text{Standard error of the predicted value}$$

$$se_{n+1} = s,$$

hence

$$se_{\overline{X}-X_{n+1}} = \sqrt{\left(\frac{s}{\sqrt{n}}\right)^2 + s^2} = s\sqrt{1+\frac{1}{n}}$$

Using the t-statistic here . . .

$$-t_{1-\alpha/2} \leq \frac{\overline{X} - X_{n+1}}{s\sqrt{1+\frac{1}{n}}} \leq t_{1-\alpha/2},$$

which becomes the prediction interval

$$\overline{X} \pm t_{1-\alpha/2} s\sqrt{1+\frac{1}{n}}.$$

3. TESTS FOR MEANS, VARIANCES, AND PROPORTIONS

Hypothesis Testing for Means

Equation (VI.5) shows the formulae for calculating the Z and the t-test values, respectively. Typically, we will ascertain an observed value for Z or t and then compare that with an expected value for Z or t. Keep in mind that Z values apply to sample or population sizes of 30 or greater and t values apply to sample sizes smaller than 30. William Gossett (whose pseudonym was "Student") developed the t-distribution particularly for the purpose of analyzing small samples.

$$Z = \frac{X - \mu}{\sigma},$$ standard deviation and mean for population MUST be known

$$Z = \frac{X - \overline{X}}{s},$$ standard deviation and mean for large sample MUST be known

$$t = \frac{\overline{X} - \mu_0}{s / \sqrt{n}},$$ standard deviation MUST be estimated from the sample.

X is some variable under study.   (VI.5)

$\overline{X}$ is the sample mean.

μ_0 is the hypothetical population mean.

σ is the population standard deviation.

s is the sample standard deviation.

n is the sample size.

The difference between the two is that with the t-test we use degrees of freedom = $n - 1$. (Also note the standard deviation.)

Calculate a Z or t value and compare with the table. Equation (VI.6) presents an example using a simple t-test.

$$n = 16$$

$$pay = \$33,000$$

$$s = \$1000, \text{ estimate true mean value of pay over interval}$$

confidence interval at 99% = 0.99, $\alpha = 0.01$ (VI.6)

$$\frac{s}{\sqrt{n}} = 250$$

$$v = 16 - 1 = 15$$

Two-tailed because pay can go up or down . . .

$$t_{\alpha/2,15} = t_{0.01/2,15} = t_{0.005,15} = 2.947,$$

which is the critical value.

We know that the mean salary at 99% confidence, then, is

$$33,000 \pm 2.947 \times 250 = 33,000 \pm 736.75$$

What if the original sample mean were \$33,000, but some say it is now \$33,500? Can we say with 99 percent confidence that it has changed?

$$t = \frac{\overline{X} - \mu_0}{s / \sqrt{n}} = \frac{33500 - 33000}{1000 / \sqrt{16}} = \frac{500}{250} = 2$$

We already know the critical t = 2.947 and we do not fall to the right of this value; therefore, we cannot reject the null hypothesis, H_0 at 99 percent confidence.

Hypothesis Testing for Variances

The chi-squared distribution and its associated tests and calculations are some of the most powerful in statistics. It is chi-squared that is the primary tool of choice when analyzing nominal and ordinal data. Chi-squared is also a good first choice when testing between observed and expected variances.

$$\chi^2 = \frac{(n-1)s^2}{\sigma_x^2} \qquad \text{(VI.7)}$$

Calculate the value and compare as we did with the Z and t calculations.

Hypothesis Testing for Proportions

$$Z = \frac{x - np_0}{\sqrt{np_0(1-p_0)}}, \qquad \text{(VI.8)}$$

where p_0 is a fixed comparison value.

Solve the same way as with the Z and t calculations: Calculate value for actual data, go to the table, and compare value with table value.

4. PAIRED-COMPARISON TESTS

Parametric Comparison Hypothesis Testing

The tests in Equation (VI.9) are executed analogously to those for single values. We assume the variances of the two groups are equal:

$$H_0 : \mu_1 = \mu_2$$

$$t = \frac{\overline{X}_1 - \overline{X}_2}{S_p \sqrt{\dfrac{1}{n_1} + \dfrac{1}{n_2}}} \qquad (VI.9)$$

$$S_p = \sqrt{\frac{(n_1 - 1)s_1^2 + (n_2 - 1)s_2^2}{n_1 + n_2 - 2}},$$

Calculate the pooled standard deviation by calculating the pooled variance. We cannot do statistical calculations with the standard deviation. Always use variance for internal calculations.

$$\text{Degrees of freedom} = v = (n_1 - 1) + (n_2 - 1) = (n_1 + n_2) - 2$$

If we have unequal variance, the formula for df is 1:

$$v = \frac{1}{\dfrac{\left(\dfrac{s_1^2}{n_1}\right)}{\dfrac{s_1^2}{n_1} + \dfrac{s_2^2}{n_2}}}{n_1 - 1} + \dfrac{\left(\dfrac{s_2^2}{n_2}\right)}{\dfrac{s_1^2}{n_1} + \dfrac{s_2^2}{n_2}}}{n_2 - 1}}$$

See Equation (VI.10) for a similar description of the F-test.

$$F = \frac{s_1^2}{s_2^2}, \qquad (VI.10)$$

where s_1^2 is always larger than s_2^2.

$$\text{Degrees of freedom}_1 = v_1 = n_1 - 1$$

$$\text{Degrees of freedom}_2 = v_2 = n_2 - 1$$

In the tables, v_1 is the row across the top and v_2 is the column down the left-hand side.

Let us say we ran a set of 8 tests in 2002 with a standard deviation of 300 and another set of 7 tests in 2003 with a standard deviation of 100.

$$F = \frac{s_1^2}{s_2^2} = \frac{300^2}{100^2} = \frac{90,000}{10,000} = 9$$

If we look at a table, we can see that for $v_1 = 7$ and $v_2 = 6$, the critical value for F is 4.21.

$$F_{calc} > F_{tabular} = 9 > 4.21$$

Hence, we can reject the null hypothesis.

Non-parametric Comparison Hypothesis Testing

See Table VI.6 further on, which lists the non-parametric tests. These tests are analogous to the parametric tests without the assumption of normality.

5. GOODNESS-OF-FIT TESTS

Chi-squared

Since the basis for the chi-squared statistic is the ratio of the population variance to that of a sample, the chi-squared test, shown in Equation (VI.11), can be used for goodness of fit between theoretical distributions (normal, binomial, Poisson, and so on) and empirical distributions derived from data. As noted earlier, chi-squared is a useful tool and is frequently the first choice for comparison tests between observed and expected results, particularly with data that involve integer counting (nominal and ordinal).

The method is very simple:

1. For each experiment, calculate the expected value based on the appropriate distribution.

2. For each experiment, measure and record the observed value.

3. Use the basic chi-squared formula to calculate a value.

$$\chi^2 = \sum_j \frac{\left(observed_j - expected_j\right)^2}{expected_j} \tag{VI.11}$$

4. Compare the result with the tabular value for the appropriate degrees of freedom.

5. Degrees of freedom for binomial would be:

   number of experiments -1 $-$ parameter count($=1$) = # experiments $- 2$

See Table VI.1 for a goodness-of-fit example.

Table VI.1   Goodness-of-fit example.

Outcomes	Probabilities	Expected	Observed	Chi-squared	CumProb	P-value
0	0.03125	31.25	35	7.68	0.895971	0.174776
1	0.15625	156.25	180			
2	0.31250	312.50	300			
3	0.31250	312.50	320			
4	0.15625	156.25	140			
5	0.03125	31.25	25			

Expected heads for coin tosses of five coins and 1000 experiments.

Chi-squared tabular value = 9.49.

7.68 < 9.49, so we cannot reject the null hypothesis. On the other hand, the p-value could be lower, so the results are not too good to be true.

6. ANALYSIS OF VARIANCE (ANOVA)

One-Way ANOVA

One-way ANOVA is used to check for differences among three or more means of one factor.

$$Grand\ mean = \overline{X}_{GM} = \frac{\sum X}{N} \tag{VI.12}$$

Sum of squares total is the total variation:

$$SS_T = \sum \left(X - \overline{X}_{GM} \right)^2$$

Between-group variation:

$$SS_B = \sum n \left(\overline{X} - \overline{X}_{GM} \right)^2$$

Mean square between groups:

$$MS_B = \frac{SS_B}{k-1}$$

Within-group variation:

$$SS_W = \sum (N-k)s^2 = SS_E$$

Mean square within groups is variation over degrees of freedom:

$$MS_W = \frac{SS_W}{(N-k)} = MS_E$$

Calculate F:

$$F = \frac{s_b^2}{s_w^2} = \frac{MS_B}{MS_W} = \frac{MS_B}{MS_E},$$

then compare to F for $N-1$ total degrees of freedom.
    Here is the simplifying tableau:

	SS	df	MS	F
Between	SS_B	$k-1$	$\frac{SS_B}{k-1}$	$\frac{MS_B}{MS_W}$
Within	SS_W	$N-k$	$\frac{SS_W}{N-k}$	
Total	$SS_W + SS_B$	$N-1$		

This is also a very common format for printouts of results from software!
    Table VI.2 shows a typical data arrangement for a one-way ANOVA. MINITAB was the tool of choice in this example, but a calculator or a spreadsheet could also be used.
    The key idea is that we are dealing with one dimension: type of carpet. That is why we call this analysis a one-way ANOVA.

Analysis of Variance for Durability

Source	DF	SS	MS	F	P
Carpet	3	111.6	37.2	2.60	0.101
Error	12	172.0	14.3		
Total	15	283.6			

If alpha = 0.10 for significance, then we cannot conclude that there is a significant difference in the means of these carpets because the p-value exceeds the 0.10 limit.

Table VI.2   MINITAB example of a one-way ANOVA for carpet types.

Durability	Carpet
18.95	1
12.62	1
11.94	1
14.42	1
10.06	2
7.19	2
7.03	2
14.66	2
10.92	3
13.28	3
14.52	3
12.51	3
9.30	4
21.20	4
16.11	4
21.41	4

Two-Way ANOVA

Two-way ANOVA, shown in Equation (VI.13), functions analogously to one-way in terms of how the formulae work. We are at the brink of DOE. The tableau for two-way ANOVA is:

$$
\begin{array}{lcccc}
 & SS & DF & MS & F \\
\text{Factor A} & SS_A & a-1 & MS_A = \dfrac{SS_A}{a-1} & \dfrac{MS_A}{MS_E} \\
\text{Factor B} & SS_B & b-1 & MS_B = \dfrac{SS_B}{b-1} & \dfrac{MS_B}{MS_E} \\
\text{Interaction} & SS_{AB} & (a-1)(b-1) & MS_{AB} = \dfrac{SS_{AB}}{(a-1)(b-1)} & \dfrac{MS_{AB}}{MS_E} \\
\text{Error} & SS_E & ab(n-1) & MS_E = \dfrac{SS_E}{ab(n-1)} & \\
\text{Total} & SS_T & abn-1 & &
\end{array}
\qquad \text{(VI.13)}
$$

See Table VI.3 for a MINITAB example of a two-way analysis.

Table VI.3 Data table for a two-way ANOVA from MINITAB example.

Zooplankton	Supplement	Lake
34	1	Rose
43	1	Rose
57	1	Dennison
40	1	Dennison
85	2	Rose
68	2	Rose
67	2	Dennison
53	2	Dennison
41	3	Rose
24	3	Rose
42	3	Dennison
52	3	Dennison

In this example, we have two factors: different supplements and different lakes.

Analysis of Variance for Zooplankton

Source	DF	SS	MS	F	P
Supplement	2	1919	959	9.25	0.015
Lake	1	21	21	0.21	0.666
Interaction	2	561	281	2.71	0.145
Error	6	622	104		
Total	11	3123			

There are no significant interaction effects, but there are definite effects from the supplement. The zooplankton population is the response. Note how the p-value for the supplement is quite small compared to the lake and the supplement-lake interaction.

7. CONTINGENCY TABLES

Building a Contingency Table

Contingency tables are one use for the chi-squared statistic; see Equation (VI.14). These tables are also known as classification tables. The total value for each row or column is known as the marginal frequency. Degrees of freedom are calculated from the product of the number of rows less 1 and the number of columns less 1 $(r–1)(c–1) = DF$.

$$\chi^2 = \sum_j \frac{\left(observed_j - expected_j\right)^2}{expected_j}$$

$$Expected\ cell_{ij} = \frac{\sum_i observed_i \sum_j observed_j}{\left[\sum_j\left(\sum_i observed_i\right)_j\ or\ \sum_i\left(\sum_j observed_j\right)\right]},$$ (VI.14)

where i is a row and j is a column.

A simpler statement of the formula is:

$$Expected\ cell_{ij} = \frac{total\ for\ column\ j \times total\ for\ row\ i}{sample\ size}$$

$$Degrees\ of\ freedom = v = \left(rows - 1\right) \times \left(columns - 1\right)$$

Using a Contingency Table

To use a contingency table, do the following:

1. Put the different "situations" in columns.

2. Put condition 1 in the first row, condition 2 in the second row, and so on.

3. Observe real data and record into the table.

4. Unless expected values are known, calculate the expected values as shown in tables VI.4 and VI.5.

5. Do the chi-squared calculation and then compare the results with the tabulated chi-squared value for the degrees of freedom.

   –If calculated chi-squared < tabular chi-squared, we cannot reject the null hypothesis.

   –If calculated chi-squared > tabular chi-squared, we can reject the null hypothesis.

Chi-squared and Statistical Significance

Tables for chi-squared are typically expressed in terms of the 95 percent confidence interval, which automatically translates into a significance of 5 percent or 0.05. That is why we would look for a p-value < 0.05 to be able to reject the null hypothesis (see tables VI.4 and VI.5).

Contingency Table Example

In Table VI.4, expected counts are printed below observed counts.

Table VI.4   2×2 contingency table example.

	Work	Not work	Total
With snibble (observed)	75	25	100
(Expected)	(140 × 100) / 200 = 70.00	(60 × 100) / 200 = 30.00	
Without snibble (observed)	65	35	100
(Expected)	(140 × 100) / 200 = 70.00	(60 × 100) / 200 = 30.00	
Total	140	60	200

In short, the expected value for any cell is equal to (the sum of that row times the sum of that column) divided by either the sum of the rows' sums or the sum of the columns' sums.

$$\text{Chi-Sq} = 0.357 + 0.833 + 0.357 + 0.833 = 2.381$$

DF = 1, P-value = 0.123. The table chi-squared for 1 degree of freedom is 3.84. Since $2.381 < 3.84$, we cannot say there is a significant difference in working and not working between with or without snibbles. We *cannot* reject the null hypothesis.

The next example is a 2×3 contingency table. Again, expected counts are printed below observed counts.

Table VI.5   2×3 contingency table example.

	C1	C2	C3	Total
With (observed)	50	47	56	153
(Expected)	(55 × 153) / 180 = 46.75	(61 × 153) = 51.85	(64 × 153) / 180 = 54.40	
Without (observed)	5	14	8	27
(Expected)	(55 × 27) / 180 = 8.25	(61 × 27) / 180 = 9.15	(64 × 27) / 180 = 9.60	
Total	55	61	64	180

$$\text{Chi-Sq} = 0.226 + 0.454 + 0.047 + 1.280 + 2.571 + 0.267 = 4.844$$

DF = 2, P-value = 0.089. For 2 degrees of freedom, chi-squared = 5.99 (at 95 percent confidence). We *cannot* reject the null hypothesis that with and without are different.

8. NON-PARAMETRIC TESTS[40]

Mood's Median Test

The Mood's Median test is used to test the equality of medians from two or more populations and, similar to the Kruskal-Wallis Test, provides a non-parametric alternative to the one-way ANOVA. Also called the median test.

Levene's Test

Levene's test is used to assess the homogeneity of variance (homoscedasticity) between sets of values. Levene's test outputs an F-value.

Kruskal-Wallis Test

The Kruskal-Wallis test compares three or more samples. It tests the null hypothesis that all populations have identical distribution functions against the alternative hypothesis that at least two of the samples differ only with respect to location (median)—if, in fact, there is any difference at all. It is the non-parametric analogue to the F-test used in ANOVA. While ANOVA tests depend on the assumption that all populations under comparison are normally distributed, the Kruskal-Wallis test places no such restriction on the comparison. It is the variance version of the Mann-Whitney U Test.

Mann-Whitney U Test

The Mann-Whitney U test is used to perform a hypothesis test of the equality of two population medians and to calculate the corresponding point estimate and confidence interval. Use this test as a non-parametric alternative to the two-sample t-test. Assume the distributions for the samples are the same.

Table VI.6 summarizes many of the non-parametric tests.

Table VI.6   List of non-parametric tests.

Type of test	Type of data	Type of use
Kruskal-Wallis	Ordinal Hypothesis: means	Analogue of ANOVA
Kendall Coefficient of Concordance	Ordinal Hypothesis: independence	Degree of association among classifications
Cramér's Contingency Coefficient	Nominal Hypothesis: dependence and independence	Association between two classifications
Mood's Median	Ordinal Hypothesis: medians	Tests equality of sample medians scoring samples against population
McNemar	Nominal Hypothesis: means or medians	Significance of change in before/after designs
Cochran Q	Nominal Hypothesis: means or medians	Tests if three or more sets of proportions differ
Friedman	Ordinal Hypothesis: means or medians	Two-way ANOVA for k matched samples—another analogue to ANOVA
Spearman rank correlation coefficient	Ordinal Hypothesis: independence	Measure of association using r
Kendall rank correlation coefficient	Ordinal Hypothesis: independence	Similar to Spearman, but allows partial correlation coefficient
Levene's	Interval Hypothesis: equal variance	Tests for homogeneity of variances across k samples. Alternative to F or t. (Homoscedasticity). Distribution must be continuous.
Mann-Whitney U	Ordinal Hypothesis: means	Tests if two independent groups come from the same population. Analogous to t test—hypothesis testing.
Kolmogorov-Smirnov 1-sample	Ordinal Hypothesis: goodness of fit	Goodness of fit. Used often as alternative to chi-squared.
Kolmogorov-Smirnov 2-sample	Ordinal Hypothesis: identical distributions	Two independent samples from same distribution
Fisher Exact Probability	Nominal Hypothesis: independence	Two groups differ in proportion in two classifications
Runs	Sequence Hypothesis: independence	Many control chart tests are runs tests. These tests are relatively weak.
Walsh	Ordinal	Matched pair randomization test; used in decision making. n < 7

FURTHER READING

Conover, W. J. 1999. *Practical Nonparametric Statistics*. 3rd ed. New York: John Wiley & Sons.

Section VII

Six Sigma Improvement Methodology and Tools—*Improve* (22 Questions)

Contents

A. Design of Experiments (DOE)

1. TERMINOLOGY[41]

Independent Variables

The independent variable in an experiment is most commonly an input. An independent variable, as the name suggests, does not have interactions with other variables. A typical example of an independent variable is time in a time series.

Dependent Variables

A dependent variable does not change unless the independent variable upon which it relies also changes. In Equation (VII.1), x is the dependent variable—it is an observation.

$x_{ijt} = \mu + \alpha_i + \beta_j + e_{ijt}$, where

μ = overall mean

α = mean effect for factor 1 at level i (VII.1)

β = mean effect for factor 2 at level j

e = random deviation from the mean position of tth item receiving treatment ij.

Factors and Levels

In DOE language, a factor is the variable (or treatment) controlled by the experimenter. A factor could be viewed as a stimulus. *Level* refers to the setting at which the experimenter puts a factor during the progress of the experiment.

Response

The response is the outcome of the experiment as a result of controlling the levels, interactions, and numbers of factors.

Treatment

Although a treatment can be viewed as a factor in a single-factor experiment, it more commonly refers to an experimental run.

Error

The error is the response value less the values of the mean, factor 1, and factor 2 and summed up for all treatments. The error must be calculated by subtracting the other values from the response.

Replication

Each and every repetition of an experiment (treatment) is called a *replication*. Replication is a technique for increasing the reliability of the technique.

Tables VII.1, VII.2, and VII.3 show typical formats for various DOE arrays.

Table VII.1 Full factorial, 2-level, 3-factor.

Trial	Factor 1	Factor 2	Factor 3	Response
1	+	+	+	R1
2	+	+	−	R2
3	+	−	+	R3
4	+	−	−	R4
5	−	+	+	R5
6	−	+	−	R6
7	−	−	+	R7
8	=	−	−	R8

Table VII.2 Fractional factorial (one example), 2-level, 3-factor.

Trial	Factor 1	Factor 2	Factor 3	Response
1	+	+	−	R1
2	+	−	+	R2
3	−	+	+	R3
4	−	−	−	R4

Table VII.3   Full factorial, 2-level, 3-factor with interactions.

Trial	A	B	C	AB	BC	AC	ABC	Response
1	+	+	+	+	+	+	+	R1
2	+	+	−	+	−	−	−	R2
3	+	−	+	−	−	+	−	R3
4	+	−	−	−	+	−	+	R4
5	−	+	+	−	+	−	−	R5
6	−	+	−	−	−	+	+	R6
7	−	−	+	+	−	−	+	R7
8	=	−	−	+	+	+	−	R8

2. PLANNING AND ORGANIZING EXPERIMENTS

Planning

Experiment planning involves understanding what it is we are trying to do and the associated cost of doing so. We must consider resources, time, cost, procurement of experiment material, schedule, and all the normal factors present in project management.

Organizing

Experiments can involve substantial organizational requirements, particularly if a large number of factors are under study. Additionally, if the manufacturing line has special requirements for a production experiment, we need to consider the impact on the customer.

Objectives

Objectives for the experiment should be defined and explicit.

Factor Selection

Unless we are doing an exploratory experiment with a huge number of factors, we want to pick factors that we reasonably expect to have an effect on the response.

Response Expectation

We need to know the range of our response values so that we have appropriate measuring equipment available.

Measurement Methods

To a large extent, measuring methods will control the level of experimental error present (the level of equipment uncertainty). This requirement explains why we have emphasized the calibration and maintenance of measurement equipment.

Appropriate Design

If we are doing exploratory experimentation, we want to choose a design (for example, Plackett-Burman) that will give us the most efficient result—the biggest bang for our buck.

If we are looking at experiments where interactions among factors may be significant, we need to use experimental designs that allow us to account for those factors.

Table VII.4 shows the various resolution levels and what they mean.

Table VII.4   Resolution levels.

Resolution	Description
I	Unable to estimate the main effects
II	Some main effects are confounded with other main effects
III	The main effects are confounded with two-factor interactions
IV	The main effects are confounded with three-factor interactions
V	The main effects and two-factor interactions have no confounding
VI	Four-factor interactions are confounded with main effects and two-factor interactions

Note that full factorial designs are frequently described as

$$\text{Levels}^{\text{Factors}}$$

3. DESIGN PRINCIPLES

Principles of Power

The higher the power, the more complex the surface. See the "Order" section further on.

Sample Size

Sample size is determined by the type of experiment chosen. Frequently, one of the goals of experimentation is efficient consumption of samples, which leads to fractional factorial designs, culminating with Plackett-Burman—which can deal with main effects with four factors at a time.

Balance

A balanced design occurs in a fractional factorial design when an equal number of trials at every level occurs for each factor.

Order

Order is defined as the polynomial that represents the surface involved in the experiment. First-order experiments cannot represent curvature. The following is first-order:

$$Y = B_0 + B_1 X_1 + B_2 X_2 + \varepsilon \text{,}$$ (VII.2)

where ε is the error term.

A first-order equation will produce a plane in space. A second-order equation will produce a more complex surface.

Efficiency

An estimator is more efficient than another if its variance is smaller.

$$\frac{\sigma_{minimum\ estimator} \times 100}{\sigma_{estimator\ in\ question}} = \text{percentage of efficiency}$$ (VII.3)

Randomization and Blocking

Blocking attempts to mitigate the effect of variables that we are trying to eliminate or avoid. Randomization allows us to spread the effect of these variables through the error term. The other method of dealing with blocking involves accounting for it explicitly in the design of the experiment.

Interaction

An interaction occurs when one or more factors have an influence on the behavior of another factor. Graphically, we see non-parallel slopes for the factors.

Confounding/Aliasing

Confounding occurs when a factor interaction cannot be separately determined from a major factor in an experiment.

Screening Experiments

Some fractional experiments (arrays) are primarily used to screen for significant factors. Tables VII.5, VII.6, and VII.7 are effectively restatements of the same array. Any one of them can be used to screen out insignificant factors.

Section VII.A.3

Table VII.5   Plackett-Burman design for seven factors.

+	−	−	+	−	+	+
+	+	−	−	+	−	+
+	+	+	−	−	+	−
−	+	+	+	−	−	+
+	−	+	+	+	−	−
−	+	−	+	+	+	−
−	−	+	−	+	+	+
−	−	−	−	−	−	−

Table VII.6   Taguchi design for seven factors.

−	−	−	−	−	−	−
−	−	−	+	+	+	+
−	+	+	−	−	+	+
−	+	+	+	+	−	−
+	−	+	−	+	−	+
+	−	+	+	−	+	−
+	+	−	−	+	+	−
+	+	−	+	−	−	+

Table VII.7   A fractional design for seven factors.

−	−	−	−	−	−	−
+	−	−	+	+	−	+
−	+	−	+	−	+	+
+	+	−	−	+	+	−
−	−	+	−	+	+	+
+	−	+	+	−	+	−
−	+	+	+	+	−	−
+	+	+	−	−	−	+

4. DESIGN AND ANALYSIS OF ONE-FACTOR EXPERIMENTS

Completely Randomized

A completely randomized experiment occurs when no tests are omitted and the order is completely random. Randomization is used as a countermeasure to undesirable variables or effects.

Randomized Block

If we take a factor in each treatment and make exactly one measurement, we are executing a randomized block experiment. We could block out some behavior at 10 a.m. by running the experiments only at 10 a.m. each day. This would block out the 10 a.m. effect.

Latin Square

See Table VII.8 for a representation of a Latin square. The principal failing of the Latin square and the related Graeco-Latin square is that it is oblivious to interactions among factors.

Table VII.8   Observe the simple layout and regularity of the Latin square.

Treatment C in Matrix		Treatment A				
		1	2	3	4	5
Treatment B	1	e	a	b	c	d
	2	d	e	a	b	c
	3	c	d	e	a	b
	4	b	c	d	e	a
	5	a	b	c	d	e

Computation Methods

Use the ANOVA computation supplied in Section VI.B, "Hypothesis Testing."

Graphical Methods

See Figure VII.1 for examples of typical graphs used in Design of Experiments.

Note the internal consistency of the results: It is obvious that time and temperature are dramatically more significant factors than the catalyst. In the normal probability plot, we look for values that deviate seriously from linearity as a help in selecting significant factors and interactions.

Analyzing/Evaluating Results

With ANOVA, we are always looking for the values that exceed the F statistic, since the F statistic is derived from the variances of samples, and that is what we are dealing with in an ANOVA study.

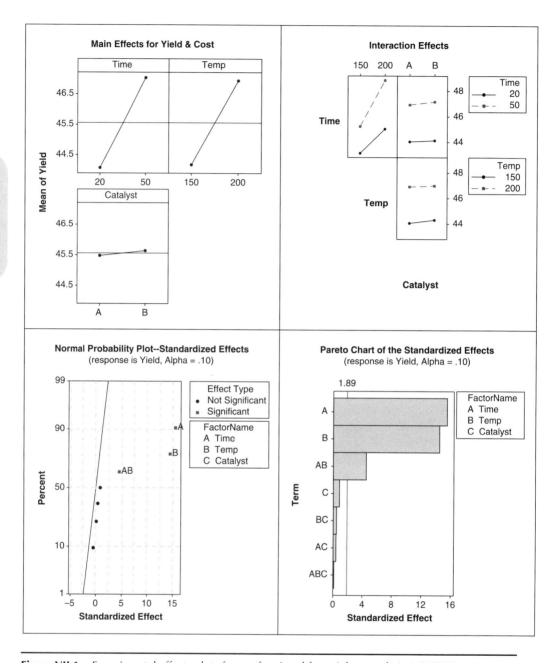

Figure VII.1   Experimental effects plots from a fractional factorial example in MINITAB.

5. DESIGN AND ANALYSIS OF FULL-FACTORIAL EXPERIMENTS

What They Are

A full-factorial experiment looks at every possible combination. If we want to study a large number of factors at more than two levels, the test size and complexity grow exponentially.

Why Do Them

In order to complete a full study of interactions, we *must* conduct full-factorial experiments. That is why it is extremely important to assess interactions ahead of time. It is not uncommon to use fractional factorial experiments to determine the significant main factors and then to conduct the final runs using significant factors and study their interactions.

When to Do Them

Construct these experiments and apply computational and graphical methods in order to analyze and evaluate the significance of results.

Refer back to Figure VII.1, which shows some plots for the example (Table VII.9).

Another Benefit

If a two-level full factorial design produces results that are not very good predictors of process performance, all is not lost. The full factorial results can be retained and the design can be converted into a central composite design (Section VII.B), where a non-planar surface can be generated.

6. DESIGN AND ANALYSIS OF TWO-LEVEL FRACTIONAL FACTORIAL EXPERIMENTS

What They Are

Fractional factorial experiments occur when we do *not* examine every possible combination. We frequently do our experiments with fractional factorials to (1) save money and (2) save time.

Why Do Them

Fractional factorial experiments can be extremely efficient. They can also miss interactions. Use the full factorial method to capture interactions.

When to Do Them

Fractional factorial experiments can be useful at any time, but especially when:

- A quick exploratory test is desired.
- Interactions are known to be nonexistent or insignificant.
- We want to run a lot of tests very quickly.

Confounding

In the tableau for every possible case in a fractional factorial experiment (Table VII.9), the interaction test setup will exactly parallel that of certain main factors. That means we cannot discern the effects of the interaction separately from those of the main factor.

Table VII.9   MINITAB data for Figure VII.1 and tables VII.10–VII.13.

StdOrder	RunOrder	Blocks	Time	Temp	Catalyst	Yield	Cost
9	1	2	20	150	A	43.2976	28.0646
14	2	2	50	150	B	45.1531	33.0854
15	3	2	20	200	B	45.3297	35.2461
16	4	2	50	200	B	48.6720	37.4261
10	5	2	50	150	A	45.3932	28.7501
11	6	2	20	200	A	44.8891	30.7473
12	7	2	50	200	A	49.0645	32.3437
13	8	2	20	150	B	43.0617	30.2104
1	9	1	20	150	A	42.7636	27.5306
3	10	1	20	200	A	45.1931	31.0513
6	11	1	50	150	B	45.5991	32.6394
8	12	1	50	200	B	49.2040	36.8941
2	13	1	50	150	A	44.7592	29.3841
5	14	1	20	150	B	43.3937	30.5424
7	15	1	20	200	B	44.7077	34.6241
4	16	1	50	200	A	48.4665	31.7457

In order to determine significant values, look at the P values in tables VII.10–VII.13. The lower the P value, the higher the significance of the factor or interaction. Also note that in the data in Table VII.9, the actual run order is *not* the same as the original array setup. We do this to *randomize* the treatment order.

Table VII.10 Fractional factorial fit: Yield versus time, temp, catalyst estimated effects and coefficients for yield (coded units).

Term	Effect	Coef	SE Coef	T	P
Constant		45.5592	0.09546	477.25	0.000
Block		−0.0484	0.09546	−0.51	0.628
Time	2.9594	1.4797	0.09546	15.50	0.000
Temp	2.7632	1.3816	0.09546	14.47	0.000
Catalyst	0.1618	0.0809	0.09546	0.85	0.425
Time*Temp	0.8624	0.4312	0.09546	4.52	0.003
Time*Catalyst	0.0744	0.0372	0.09546	0.39	0.708
Temp*Catalyst	−0.0867	−0.0434	0.09546	−0.45	0.663
Time*Temp*Catalyst	0.0230	0.0115	0.09546	0.12	0.907

Table VII.11 Analysis of variance for yield (coded units).

Source	DF	Seq SS	Adj SS	Adj MS	F	P
Blocks	1	0.0374	0.0374	0.0374	0.26	0.628
Main effects	3	65.6780	65.6780	21.8927	150.15	0.000
Two-way interactions	3	3.0273	3.0273	1.0091	6.92	0.017
Three-way interactions	1	0.0021	0.0021	0.0021	0.01	0.907
Residual error	7	1.0206	1.0206	0.1458		
Total	15	69.7656				

Table VII.12 Estimated effects and coefficients for cost (coded units).

Term	Effect	Coef	SE Coef	T	P
Constant		31.8928	0.09085	351.03	0.000
Block		−0.0914	0.09085	−1.01	0.348
Time	1.7815	0.8907	0.09085	9.80	0.000
Temp	3.7339	1.8670	0.09085	20.55	0.000
Catalyst	3.8813	1.9407	0.09085	21.36	0.000
Time*Temp	−0.0963	−0.0481	0.09085	−0.53	0.613
Time*Catalyst	0.5740	0.2870	0.09085	3.16	0.016
Temp*Catalyst	0.6943	0.3471	0.09085	3.82	0.007
Time*Temp*Catalyst	−0.0342	−0.0171	0.09085	−0.19	0.856

Table VII.13   Analysis of variance for cost (coded units).

Source	DF	Seq SS	Adj SS	Adj MS	F	P
Blocks	1	0.134	0.134	0.1336	1.01	0.348
Main effects	3	128.722	128.722	42.9074	324.88	0.000
Two-way interactions	3	3.283	3.283	1.0944	8.29	0.011
Three-way interactions	1	0.005	0.005	0.0047	0.04	0.856
Residual error	7	0.924	0.924	0.1321		
Total	15	133.068				

7. TAGUCHI ROBUSTNESS CONCEPTS

Apply Taguchi robustness concepts and techniques such as the following.

Signal-to-Noise Ratio

Calculated by using equations derived from the quality loss function:

Larger is better (maximize the response):

$$\frac{S}{N} = -10\log\left(\frac{\sum\frac{1}{Y^2}}{n}\right)$$

Nominal is best (target the response):   (VII.4)

$$\frac{S}{N} = 10\log\left(\frac{\overline{Y}^2}{s^2}\right)$$

Smaller is better (minimize the response):

$$\frac{S}{N} = -10\log\left(\frac{\sum Y^2}{n}\right)$$

Controllable Factors

In dynamic analyses, a very strong influencing factor is called a "signal factor." Signal factors affect the response mean. In some cases, the signal factor might be considered the energy put into the system (for example, fanning the accelerator pedal).

Noise Factors

Noise factors can be blocks or uncontrollable factors. We are trying to reduce the sensitivity of our product or process to noise.

Robustness

Robustness occurs when a given response remains relatively immune to variations in treatments.

P-diagram

The P-diagram (Figure VII.2)[42] is the traditional Taguchi-style representation of the items affecting a system. Not all items under study will have a signal factor.

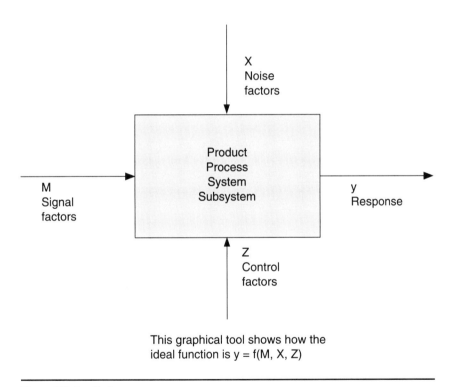

Figure VII.2   P-diagram.

FURTHER READING

Montgomery, Douglas C. 2000. *Design and Analysis of Experiments.* 5th ed. New York: John Wiley & Sons.

B. Response Surface Methodology

1. STEEPEST ASCENT/DESCENT EXPERIMENTS[43]

The path of steepest ascent/descent is the most efficient method of looking for a response optimum. We call this the steepest ascent method because we want to find the optimum quickly by "climbing" quickly. Therefore, we desire to find this path of steepest ascent so that we can bring ourselves into the region of the optimal response as quickly as possible and then perform a more detailed analysis in order to more fully characterize the behavior in the optimal region. Some prerequisites for the response surface methodology (RSM) exist:

- We should have some idea of the major factors influencing the response (exploratory DOE could be used with something like a Plackett-Burman filter to discover this).

- The response and the factors should have some relevance with respect to either manufacturing, parameter design, or tolerances.

- Some relationship must exist between the factors and the response or we are wasting our time.

- The response surface needs to be reasonably regular and relatively uncomplicated (a "bumpy" surface will make the discovery of an optimum difficult).

Response surfaces are frequently represented in both a three-dimensional and a contour format. Figure VII.3 shows some contours and Figure VII.4 shows the actual surface from an example using MINITAB.

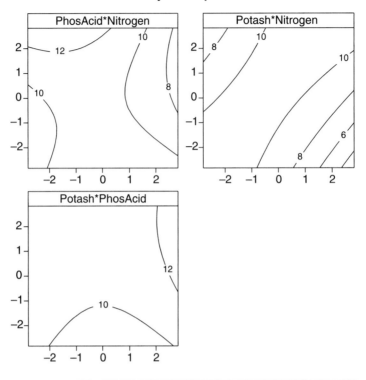

Figure VII.3   Contour plots for a response surface from a MINITAB example.

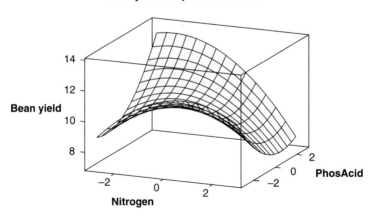

Figure VII.4   Surface plot for a response surface from a MINITAB example.

2. HIGHER-ORDER EXPERIMENTS

Central-Composite Design (CCD)

The CCD requires five levels for each factor. The design is rotatable if the variance of the response is a function of distance from the center of the surface under study. A conversion allows for the variance of the response at the origin to be equal to the variance of the response at unit distance from the origin, which can assist in eliminating experimental or measurement bias. Three kinds of CCD exist:

- Central-composite circumscribed (CCC)—five levels for each factor with a circular, spherical, or hyperspherical geometry

- Central-composite inscribed (CCI)—five levels for each factor with a circular geometry (CCC junior)

- Central-composite face-centered (CCF)—three levels for each factor

Box-Behnken Design

The Box-Behnken design requires only three levels and is thus more efficient than the CCD, which requires five levels. The test format is not *necessarily* rotatable, nor is it block orthogonal. Treatment combinations use the midpoints of the cubic geometric representation as if a sphere were tangential to the cubic surface at just those midpoints.

Mixture Design

Mixture designs are a perfect example of a form for which consideration of interactions is absolutely required. Mixture designs are most commonly used in chemical studies, where interaction is sought and is therefore significant.

Simplex Lattice Design

As the name suggests, the lattice can be represented by a geometric figure—it is used for experiments with mixtures. These figures can be equilateral triangles, pyramids, squares, or cubes depending on the number of factors under study and the characteristics of the response. The vertices of the geometrical figure can represent limiting extreme values on the proportions in the mixture. The composition of the mixture is always 100 percent, so we are truly dealing with proportions.

Figure VII.5 is a MINITAB example of a simplex design.

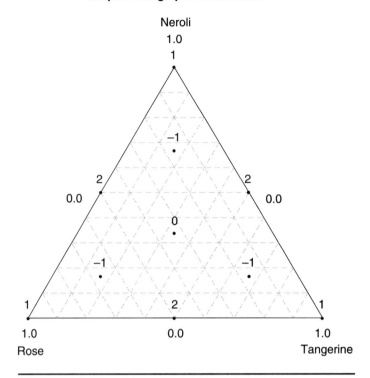

Figure VII.5   Design plot for a mixture-style designed experiment using a MINITAB example.

C. Evolutionary Operations (EVOP)

Because DOE experiments can produce large amounts of scrap in some scenarios related to production, George Box and Norman Draper developed a method called evolutionary operations (EVOPs). The general idea of EVOPs is that we can nudge a running process in one direction or another and measure the effect on the response, just as we would with ordinary DOE.

EVOPs is an iterative process, a form of high-technology kaizen. Data are normally taken over multiple cycles so the data are cumulative in nature. Where we might use a response surface in the beneficent environment of the laboratory, we use EVOPs in the real environment of the product line. At every point during the EVOPs process, we are still producing acceptable product. Experiments with two factors at two levels can be done, as can more complicated experiments. Box and Draper concentrated on the two-factor, two-level experiment as their prime tool.

In *Evolutionary Operations*, Box and Draper made it clear that the EVOPs technique was designed to be readily applicable by line operators with only a minimum of training in the necessary data recording. The Box-Draper idea was to bring the power of designed experiments to the production line so that continuous improvement would have a scientific grounding. The book is very readable and supplies numerous recommendations for worksheets and charts for use by operators, technicians, and line managers.[44]

To keep the lines running, EVOPs changes are typically very small. As we iterate, we are, in fact, creating a response surface over time. The Black Belt needs to remember that the process is changing even as we run our experiments; that is, the final cycle may not resemble the first cycle very much at all.

Normal ANOVA methods can be calculated to determine the significance of the factors, and the interactions can be analyzed in the same way that we would perform a normal off-line experiment.

Figures VII.6 and VII.7 show the simple geometric representations of the experiments recommended by Box and Draper. Variables 1 and 2 are two significant variables (factors) from our operation. The dots represent the response map, which is yield. We will measure the yield and then decide on the direction of the factor manipulations.

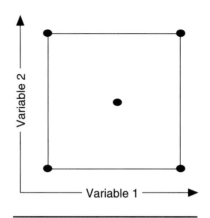

Figure VII.6 EVOPs geometry for a 2×2 experiment.

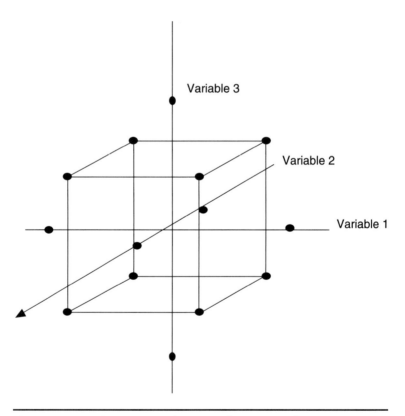

Figure VII.7 EVOPs geometry for a central composite design.

What is the point of this simple diagram? What we are saying is that simple 2×2 experiments can be sufficient to drive a process toward optimal results. Obviously, we can run more complex experiments if desired. If we use a full factorial design, we can mutate into a central composite design without losing any of our work. Indeed, the central composite design is an expansion of the graph in Figure VII.6, with quadratic terms added to account for curvature that would never be captured by the regular 2×2 design. Figure VII.7 shows what the geometry looks like for three factors.

FURTHER READING

Montgomery, Douglas C. 2002. *Response Surface Methodology: Process and Product Optimization Using Designed Experiments.* 2nd ed. New York: John Wiley & Sons.

Section VIII

Six Sigma Improvement Methodology and Tools—*Control* (15 Questions)

Contents

Section VIII

A. Statistical Process Control

1. OBJECTIVES AND BENEFITS

Controlling Process Performance

Statistical = sampling

Process = coordinated activity

Control = modification of behavior by comparing desired response with actual output

The ultimate goal is reduction of variation. Simply gathering data and putting it on a chart is insufficient.

Figure VIII.1 shows some sample control charts. Notice the smoothing achieved with the averaging in the Xbar-R and the Xbar-S charts. The various kinds of control charts are discussed later in this section.

Special versus Common Causes

A special cause is an assignable cause. We use a special tool called a control chart in order to separate the assignable causes from those expected from normal random variation. In fact, common causes lie behind the random variation.

Of the two cause, the special cause is easier to handle because we can assign a reason for it. Reducing the effect of a common cause, on the other hand, frequently requires a profound knowledge of the process being measured.

Type I SPC errors occur when we treat a behavior as a special cause when no change has occurred in the process. This item is sometimes called *overcontrol*.

Type II SPC errors occur when we *don't* treat a behavior as a special cause when in fact it *is* a special cause. This situation is sometimes called *undercontrol*.

Tampering

Tampering is when an operator or technician nudges a device or process in a direction that they believe will reduce the variation. Deming was able to show time and again that tampering makes the situation worse!

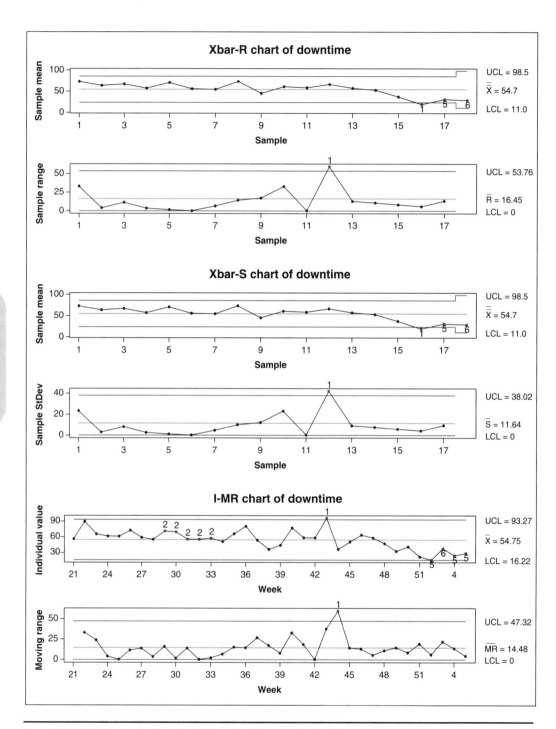

Figure VIII.1 Three sets of control charts for the same basic data.

Tools exist that do permit changes to common causes. Two related examples come out of the work of Box and Jenkins and Box and Luceño. These studies were initially used as forecasting tools, predictive indicators of observed patterns. However, engineers released very early on that the tools could also be used in a control scenario and they have been applied to dynamic control with control charts.

Box-Luceño

A powerful alternative to the woes of tampering lies in the technique advocated by Box and Luceño in their book on control of processes.[45] First, they look at detecting small shifts in process performance. They recommend either the exponential weighted moving average (EWMA) control chart or the accumulated sum (CuSum) control chart because both of these are more sensitive than Shewhart control charts. Then they propose a control system where the deviation of the process from the desired value is adjusted using a gain (a percentage of the total deviation opposite in value to the deviation itself). Then they present data to support the benefits of using this technique.

2. SELECTION OF VARIABLE

Variables selected for variable control charts should be critical to quality (CTQ). A variable is critical to quality if:

- It is important to customer perception.

- It can be counted or measured.

- We can tell whether we are achieving it.

If we have performed a Quality Function Deployment (QFD), we will have an idea of the items that are of concern to the customer. Alternatively, we can construct a hierarchical CTQ tree to try to clarify the items that are critical to quality.

If we are in a true process control situation, we can also measure the control variables—that is, which variables contribute to the ability of the process to remain on target?

Other Considerations

A process that is utterly out of control is not a good candidate for control charts. An out-of-control process will have mostly special causes. Hence, in order to use the control charts, we want to bring the process under some kind of reasonable control. In the beginning, it may make more sense to track the data of interest with a simple run chart, which will show the variation without requiring control limits.

Once we have chosen the variable of interest, what will be our sampling plan? Keep in mind that although variable control charts are incredibly efficient with regard to information, they really don't tell us a whole lot about reject rates. An attribute chart is more appropriate when the topic of concern is the level of product rejection. Additionally, attribute-based sampling schemes have a substantial literature: ANSI Z 1.4, MIL-STD-1235C (continuous sampling), Dodge-Romig, and various other sampling schemes.

Table VIII.1 compares attribute and variable control charts and—no surprise!—trade-offs exist when making a choice.

Table VIII.1   Differences between variable- and attribute-based control charts.

Variable	Attribute
Measured data	Counted data
Specific to the CTQ characteristic	Overall quality
Sensitive to process change	Not as sensitive to process change (we are using integers here!)
Small sample size (frequently only 5)	Sample sizes from 25 to 200, depending on the number of defectives and the underlying statistical process
Requires higher level of skill to interpret	Simple to interpret
May provide enough information to assist in improving process	Probably will *not* provide enough information for process improvement
Can be used for true process control using Box-Jenkins or Box-Luceño	Typically not satisfactory for dynamic process control. Counts of defectives do *not* tell us which way the process is drifting from a control point of view

3. RATIONAL SUBGROUPING[46]

Meaning

A rational subgroup is a sample that is sufficient to define the common cause scenario such that special causes appear as differences between subgroups. Normally, the average of a subgroup is the measurement used, especially in variables control charts.

Attributes

Attributes data is typically *qualitative*. This qualitative data can be counted, recorded, and analyzed. The count is always expressed as an integer. Typical items for count are nonconformities, nonconforming units, percent nonconforming, and so on. Subgroups for attributes frequently require 50 to 200 sample units per subgroup to provide meaningful information. Equation (VIII.1) shows a quick calculation of sample size for a subgroup falling under the binomial distribution (Bernoulli process).

$$\gamma = 0.95$$

$$probability = 0.01$$

$$\frac{-\ln(1-\gamma)}{probability} = 299.573 \ or \approx 300 \ units \ in \ sample \qquad \text{(VIII.1)}$$

Note the large sample size required under the stated conditions. This is typical of attribute-based control charts. The example shows a calculation using the binomial distribution. Since the Poisson distribution is an approximator of the binomial at low probabilities and large sample sizes, the same kind of situation applies.

Why can we use such small samples for the charts like the x-bar R?

The answer lies in the fact that we are using small sample size statistics, which allows the use of the t distribution and, furthermore, a strong assumption of normality derived from the fact that the distribution of the mean follows a normal distribution regardless of the underlying distribution. Remember that the central limit theorem always refers to the mean of the sample data and not to the individual values of the sample data. The fact that we can use the normal and standard normal distributions with sample means gives a tremendous incentive for doing just that.

Variables

The classic variables control chart is the X-bar R-chart, which is actually two charts. Variable is normally expressed as a floating point or real value. Other variables control charts are the X-bar S, the median, and the individuals and moving range charts. Variable data is always *quantitative*. Variables control charts can have subgroups as small as individual units, although sampling allows a more common value like five to six units per sample.

Another Consideration

Also keep in mind that you will normally take 25 subgroups before constructing the control chart in order to provide sufficient history to have meaning.

4. SELECTION AND APPLICATION OF CONTROL CHARTS

Equations (VIII.2)–(VIII.8) show control limit calculations. Figure VIII.2 shows how to select a control chart.

X-bar R and X-bar S

For the $\bar{X}$ chart,

$$\bar{R} = \frac{R_1 + R_2 + \cdots + R_n}{n}, \bar{\bar{X}} = \frac{\bar{X}_1 + \bar{X}_2 + \cdots + \bar{X}_n}{n},$$

$$n = \text{number of subgroups} \qquad\qquad (VIII.2)$$

$$CL = \bar{\bar{X}} \pm A_2 \bar{R}; A_2 = 3\sigma_X; \sigma_X = \frac{\sigma}{\sqrt{n}}; \text{center line} = \bar{\bar{X}}.$$

For the R chart,

$$UCL = \bar{R}D_4; LCL = \bar{R}D_3; \text{center line} = \bar{\bar{X}}$$

For the S chart, the center line is $\bar{\bar{X}}$ and $UCL - LCL = \pm 3\sigma$

Individual/Moving Range (Im/R)

For the *I* chart,

$$CL = \overline{X} \pm E_2 \overline{Rm}; center\ line = \overline{X} \qquad \text{(VIII.3)}$$

For the *R* chart,

$$UCL = \overline{R}D_4 ; LCL = \overline{R}D_3 ; center\ line = \overline{R}$$

For the *S* chart, the center line is $\overline{\overline{X}}$ and $UCL - LCL = \pm 3\sigma$

Median

For the median control chart, $\widetilde{\widetilde{X}}$ is the median of the medians. Hence,

$$CL = \widetilde{\widetilde{X}} \pm \widetilde{A}_2 \overline{R} \qquad \text{(VIII.4)}$$

p

For the *p* chart,

$$CL = \overline{p} \pm 3\sqrt{\frac{\overline{p}(1-\overline{p})}{n}}; \qquad \text{(VIII.5)}$$

when *n* varies, use $\overline{n}$.

np

For the *np* chart

$$CL = n\overline{p} \pm 3\sqrt{np(1-\overline{p})}, \qquad \text{(VIII.6)}$$

n being constant.

u

For the *u* chart,

$$CL = \overline{u} \pm 3\sqrt{\frac{\overline{u}}{n}}; \qquad \text{(VIII.7)}$$

when *n* varies, use $\overline{n}$.

c

For the *c* chart,

$$CL = \bar{c} \pm 3\sqrt{\bar{c}} \qquad\qquad (VIII.8)$$

with *n* constant.

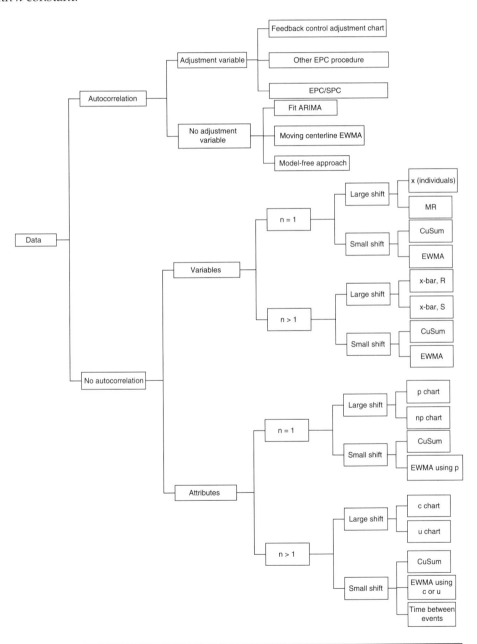

Figure VIII.2   Choosing a control chart.

5. ANALYSIS OF CONTROL CHARTS

Analyzing for Special Cause

To analyze for statistically significant events, we can use any one or all of eight tests applied to the control chart.

1. One point more than three sigmas from the center line

2. Nine points in a row on same side of the center line

3. Six points in a row, all increasing or all decreasing (trending)

4. Fourteen points in a row, alternating up and down (cyclic or two processes)

5. Two out of three points in a row more than two sigmas from the center line (same side)

6. Four out of five points in a row more than one sigma from the center line (same side)

7. Fifteen points in a row within one sigma of the center line (either side)

8. Eight points in a row more than one sigma from the center line (either side)

Use tests 1–4 for R chart, S chart, moving range chart, and the attributes control charts (p, np, c, and u charts).

Analyzing for Common Cause

Finding common causes is much more difficult than finding special (assignable) causes because the behavior of the common cause is the intrinsic variation in the process itself. An improvement in common cause means modifying the very heart of the process.

The control chart in Figure VIII.3 shows the results of some control chart testing using MINITAB, which has a very nice implementation of the eight AIAG criteria for statistically significant events.

The following list summarizes the specific tests "triggered" in Figure VIII.3:

Test 1: 1 point more than 3σ from center line

Test 2: 9 points consecutively on same side of mean

Test 5: 2 out of 3 points > 2σ from center line (same side)

Test 6: 4 out of 5 points > 1σ from center line (same side)

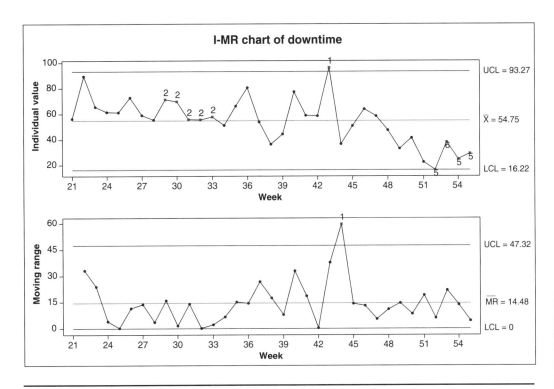

Figure VIII.3   Testing for special causes.

6. PRE-CONTROL[47]

What It Is

A mere three units and an assumption of a normal distribution are sufficient to provide control information using the pre-control technique. It is *not* statistically based.

When to Use It

Pre-control can be used if the following applies:

$$specification\,limits > \mu \pm 3\left(\sigma + \frac{\sigma}{\sqrt{n}}\right) \qquad\qquad (VIII.9)$$

Typical Guidelines

1. Commence the process. If the first item is outside spec, reset and start over.

2. If the item is inside spec but outside the pre-control line, reset the process.

3. If the second item is outside the same pre-control line, check the next item.

4. If the second item is inside the pre-control line, continue. Reset the process only when two consecutive items are outside a specific pre-control line.

5. When one item is outside a pre-control line and the next item is outside the other pre-control line, process variation is *out of control*.

6. If five consecutive units are inside the pre-control lines, change over to frequency gaging.

7. If using frequency gaging, make no adjustments unless the item goes outside a pre-control line. Examine the next item and proceed from step 4.

8. If the process is reset, step 6 applies.

9. If the operator goes more than 25 times without a process reset, decrease the gaging frequency to increase units between samples; if fewer than 25 times, increase the gaging frequency. The situation is satisfactory when running 25 samples to a reset.

See Figure VIII.4 for a representation of the pre-control limits.

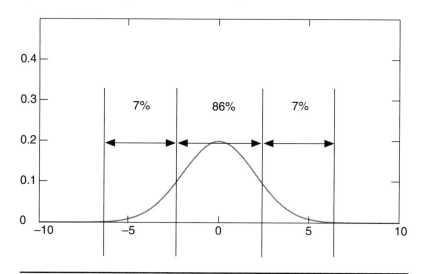

Figure VIII.4 An illustration of pre-control limits (not to scale).

Bottom of left 7 percent is lower specification limit

Top of left 7 percent is lower pre-control limit (1/4)

Bottom of right 7 percent is upper pre-control limit

Top of right 7 percent is upper specification limit

Downsides

The following are some downsides to using pre-control:

- No pattern recognition.
- Small sample size reduces discrimination.
- No real control information.

FURTHER READING

Montgomery, Douglas C. 2004. *Introduction to Statistical Quality Control.* 5th ed. New York: John Wiley & Sons.

Section VIII.A.6

B. Advanced Statistical Process Control

SHORT-RUN[48]

Why Is It Called "Short-Run"?

Short-run SPC is an extension of the SPC concept. A short-run SPC can be used for the following reasons:

1. We have no choice but to use a *very small lot size*, say, 1 to 15 pieces per lot. We could be in a situation where not very many of these items are built (aircraft carriers) or where each one is unique (major river dams).

2. The lot size may be large enough, but *relatively few subgroups* are collected. It may be extremely inconvenient to collect subgroups; for example, we might have process dealing with medical supplies that is highly regulated for hygiene.

Coding Data—A Partial Solution

One form of coding data occurs when we only record the variation from a common reference point. This technique can be extremely convenient because we only have to record the difference. The benefit of this method is that it allows us to begin evaluating the behavior of the process as soon as we start collecting data. The standard formula for coding is as follows:

Coded data value = (actual measurement – reference)/(measurement unit)

Other Kinds of Variables Charts

Nominal Xbar R. Code using the nominal specification. Plot the average and range. Subgroups are two to five sample units, frequently three.

Target Xbar R. Use when a nominal value doesn't exist for a limit. This situation occurs when you have a maximum with a minimum, or vice versa. Substitute a target Xdouble bar. Code off of the Xdouble bar derived from the process itself.

259

Short-run Xbar R. This method adjusts data for changes in both centering and variation. Use an Xdouble bar and a target Rbar.

There are many other variations of the variables charts.

Short-Run Attributes

Short-run versions of the standard charts exist using the formulas in Equation VIII.10. The following rules apply in all short-run attributes charts:

- Center line = 0 in *every case.*

- Upper control limit = +3 in *every case.*

- Lower control limit = –3 in *every case.*

These look like a Z chart (standard normal distribution) and function in the same way.

Variables

$$\text{Nominal } \overline{X} \text{ and } R$$

$$Center\ line_{\overline{X}} = \frac{\sum_{i=1}^{n} \overline{X}_i}{k};$$ (VIII.10)

$$Center\ line_{\overline{R}} = \frac{\sum_{i=1}^{n} \overline{R}_i}{k};$$

where k = number of plot points. Control limits are plotted as with standard $\overline{X}$ and R chart. Target $\overline{X}R$ and short-run $\overline{X}R$ use similar formulas.

Attributes

$$\text{Short-run np plot point} = \frac{np - Target\ n\overline{p}}{\sqrt{Target\ n\overline{p}(1 - \frac{Target\ n\overline{p}}{n})}}$$

$$\text{Short-run p plot point} = \frac{p - Target\ \overline{p}}{\sqrt{Target\ \overline{p}(1 - \frac{Target\ \overline{p}}{n})}},$$

where

$$\bar{p} = \frac{np}{n}.$$

$$\text{Short-run c plot point} = \frac{c - Target\,\bar{c}}{\sqrt{Target\,\bar{c}}}$$

$$\text{Short-run u plot point} = \frac{u - Target\,\bar{u}}{\sqrt{\dfrac{Target\,\bar{u}}{n}}},$$

where

$$\bar{u} = \frac{c}{n}.$$

EWMA

One of the topics of concern in the use of control charts once a process is under a very high level of control is the ability to detect small shifts in process behavior. The exponential weighted moving average (EWMA) chart is one solution to this problem.

The standard EWMA function is:

$$z_t = r\bar{x}_t + (1-r)z_{t-1}, \tag{VIII.11}$$

where $0 < r \le 1$ and r is a constant, and at $t = 1$, the starting value is $z_0 = \bar{\bar{x}}$.

Control engineers may recognize that this formula is an abstract definition of a filter they use for noisy analog data. If we look at this carefully, we realize that more recent values of data are given more weight and earlier values are given less weight. This makes sense if we give the greatest credence to the most recent data. If we weight the data farther back in time, we increase the smoothing on the filter and increase the lag between the real value and the filtered value—not necessarily desirable.

Our variance becomes:

$$\sigma_{z_t}^2 = \frac{\sigma^2}{n}\left(\frac{r}{2-r}\right)\left[1-(1-r)^{2t}\right], \tag{VIII.12}$$

but as t increases, we have

$$\sigma_z^2 = \frac{\sigma^2}{n}\left(\frac{r}{2-r}\right),$$

leading to control limits of

$$(U \text{ or } L)CL = \overline{\overline{x}} \pm 3\sigma \sqrt{\frac{r}{(2-r)n}}.$$

As r approaches the value of 1, the EWMA approaches a standard Shewhart control chart. Figure VIII.5 shows an example EWMA chart. Note how the control limits reflect the increased resolution of the data over time. This feature also makes the EWMA chart fairly usable for individual measurements.

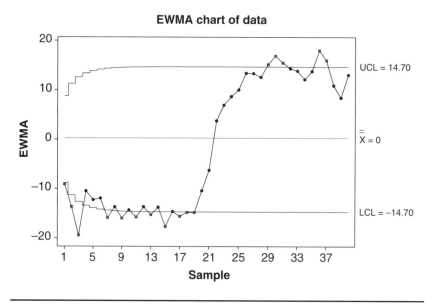

Figure VIII.5   An example of an EWMA control chart using a file called "Data." Output from MINITAB.

CUSUM

CuSums are another solution to the small change problem. They have been around since the mid-1950s. They are capable of detecting shifts in a process that are invisible to the standard Shewhart-style control chart.

Older versions of the CuSum chart use a control limit tool called a V-mask. The dimensions of the V-mask depend on the degree of sensitivity you might desire regarding the detection of the process shift as well as the confidence level.

So why do we call it a CuSum? The calculations are based on the accumulated sum of the differences. The first value is the difference between the measured value and some target value. This idea continues throughout the run. Differences can be negative, which affects the ongoing cumulative result. Figure VIII.6 shows the CuSum for the same data used in Figure VIII.5 (using Air Academy's SPC XL product). Which one do you find easier to interpret? Note also how negative data slows down the rate of accumulation but does not cause it to drop in this example. We might interpret this CuSum to mean that our deviations are getting progressively worse.

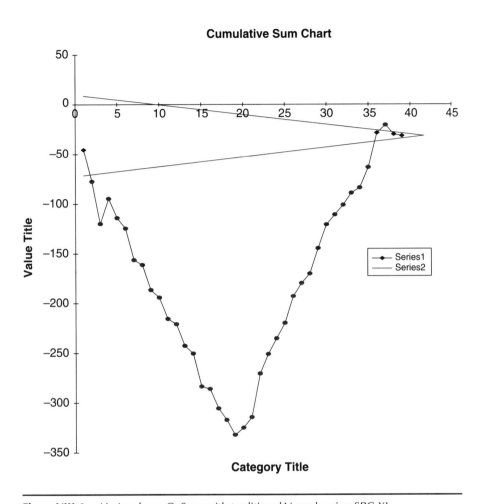

Figure VIII.6   Air Academy CuSum with traditional V-mask using SPC XL.

Look also at MINITAB's output of a CuSum (Figure VIII.7), which takes an alternate approach to using the chart—MINITAB can establish control limits that resemble those of a standard Shewhart control chart. With the V-mask, any point outside the "V" is out of control; with the control limits, any point outside of the control limit is out of control.

MOVING AVERAGE

Moving averages are typically used to smooth extremely noisy data. The more components to the moving average calculation, the greater the smoothing until the data become virtually unrecognizable. On the other hand, as with stock market data, long-term trends can be observed with careful use of extreme smoothing.

Moving average charts can be used for individual or subgroup data because the average values determined are based on artificial subgroups to begin with. Generally, the weighting of a moving average chart is less sophisticated than that of the EWMA and, hence, this chart is probably less desirable than the EWMA.

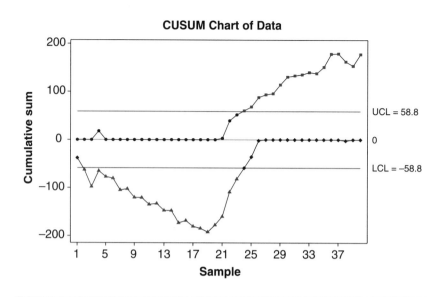

Figure VIII.7   MINITAB CuSum with control limits.

We pick a finite interval as our standard for the moving average and we calculate it with the following formula:

$$MA = \frac{\left[\overline{X}_t + \overline{X}_{t-1} + \cdots + \overline{X}_{t-w+1}\right]}{w}, \tag{VIII.13}$$

where we measure $\overline{X}$ at some time t in the past and divide by the number of X's that we have.

As we move across time, the oldest measure drops off the left side and a new measurement is added to the right side of the equation. The moving average must be recalculated with each new point. If the number of values is large, this calculation can be very computationally intensive.

The variance of the moving average turns out to be:

$$\sigma^2_{MA} = \frac{1}{w^2} \sum_{i=t-w+1}^{t} \frac{\sigma^2}{n} = \frac{\sigma^2}{nw}, \tag{VIII.14}$$

where σ is the variance of the base data.

The control limits for this chart are:

$$(U \, or \, L)CL = \overline{\overline{X}} \pm \frac{3\sigma}{\sqrt{nw}} \tag{VIII.15}$$

Use caution if you must use one of these control charts—longer moving averages reduce the response to large shifts. See Figure VIII.8 for a small moving average control chart that uses the same data shown in the EWMA and CuSum charts we have displayed so far.

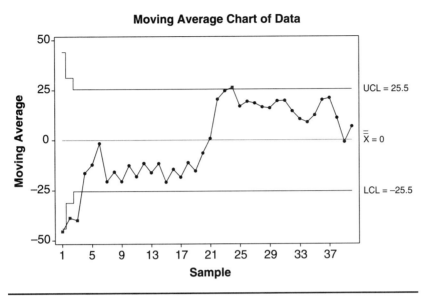

Figure VIII.8   Moving average control chart.

In general, the EWMA is a better choice because of the minimal calculational requirements. It is very easy to adjust the sensitivity of an EWMA just by changing the value of two parameters.

FURTHER READING

Montgomery, Douglas C. 2004. *Introduction to Statistical Quality Control*. 5th ed. New York: John Wiley & Sons.

C. Lean Tools for Control

5S[49]

A 5S program focuses on organization, cleanliness, and standardization to improve profitability, efficiency, and safety. It does this by reducing wasted time and materials, improving manufacturing line and office setups, reducing maintenance and downtime, improving efficiency and productivity, improving employee morale, and simplifying the work environment. Any organization, profit or nonprofit, large or small, can derive benefit from implementing a 5S program. The following list shows the Japanese words that define the 5S system:

1. Sort (*Seiri*): What is needed stays; what is not needed leaves; what is temporarily needed is stored.

   –Sorting improves search and retrieval time as well as creating more space in storage locations. Sorting is a good way to regain precious floor space and discard dysfunctional tools, obsolete equipment and fixtures, out-and-out scrap, and surplus raw material. The basic idea is to remove the unnecessary so that it doesn't need to be managed, liberating both time and space.

2. Straighten (*Seiton*): Simplify access and efficiency.

   –Simplifying access implies some level of systematic arrangement for the most efficient and effective retrieval. This "S" goes beyond the simple sorting of *seiri*. Examples include painting floors to more readily disclose the presence of grime, marking work areas and specific locations by tagging or outlining the area, and shadow tool boards, where the outline of the tool is marked on the pegboard.

   –*Seiton* is also a key concept in setup reduction time and preventive maintenance efficiency. Additionally, intelligent site selection for tools can reduce excessive movement of employees and reduce one of the seven wastes.

3. Shine (*Seiso*): No trash or dirt in the workplace.

   –Daily follow-up cleaning is necessary in order to sustain improvements gained from removing excess and relocating the remainder. A spotless workplace also helps to expose damaged equipment experiencing seepage, breakage, and misalignment of component machine pieces. Seemingly minor issues can grow into major problems, leading to production downtime and opportunity cost or customer fines. Regular cleaning serves as an audit function. In the experience of the author, no filthy workplace has ever been a well-managed workplace.

4. Standardize (*Seiketsu*): Systematize organization.

   –The goal is to reinforce the first three S's such that it becomes second nature for the workers to employ them. When this culture shift does not occur, the work will rapidly drift in the direction of increased entropy. Employees backslide into their previous behavior. Straightforward, frequently audited standards support a controlled, clean, and safe workplace. If employees develop the standards themselves, they participate in increased ownership of their work area and enhance the probability of the 5S culture's success.

5. Sustain (*Shitsuke*): Adherence to standards established for the four components.

   –In order to retain the vigor of a good 5S program, management must train and reinforce the staff in standards and expectations. Respectful coaching, when necessary, can reinforce the desired cultural changes as well as serve as part of the auditing procedure. In this age of the digital photograph, it is very easy to disseminate illustrations of before and after—what you don't want to see and what you do want to see. 5S is not a one-shot program from which the employee can walk away—it is a complete change of viewpoint about the nature of the workplace.

The Program

Inculcation of the 5S philosophy and way of life can be managed like any other project with the caveat that it is a *never-ending* project. Because the program can be run as a project, it must have objectives, milestones, and schedules. As discussed earlier in this book, we normally select a team and a team leader to provide the initial level of ownership. The team should be composed of the employees/members of the work area under consideration, up to and including an entire office complex or plant. The project should also have a Champion to represent the team to executive management as well as frequent executive oversight. The team should report their progress to management on a regular schedule. One approach to implementing a 5S program could be the following:

Groundwork	Create the project team and select the first improvement area sensibly. Early victories can provide inspiration to the project team.
Early coaching	The team leader must clarify goals and provide examples of correct and incorrect 5S.
Kick-off	Implement a thorough 2S action: sort and straighten.
Improvement	Continue the "straighten" S (*seiton*) by selecting appropriate storage space for equipment, tools, and resources. In some cases, the team may want to measure the actual usage of some of the equipment to see if it is ripe for removal.
Revelation	Every setback must be clearly visible, even jarring to the eye. Avoid pointing fingers at individuals. The idea is to cause a kind of culture shock.
Institutionalize criteria	Audit teams should be a mix of all levels of staff as well as members from different areas of the organization. The audits should use an audit checklist to maintain consistency and avoid missing any items. Audit results are part of the presentation of the team to management: "What gets measured is what gets done."
Kaizen attitude	Management must ensure that even after the team has disbanded, audits continue, individuals are rewarded for special efforts, and the program does not shrivel away and die.

VISUAL FACTORY

The visual factory is a logical extension of 5S, set up so anyone can promptly know the status of the process, comprehend the process, and discern if the process if functioning properly.

There are two types of application in the visual factory: displays and controls.

Visual Displays

Visual displays are typically informative. Examples are:

- Profitability charts
- Line quality charts
- Attendance run charts

Visual Controls

Visual controls direct behavior. Examples are

- Stop signs
- No smoking signs
- Color-coded directional arrows or keep-out areas

In some factories, a special electronic board called an "andon" signals the status of a process with lights or sounds. All workers can see the andon and keep track of the status in real time.

Some more examples:

- Color-coded pipes and wires (also 5S)

- Painted floor areas for good stock, scrap, trash, and so on (also fits in with kanban, discussed later in this section)

- Indicator lights (can use LEDs or ticker tape to send messages)

- Workgroup display boards with procedures and metrics

Figure VIII.9 shows usage in the visual factory. This photo is used to help keep the tools in order as well as giving a quick idea of tool inventory status. In other words, not only is this a photograph of the tools, it is also the device for showing the user how to locate the tools on the pegboard.

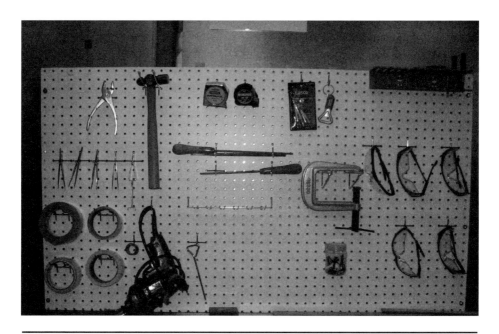

Figure VIII.9   Photograph used to show employees the proper location of tools.

This method is very easy to accomplish with a camera. Another technique for showing the location of tools uses the outline or "shadow" of the tool to indicate the proper location.

KAIZEN[50]

Classical Kaizen

Kaizen is the principle of continuous improvement. It can cover improvements in the factory, the office, business life, and personal life. It encapsulates most lean concepts and some of the tools and concepts of Six Sigma.

What distinguishes true kaizen from other philosophies is the lack of emphasis on breakthrough improvements; rather, kaizen has a philosophy of low-cost, gradual improvement—a sort of tortoise and hare approach to quality. Imai has used terms like the following:

- Small steps

- Continuous and incremental

- Gradual and constant

- Group effort

- Maintenance and improvement

- People over technology

- Low financial investment

- Still works in slow economies

Another term frequently used in kaizen activities is "gemba." The gemba is where the action is in the organization. Masaaki Imai's point was that this is where the value is added.

Another unusual emphasis in kaizen is the concept of employee suggestions. Imai and others have felt that many, if not most, of the continuous improvement suggestions most effectively arise from the people in the gemba.

Figure VIII.10 contrasts the benefits of kaizen with innovative programs. Masaaki Imai's point: The tortoise wins!

Kaizen Blitz

In recent years, another kind of kaizen has been popularized: kaizen blitz. Kaizen blitz is a contradiction in terms. The idea behind a kaizen blitz is to (1) set aside five working days, (2) gather a small team, (3) pick a small area to work on, (4) put concentrated effort to improve only that small area (scope control), and (5) review the results at the end of the session. It is not that the kaizen blitz is bad, but rather that it is an inept choice of terms for a gradual philosophy of continuous improvement.

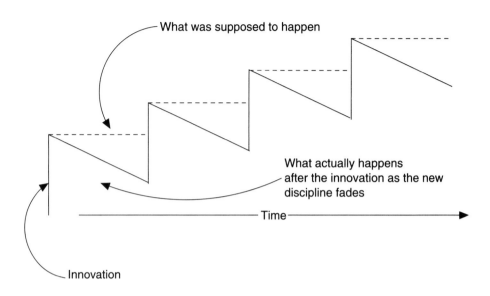

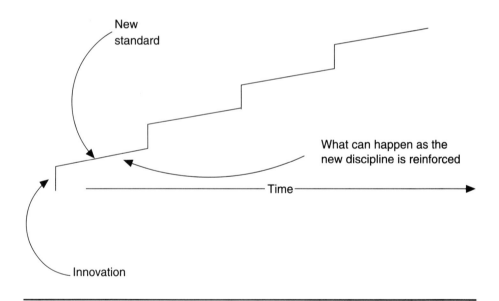

Figure VIII.10 Comparison of kaizen's gradual method versus that of fading innovation.

KANBAN

A "kanban" is simply a signal to do something. This can be very simple or very complex. The purpose of a kanban is to promote an inventory pull system in manufacturing or any other venue where material moves in a flow.

In the office or on the floor, the kanban can function as a work order. It can contain the information necessary in order to do the job. A new kanban is not pulled until the old one is complete and overall work becomes regulated.

Production Kanban

A production kanban can authorize the manufacture of one or more pieces of product (for example, office forms or manufacturing stock). Production kanban typically have information about details of the manufacture and sometimes explicitly define the flow.

Withdrawal Kanban

Withdrawal kanban authorize the movement of material and represent the truest form of the pull system. Raw material kanban are usually represented by a triangular, colored plate that signals a reorder when reached.

Ohno's Rules for Use

1. The downstream process can only pick up the number of pieces indicated on the kanban.

2. The upstream process can only create the number of pieces indicated on the kanban.

3. No item may be made or moved without a kanban.

4. The kanban must be *attached* to the pieces.

5. No defective product/piece passes on to the subsequent process.

6. The sensitivity of the system is inversely proportional to the number of kanban.

Reducing the number of kanban is known as "stressing the system." This technique is used to reveal problems in the system.

Kanban without Cards

Because kanban really represents a signaling system, anything that sends a signal can become a kanban:

- A special place marked out in color on the floor, with emptiness signaling the need for replenishment

- Double bin systems, where the emptiness of one bin signals the order for replenishment

- Electric kanban using computers

See Equation VIII.16 for an overview of kanban calculations.

Section VIII.C

Re-order point = average usage during lead time + safety stock
– order placed but not yet received

$$Total\ number\ of\ kanban = \frac{(economic\ lot\ size) + (daily\ demand \times safety\ coefficient)}{container\ capacity}$$ (VIII.16)

or

$$Total\ number\ of\ kanban = \left(\frac{monthly\ demand}{monthly\ number\ of\ setups}\right) + (daily\ demand \times safety\ coefficient)$$

$$Maximum\ inventory = daily\ demand \times (order\ cycle + lead\ time) + safety\ stock$$

$$Order\ cycle = \frac{economic\ lot\ size\ for\ expected\ demand}{daily\ average\ demand}$$

$$EOQ = \sqrt{\frac{2AR}{ic}},$$

where $A = \dfrac{ordering\ cost}{lot}$

R = monthly estimated demand quantity

$i = \dfrac{carrying\ cost}{\$item}$

c = unit cost

$$Order\ quantity = (standard\ quantity - existing\ inventory) - (orders\ placed\ but\ not\ yet\ received)$$

$$Total\ kanban = \frac{daily\ demand \times (order\ cycle + lead\ time + safety\ period)}{container\ capacity}$$

In some plants, the kanban count will be reduced occasionally as a means of stressing the system, which will reveal weaknesses in the process.

POKA-YOKE

Poka-yoke simply means "mistake-proofing." When poka-yoke is implemented correctly, a mistake *cannot happen*. That is why Shingo used the term "zero quality control." He felt that creating a situation in which mistakes didn't happen in the first place was significantly superior to allowing a certain level of error and defects and controlling them.

Poka-yoke only works well in one-piece flow systems, where no more than one defective part can occur. It can, however, be used in batch systems so that only one batch will produce defective parts.

Inspection

Inspection in the normal sense of special inspectors performing a quality policing function is *not* poka-yoke. Inspection in the sense of the operator/technician inspecting their own work and refusing to send it downstream if it is defective *is* poka-yoke. When this method works properly, the piece is inspected by the operators/technicians at each workstation, providing a much higher level of inspection than what can be achieved using inspectors working with a sampling plan.

Mistake-Proofing Devices

The classical poka-yoke involves the installation of devices that prevent error from occurring on the line. Some of these devices control by means of a sizing device (an opening) and others use a limit switch—for example, an oversized box might strike the switch and stop the conveyor. This use of limit switches is called autonomation and was piloted by Taiichi Ohno at Toyota Motors. Some safety devices use a system where the operator working a press must push two buttons on either side of the machine to make it work, thus forcing the operator to remove his or her hands from the press area.

Immediate Feedback

The poka-yoke system should send out an alarm that an event has occurred, allowing the engineers or supervisors to intervene immediately to get at the root cause of the error. Feedback can be visual (visual factory), audible (horn or klaxon), or by computer messaging.

Food for Error

1. Unusually high quantities of work, as in end-of-month all-out frenzies, can cause the operator to bypass the standard operating procedures.

2. Too many parts means too many decisions at a workstation. Even a visual can be confusing under these circumstances. Kitting can help here.

3. Parts that are rarely produced can lead to error because the operators basically forget how to make the product. This situation may require retraining.

4. Machinery wear can cause defective parts.

5. Failure to understand the reason for geometric dimensioning and tolerancing can lead to problems as the wrong sizes are used.

6. Lack of Gage R&R activities can lead to incapable manufacturing devices. The purpose of Gage R&R is to satisfy ourselves about the ability of the machine to actually make the product.

7. Infrequent calibration can lead to shifting or drifting values in the measurements.

8. Lack of standards gives workers no direction.

9. If a product lacks asymmetry, the operator can confuse the top and bottom or sides. This is why automotive harness manufacturers use connectors that only fit one way.

10. Tampering with a process under control can cause even greater variation.

TPM

TPM = total productive maintenance. Who cares? We do. A good TPM system:

- Improves equipment performance, much as the performance of your personal automobile can be improved by maintaining the lubricants, the battery water, the various fluids, the belts, the hoses, and so on.

- Is a planned system. Because the TPM schedule is known ahead of time, downtime can be planned for. This situation is much better than that in which the machine breaks down at random intervals.

- Causes yields to go up because the machine is always in proper adjustment. Better yields mean less scrap and a nice move in the Six Sigma direction, which is what this is all about.

- Improves ownership of problems, because the involved operators normally perform the TPM instead of some special group.

- Extends the life of the machinery, reducing opportunity cost and improving return on investment.

- Reduces firefighting because unexpected downtime disappears.

The pillars of TPM are:

1. Autonomous maintenance with seven steps
    –Do initial cleaning and inspection
    –Establish controls for the causes of dirt and dust
    –Create cleaning and lubrication standards
    –Supervise inspection training
    –Perform equipment inspections
    –Implement workplace management and control
    –Promote continuous improvement

2. Equipment and process improvement

3. Planned maintenance—breakdown, corrective, preventive, predictive, productive maintenance, and establishment of maintenance calendar

4. Education and skill training
    –"Soft" skills
    –"Hard" or quantitative skills

5. Initial flow control (production and equipment), especially new equipment

6. Process quality maintenance

7. Office TPM
    – These departments have processes, too
    – Process analysis can be used to streamline the flow (transactional Six Sigma)

8. Safety, hygiene, and environmental

Significant TPM measures can include:

- Availability = (operating time) / (available time)

- Performance efficiency = (total parts run × ideal cycle time) / (operating time)

- Quality = (total parts run – total defects) / (total parts run)

- Overall equipment effectiveness = equipment availability × performance efficiency × quality

- Downtime due to breakdown

- Setup and adjustment time

- Inefficient setup time

- Production of defective components

- Operating at less-than-ideal speed

- Cycles lost to tooling (opportunity cost)

- Work stoppage time

STANDARD WORK

Standard work means we have calculated the most efficient possible operations. The process is documented and becomes a standard operating procedure. Whenever possible, this standard operating procedure should be available at the operator workstation, creating a visual workplace.

Figure VIII.11 shows a bad copy of page one of DD-1723, a government form for analyzing processes that can be used in the office or on the factory floor.[51] (As of this writing, a clean copy can be found at http://www.dior.whs.mil/forms/DD1723.PDF).

In a manufacturing study, you might also see charts like:

- Process capacity tables

- Standard Operations (combination) Chart

- Standard workflow diagrams

- Standard Operations sheets

Once the work is studied and standardized and standard work is known, the organization can begin to realistically calculate the two most common capacity values: (1) rough cut capacity planning (RCCP) and (2) capacity resource planning (CRP).

FLOW PROCESS CHART		1. NUMBER	2. PAGE NO.	3. NO. OF PGS

4. PROCESS	5.		SUMMARY				
	a. ACTIONS		b. PRESENT		c. PROPOSED		d. DIFFERENCE
6. ☐ MAN OR ☐ MATERIAL			NO.	TIME	NO.	TIME	NO.	TIME
	◯ OPERATIONS						
7. CHART BEGINS 8. CHART ENDS	⇨ TRANSPORTATIONS						
	☐ INSPECTIONS						
9. CHARTED BY 10. DATE	D DELAYS						
	▽ STORAGES						
11. ORGANIZATION	DISTANCE TRAVELED (Feet)						

12a. DETAILS OF ☐ PRESENT ☐ PROPOSED METHOD	b. OPERATION TRANSPORT INSPECTION DELAY STORAGE	c. DISTANCE IN FEET	d. QUANTITY	e. TIME	f. ANALYSIS WHY? WHAT? WHERE? WHEN? WHO? HOW?	g. NOTES	h. ANALYSIS CH ELIMINATE COMBINE SEQUENCE PLACE PERSON IMPROVE
1.	◯⇨☐D▽						
2.	◯⇨☐D▽						
3.	◯⇨☐D▽						
4.	◯⇨☐D▽						
5.	◯⇨☐D▽						
6.	◯⇨☐D▽						
7.	◯⇨☐D▽						
8.	◯⇨☐D▽						
9.	◯⇨☐D▽						
10.	◯⇨☐D▽						
11.	◯⇨☐D▽						
12.	◯⇨☐D▽						
13.	◯⇨☐D▽						
14.	◯⇨☐D▽						
15.	◯⇨☐D▽						
16.	◯⇨☐D▽						
17.	◯⇨☐D▽						
18.	◯⇨☐D▽						
19.	◯⇨☐D▽						
20.	◯⇨☐D▽						
21.	◯⇨☐D▽						

DD Form 1723, SEP 76 (EG)   Designed using Perform Pro, WHS/DIOR, Feb 95

Figure VIII.11   Form DD-1723 can be used as a compact way to measure process and time.

Rough cut capacity planning is a straightforward calculation that takes the workload demand in hours and divides it by the standard hours to get the number of operators required to do the work.

Capacity resource planning is an iterative algorithm that exercises different combinations and scenarios to find a good, possibly optimum, capacity plan.

In both cases, infinite loading scenarios are avoided and the organization might actually meet the promised delivery dates.

FURTHER READING

Imai, Masaaki. 1986. *Kaizen: The Key to Japan's Competitive Success.* New York: Random House.

Section VIII.C

D. Measurement System Re-analysis

MEASURING SYSTEM IMPROVEMENT[52]

The key to measurement system improvement lies in looking at the sources for measurement error after performing the study. Although a Gage R&R study is the typical tool of choice for measurement system and machine study, multi-vari charts can also be used and normally exist in a proto form on an R&R study. Please note that the kind of measurement system we discuss in this section is one in which machine calibration plays a large part. Behavioral measurement systems are significant to transactional Six Sigma; for example, we might measure the number of times a hotel desk clerk says "please" to customers during the course of a shift.

A common source of measuring system problems lies in repeatability. This factor is the ability of multiple operators to measure the same parts with the same gaging and achieve the same result within some level of confidence.

Another common issue lies in reproducibility, where we examine inter-operator variation rather than intra-operator variation. If some of these terms are reminiscent of designed experiments, this is no mistake. The Analysis of Variance plays a significant part in the determination of the quality of the measurement system.

How critical is a measurement system? In the automotive world, it is extremely important. If a supplier is required to be certified to QS-9000 or ISO/TS 16949 (the automotive quality standards), a customer may demand a recall if an audit discovers the product has been erroneously produced with devices that are not in calibration. It is not so much that a calibration due date has passed, for the device may still be in calibration—it is the fabrication of products with out-of-calibration devices that causes the problem. A product recall can be expensive for both customer and supplier.

Equation (VIII.17) shows the two most important percentage calculations in measurement systems work.

$$\%tolerance = \frac{Total\ R\ \&\ R \times 100}{USL - LSL}$$

$$\%process\ variation = \frac{Total\ R\ \&\ R \times 100}{5.15 \times \sigma_{process}}, \sigma_{process}$$

$$(VIII.17)$$

In some cases, the data are historical values from a control chart. Regardless, if either value is greater than 10 percent, then the measurement system is probably not acceptable.

MEASUREMENT SYSTEM CAPABILITY

Stability

Stable processes are free of special cause variation. The standard SPC tools are used to measure process stability. Typical contributions to variation come from the following:

- Part variation: piece to piece, raw material lot to lot, piece area to area, and so on

- Tooling variation: cavity to cavity, tool to tool, tool wear over time, and so on

- Human variation: operator to operator, supervisor to supervisor, setup lead to lead, number of other tasks performed at the same time, ergonomic conditions, and so on

- Time variation: Sample time to time, hour to hour, shift to shift, day to day, week to week, month to month, season to season, year to year, lunch and other break times, and so on

- Location variation: machine to machine, facility to facility, state to state, country to country, temperature zone to temperature zone, and so on

Note that these are all forms of process *noise*. They can also be measured using a multi-vari chart.

Bias

Bias in a sample is the influence of a factor that causes the data population or process being sampled to appear different from what it actually is, typically in a specific direction (less or more).

Linearity

Linearity refers to measurements being statistically different from one end of the measurement space to the other. A measurement process may be very capable of measuring small parts but much less accurate measuring large parts, or one end of a long part can be measured more accurately than the other end. Typical noise includes: (1) equipment not calibrated at the upper and lower end of the operating range (or across the span), (2) error in the minimum or maximum calibration master, (3) worn or deteriorating equipment, and (4) possible poor internal equipment design characteristics.

Response-to-Control (RtC) Variable Correlation and Autocorrelation

A low correlation between the control variable (which is used to control the process) and the response variable (which is being measured) can mask the time it appears to take for a process change to be implemented. RtC variable correlation is measured with regression analysis. This situation happens when the response variable is not the same as the control variable and they have differing frequencies of behavior.

Autocorrelation affects measurement when the correlation between paired values of mathematical functions taken at constant intervals incorrectly indicates the degree of periodicity of the function. The values are periodic but really out of sync.

Measurement System Capability Charts and Measures

The following are some of the tools used to determine measurement system capability:

- Linearity plots show the accuracy of the measurement system across the range of part values.

- Stability charts provide a visual display of measurement system performance as a time series. This measurement allows for time series analysis if patterns are detected.

- Control charts plot repeatability to detect sources of error (error from operator to operator is common—a byproduct of training or lack thereof).

- Box and whiskers charts show the variation of the operator's measurements and provide a quick assessment of major characteristics of the distribution.

- Gage error histograms show the distribution of measurement deviations from "true" values. This method tracks residual values and provides another way to assess patterns.

- Gage performance (operating characteristic) curves determine the probability of acceptance or rejection of parts (producer/consumer risk).

- Intraclass correlation plots depict data/products categories.

- Operator bias charts can suggest whether bias is occurring among the operators.

GAGE R&R WITH VARIABLES

Gage R&R is similar to a control chart analysis for a machine; here we are interested in determining the accuracy of our measurement system as well as our ability to remain in calibration. The most common method is to use variables; this makes a lot of sense because we are trying to assess the measuring accuracy of our gaging system.

Here is the process:

1. Assess gage stability.

2. Use Xbar-R or Xbar-S to plot a control chart.

3. Establish the control limits and look for special causes.

4. Use the standard deviation to determine whether the measurement system repeatability is appropriate for the application (that is, are we measuring very

precisely and accurately where we need to be measuring precisely and accurately?).

5. Determine bias by comparing with the reference value.

6. Determine repeatability and reproducibility (R&R!).

Gage R&R studies are complex enough that we recommend using quality software to do the analysis whenever possible. Figure VIII.12 shows a variables study using nested data.

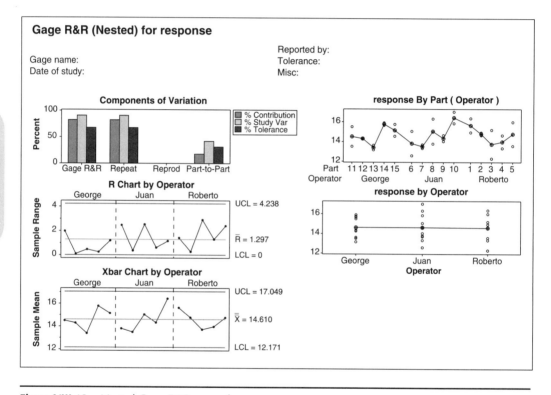

Figure VIII.12 Nested Gage R&R example.

The output is from MINITAB.

Source	VarComp	% Contribution (of VarComp)
Total Gage R&R	1.27232	82.21
Repeatability	1.27232	82.21
Reproducibility	0.00000	0.00
Part-to-Part	0.27531	17.79
Total variation	1.54763	100.00

Source	StdDev (SD)	Study Var (6 * SD)	% Study Var (% SV)	% Tolerance (SV/Toler)
Total Gage R&R	1.12797	6.76784	90.67	67.68
Repeatability	1.12797	6.76784	90.67	67.68
Reproducibility	0.00000	0.00000	0.00	0.00
Part-to-Part	0.52470	3.14818	42.18	31.48
Total variation	1.24404	7.46423	100.00	74.64

Number of Distinct Categories = 1
NOTE: this system is not acceptable—variation is way over 10 percent.

GAGE R&R WITH ATTRIBUTES

How do we do the gage study if we are looking at measurements? The system is very simple: We compare each part to a set of predetermined limits and accept or reject the part depending on whether it meets the limits. It is relatively simple to do, but it is much harder to assess than a variables type of study. While we may understand that we have accepted or rejected material based on our attribute gages (for example, feeler gages), we have learned nothing about the level of "goodness" or "badness" of a gage.

One significant prerequisite to such a study is that the process under analysis be in control, which can be ascertained from attribute control charts on the particular process under consideration. Then a set of reference parts must be selected that covers the tolerance range of interest. As we run the parts through the analysis, each part is normally measured 20 times. We count the number of times the part is accepted. There should be zero acceptances for the smallest study part and 20 acceptances for the largest part, assuming the largest part matches the largest end of the tolerance range.

Figure VIII.13 shows what an attribute Gage R&R study could look like. This particular assessment was performed using MINITAB. Other software packages are available for doing these kinds of analyses.

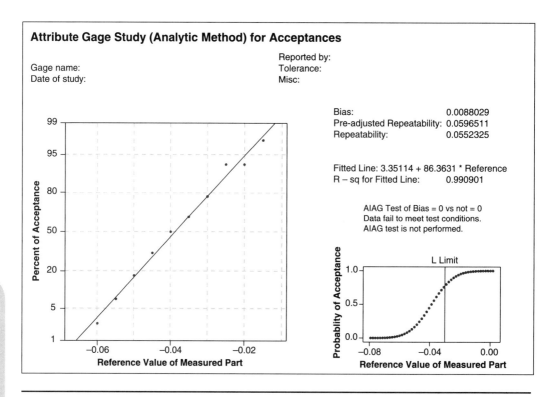

Figure VIII.13   Gage R&R using attributes.

Note that the test shown in Figure VIII.13 fails for the bias test conditions. Normally we would test the bias and the adjusted repeatability using a t-test for the data.

Following are the data for a gage system with a low-end tolerance at –0.030 units that yields the analysis shown in Figure VIII.13:

Partnumber	Reference	Acceptances
1	–0.060	0
2	–0.055	1
3	–0.050	3
4	–0.045	6
5	–0.040	10
6	–0.035	13
7	–0.030	16
8	–0.025	19
9	–0.020	19
10	–0.015	20

GAGE R&R—DESTRUCTIVE

Destructive testing of test samples presents special problems for the measurement system analyst. As the part is tested, it is damaged or destroyed, and testing reproducibility and repeatability becomes very difficult.

The only solution to this problem is to use a relatively homogeneous batch of measurable parts. These parts must resemble each other closely enough that they can be assumed to be the same part. Of course, we have the issue of knowing this throughout the very testing that is going to destroy the part! Alternative methods of measurement may be necessary to assure ourselves that the batch is reasonably homogeneous.

R&R-style crossed testing cannot be performed, so we have to use a nested model. The equation for this situation is:

$$\text{response}_{ijk} = \mu + \text{operator}_i + \text{sample}_{j(i)} + \varepsilon_{(ij)k},$$

where $i, k = 1, 2, 3$ and $j = 1, \ldots, 5$ (with respect to Figure VIII.13).

We perform analysis just like a typical R&R study by using ANOVA to ascertain the most prevalent factor or factors. We would check to see if any given component (part-to-part, repeatability, and reproducibility) is over 10 percent and whether the total Gage R&R is over 30 percent, at which point the measurement is deemed to need improvement.

Figure VIII.14 shows the typical nesting pattern used for all Gage R&R activities.

Section VIII.D

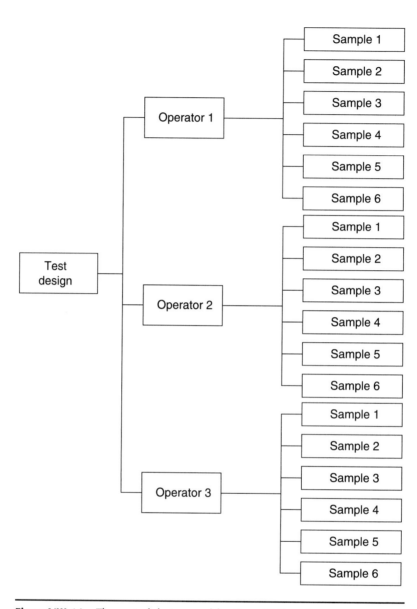

Figure VIII.14   The nested design used for Gage R&R work.

FURTHER READING

AIAG. 1998. *Measurement Systems Analysis.* 2nd printing. Southfield, MI: Automobile Industry Action Group.

Section IX

Lean Enterprise (9 Questions)

Contents

A. Lean Concepts

1. THEORY OF CONSTRAINTS[53]

Eliyahu Goldratt made an important discovery in the 1970s. He observed that if a given process had a significant constraint (often called a "bottleneck") in the system, producing more material at non-constraints would simply pile up partially finished inventory at the constraint. Consequently, he recommended a drum-buffer-rope theory, which effectively translates into a system synchronized with the constraint (the drum), buffers to keep the constraint from ever starving, and rope to pull everything along. He described his theories in a series of parable-style novels, beginning with *The Goal*. The following list is a quick overview of some of Goldratt's unique formulae for accounting.

Throughput Accounting

Throughput = the rate at which enterprise generates money through sales

Inventory = the totality of money invested in purchasing things the enterprise intends to sell

Operating expense = the totality of money invested by the enterprise in order to convert inventory into throughput

Net profit = throughput – operating expense

Return on investment = (throughput – operating expense) / inventory

Productivity = throughput / operating expense

Turns = throughput / inventory

The Five-Step Algorithm

The basic Theory of Constraints (TOC) algorithm is as follows:

1. Identify the constraint.

2. Exploit the constraint.

3. Subordinate everything else to the constraint.

4. Elevate the significance of the constraint.

5. Improve on the constraint situation if finances warrant it.

And, of course, repeat as necessary.

Local versus Global Optimization

Goldratt also had the insight that optimizing locally in a plant does not necessarily contribute to a global or systemwide optimization. In fact, his main point was that the only optimizations that make any sense are those at constraints.

Some Critiques

In some cases, increasing capacity (elevating the constraint) does not make economic sense. For example, a food processing machine can only process so much food due to regulatory reasons; buying another machine increases capacity 100 percent, which may be utterly unnecessary and result in waste.

Hopp and Spearman[54] state a law of self-interest: "People, not organizations, are self-optimizing." Because people will optimize themselves, often at the expense of the organization, achieving global optimization can be a pipe dream. Additionally, many organizations have conflicting goals, like speed of response versus low inventory.

Scheduling in TOC can become extremely complex. Goldratt's descriptions always deal with one constraint—the "master" constraint, if you will. But what about a system with enough constraints that scheduling becomes a nightmare?

2. LEAN THINKING[55]

What Is Value?

Value is anything intrinsic to or added to the product to make it more desirable and usable to the customer.

What Is a Value Chain?

A value chain is a collection of supplier-customer relationships wherein each step adds value to the product. Non-value-added activities are typically removed; if not, they should probably be called the non-value chain. In some instances, a value stream map may be used to represent the supply chain as the product proceeds from some defined point to some terminus; however, a flowchart can serve this function as well.

Flow

Flow is the movement of product down a line. Batches for flow can be the process batch, which can be huge, and the transfer batch, which can be as small as one piece, simulating one-piece flow.

Pull

Pull systems synchronize flow by only performing work after receiving a signal. A push system will supply material to the beginning of a process according to a master plan regardless of line conditions. A pull system stage "pulls" more material when the current lot (sometimes one piece) has been moved to the next stage.

Perfection

Lean is "quality at the source." Six Sigma is near perfect quality, with a little slack for random variation.

Quality at the Source

"Quality at the source" is the battle cry of the Just-in-Time movement. It means that no defective product is allowed to flow down the manufacturing line. Operators are trained to inspect every piece they make instead of relying on outside inspectors to catch the bad work. When quality at the source is coupled with one-piece flow, the worst-case scenario should be only *one* defective product.

Figure IX.1 shows a straightforward flowchart of a value chain, including a graphical analysis of non-value-added activities.

3. CONTINUOUS FLOW MANUFACTURING

One-Piece Flow

Continuous flow manufacturing (CFM) is often called one-piece flow. The beauty of CFM lies in the fact that if the operators are doing their job of inspecting every part before sending it downstream, only one part will ever be defective at a given time— unlike batch methods, where hundreds or thousands of parts can be defective at any given time.

CFM leads to many positive outcomes:

- Inventory is reduced.

- Labor devoted to storing and transporting inventory is reduced.

- Order-to-ship cycles are reduced so shipments can go to the customer sooner.

- Batch-process fiascoes are reduced.

- Operating costs go down as non-value-added work declines (especially setups).

- Because order-to-ship times diminish, order flexibility increases.

Technically, continuous flow manufacturing is not synonymous with one-piece flow—it simply means we are not batching our material flow. True continuous flow would be just that—continuous flow, like the flow of oil or water. Nonetheless, one-piece flow simulates continuous flow by reducing the batch size to exactly one piece.

CONWIP

CONWIP is continuous work in process, a relative of CFM. CONWIP systems typically have less WIP than a pure push system (manufacturing resource planning). Because of this, they have shorter cycle times than the push system. Hopp and Spearman[56] also noted other characteristics of a CONWIP system:

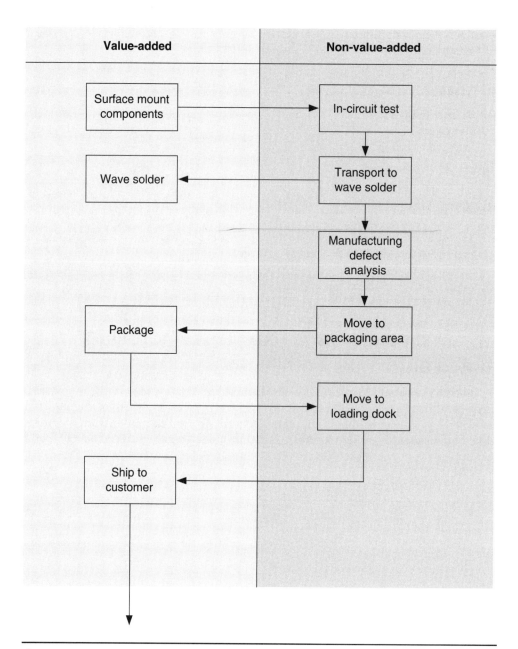

Figure IX.1   An "as-is" value stream map using the ANSI flow chart notation. Womack and
Jones use a different notation; however, no standard exists for value stream
mapping.

- CONWIP systems are more robust to errors in WIP than push systems are to errors in release rate.

- CONWIP systems can handle more complexity than kanban systems, which would otherwise be swamped with "cards."

- A CONWIP system is unlikely to proliferate unfilled demand all the way to the upstream source on demand for a low-volume product with unusual unique components held in short supply.

How Do I Make One-Piece Flow Work?

1. Choose the right kind of products. Small products may not work well in this environment; for example, small printed circuit boards intended to be sensors are frequently optimized to something like 60 boards per panel for surface mount reflow soldering. Single-sensor throughput makes no economic sense at all.

2. Changeover must be quick or else one-piece flow will not function properly. If setups take an hour, we are not going to run one piece and then switch to another product and redo the setup. That is why single-minute exchange of die (SMED) or one-touch exchange of die (OTED) is so important to product leveling and other desirable lean functions.

3. Make sure your assembly is reasonably simple. Delivery kanban doesn't work very well when a product has 600 components and all of them are different. In fact, reorder kanban won't work here, either.

4. Ensure that the capital cost of the equipment is not such that it drives the accountants to *demand* high utilization numbers. Cheaper, smaller machines allow for flexibility.

5. Train, train, and train. Employees who are used to batch operations frequently resist the move to a one-piece flow.

4. NON-VALUE-ADDED ACTIVITIES

Inventory

Inventory provides several problems:

- Opportunity cost ("we could have invested our money or bought something useful instead of having this stuff sitting on the floor")

- Potential degradation due to pilfering and deterioration of the material

- Lost inventory

- Obsolete inventory

Space

Space that isn't wasted by inefficient plant layout can be used for other things; for example, space could be rented out to another supplier or set aside for vendor-managed inventory (VMI).

Test Inspection

We don't think we made the product correctly, so we hire somebody to check it out for us. This activity adds exactly zero value to the product. Poka-yoke can make this task obsolete (see Section VIII.C). Note, however, that poka-yoke does not eliminate the need for auditing. The key concept is to use test inspection as part of a larger control system rather than trying to "inspect in quality." We have seen this done with in-circuit testing in an electronics surface mount facility. The control system allowed nearly instant feedback and produced true statistical process control.

Rework

We made a defective product, so now we have to fix it. We have to pay someone to do this, but we cannot bump up the price on the product; therefore, we are actually *reducing* the value of the product by doing rework. The key is not to make mistakes in the first place.

Transportation

Let's see how much we can move this product around with expensive transportation. The perfect example of a disaster in this area is when a factory has so little control over their processes and promise times that they have to air freight the finished goods to the customer—very expensive! In Figure IX.2, nearly all the unnecessary movement of material has been eliminated.

Storage

Why are we storing this stuff instead of selling it? When the Porsche auto company went lean, its Japanese adviser handed an electric saw to its chairman and had him saw the WIP storage racks in half. The velocity of materials correspondingly increased by a factor of two.

Figure IX.2 updates our previous simple value chain flowchart by deleting the non-value-added activities.

Non-value-added activities are frequently defined in the following mantra: defects, overproduction, transportation, waiting, inventory, motion, and overprocessing. Note, however, that the traditional seven-item list does not directly incorporate the concept of wasted space.

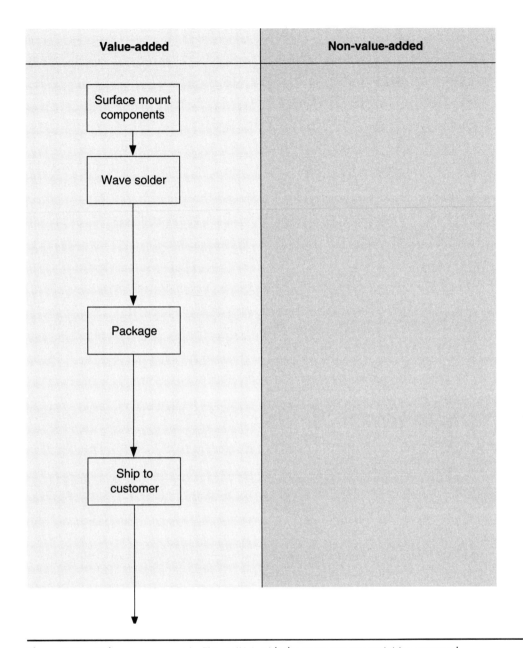

Figure IX.2   Value stream map in Figure IX.1 with the unnecessary activities removed.

5. CYCLE-TIME REDUCTION

Takt Time

$$\text{Takt time} = \frac{\text{(total available work time per shift)}}{\text{(customer demand requirements per shift)}}$$

Beware! Some takt time calculations reflect ideal time and not the real time to work the product.

For example: a customer wants 1000 frimframs. The line operates 50 minutes × 8 hours per day = 400 minutes (assuming a 10-minute break every hour). That means 2.5 frimframs per minute or a takt time of 24 seconds per frimfram.

Kaizen

The concept of kaizen is discussed in detail in Section VIII.C, "Lean Tools for Control."

Operational Improvements

An operational improvement occurs when we figure out a way to speed up an existing process. We might use single-minute exchange of die (SMED) or one-touch exchange of die (OTED), or we might increase the use of external setup to reduce the wasted time.

Process Improvements

A process improvement occurs when a portion of the process that has become irrelevant is removed from the process. Process improvement explains why we study the value flow, because it is the subprocesses that add no value that need to come out of the system.

What Is Single-Minute Exchange of Die?

Other names for this function are "one-touch exchange of die" and "quick changeover."
A possible study sequence:

1. *Define* the purpose of the study.

2. *Define* the scope of the analysis and where we are analyzing.

3. *Measure* the setup times for the various workstations in a workflow (usually a manufacturing line).

4. *Analyze* the times taken to set up the various workstations:
   – Take films of the setup.
   – Use time-motion studies to break the setup into parts.
   – Compare the calculated ideal takt times.

5. *Improve* the times taken for setup, especially at any workstation recognized to be a constraint (à la the Theory of Constraints).

   –Move as much of the setup as possible into external setup—anything that can be done ahead of time while the workstation is performing its normal function.

   –Look for opportunities to speed up the internal setup.

   –Reduce movement as much as possible.

6. *Control* the setup time by running a control chart for a period of time to determine the upper and lower control limits (real times due to random variation).

Note that some setup times at Toyota were reduced from four hours to less than three minutes!

FURTHER READING

Lareau, William. 2003. *Office Kaizen: Transforming Office Operations into a Strategic Competitive Advantage.* Milwaukee, WI: ASQ Quality Press.

Section X

Design for Six Sigma (DFSS)
(9 Questions)

Contents

A. Quality Function Deployment (QFD)

QFD MATRIX[57]

The QFD matrix was pioneered at the Japanese Kobe shipyards in the 1970s. The full QFD is much more complicated than the House of Quality, but the House of Quality is at the heart of any QFD (see Figure X.1; the figure resembles a house, hence the name Hous of Quality).

Customer Requirements

Run the "what" of the customer requirements down the left-hand side of the matrix. This can also be represented in a hierarchy if that makes sense.

Product Requirements

Across the top, list the "how" of product requirements (design ideas). These explain how your design team will meet the customer requirements already listed. In the "roof" area, show strong positive and negative correlations between the design ideas.

Market Evaluations

On the far right-hand side of the house, show the competitive evaluation between your company and company A and your company and company B. Indicate estimated customer priority as well.

You can also indicate the improvement goals and factors, highlight sales points, and assign an importance rating. The idea is to focus the attention of the design team on the items that are truly critical to customer satisfaction and product quality.

Technical Benchmarks

In the "basement," list the technical comparison with competitors. This part is a qualitative analysis, as is much of the QFD. The point is to discern which design ideas can overcome perceived dereliction on the part of our company versus our competitors.

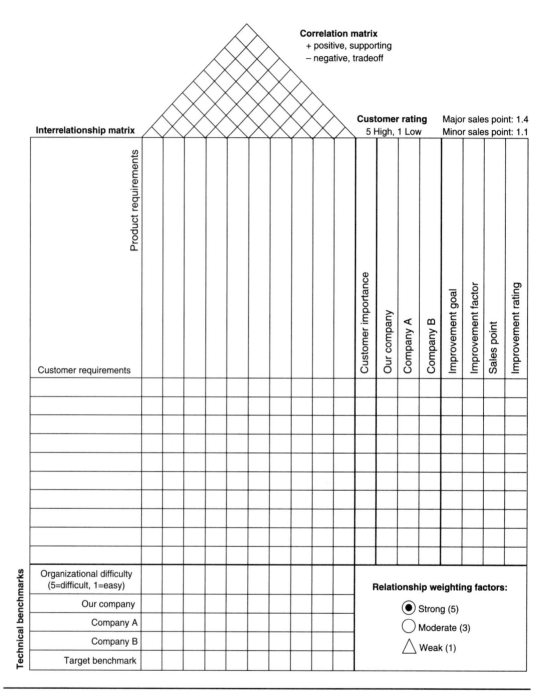

Figure X.1   A template for a House of Quality. Example in SmartDraw Business Process Management toolbox. You could also use Microsoft Visio, a spreadsheet, or dedicated software to do this.

Many QFD matrices will also show the target values for each design idea in the first row of the "basement." This is objective tolerancing information.

The ASI Model

The American Supplier Institute has a model for QFD that is multipart. They accomplish substantial linkage by making the top "how" row the next House's "what" row in the following manner:

- Customer requirements to engineering design ideas

- Engineering design ideas to parts characteristics

- Parts characteristics to key process operations

- Key process operations to machine settings, control methods, sampling, control documents, operator training, and maintenance tasks

The ASI model is very well known, and the linkage among the "houses" provides a reasonable amount of power, covering a huge part of the development life cycle.

FURTHER READING

King, Bob, et al. 1989. *Better Designs in Half the Time: Implementing QFD Quality Function Deployment in America*. Salem, NH: Goal/QPC.

B. Robust Design and Process

1. FUNCTIONAL REQUIREMENTS

The plan that follows shows a rational approach to robust design as explained by Taguchi, Chowdhury, and Taguchi.[58]

Robust Engineering Steps

Plan

1. Define project scope.

2. Define subsystem boundary.

3. Define input signal M and output response y, then the ideal function.

4. Strategize signal and noise issues.

5. Define control factors and levels in response to noise issues.

6. Formulate and prepare experiments.

Do

7. Conduct experiments and/or simulations and record data.

8. Analyze the data.

8.1. Calculate signal-to-noise ratio and sensitivity for each run.

8.2. Generate response table to values in 8.1.

8.3. Perform two-step optimization.

8.4. Predict behavior.

Check

   9. Conduct confirmation run, then evaluate the reproducibility.

Act

   10. Document and implement the results.

   11. Plan the next step.

Steps 1–3 define good requirements practice regardless of the discipline doing the design. In software, defining the subsystem boundary results in a context diagram that explicitly defines the fundamental process, the main interface constituents, and the external entities that communicate with the process.

Robustness

Robustness can generally be described as immunity to extraneous influence. Taguchi refined this concept such that the product has reduced sensitivity to noise, and variation of the response is minimized.

We can measure robustness by looking at values we have already explored in this book:

- Cpk

- Warranty returns

  - Field failures
  - Returned merchandise authorization

- Customer complaints

- Rework and scrap

- Long-term reliability data

- Testing results from both customer and supplier

- Yield and rolling throughput yield

2. NOISE STRATEGIES

Robust design primarily uses five tools:

1. The *p-diagram* (or parameter-diagram) is used to classify the variables associated with the product into noise, control, signal (input), and response (output) factors.

2. The *ideal function* is used to mathematically specify the ideal form of the signal-response relationship as embodied by the design concept for making the higher level system work perfectly (hence, ideal).

3. The *quality loss function* is used to quantify the loss incurred by the user due to deviation from target performance.

4. The *signal-to-noise ratio* is used to predict the field quality through laboratory experiments.

5. *Orthogonal arrays* are used to gather experimental data about control factors (design parameters) with an efficient number of experiments.

Of course, many other tools are available, but these five are specific to robust design. Taguchi experiments typically deal with noise using three mutually exhaustive approaches:

- Larger (higher, bigger, maximal) is better.

- Smaller (lower, lesser, minimal) is better.

- Nominal is better.

Equation (X.1) shows the formulas for Taguchi-style signal-to-noise ratios:

Larger is better (maximize the response)   (X.1)

$$\frac{S}{N} = -10 \log \left(\frac{\sum \frac{1}{Y^2}}{n} \right)$$

Smaller is better (minimize the response)

$$\frac{S}{N} = -10 \log \left(\frac{\sum Y^2}{n} \right)$$

Nominal is better (target the response)

$$\frac{S}{N} = 10 \log \left(\frac{\overline{Y^2}}{s^2} \right)$$

In all cases, Y is measured data and s^2 is the variance.

3. TOLERANCE DESIGN[59]

Tolerance design is a step beyond parameter design, with the following considerations:

- Tolerances are an economic decision.

- Tolerances are constrained by the physics of the material.

- Tolerances are an engineering design choice.

The purpose of tolerance design is to establish metrics that allow the engineer to determine which tolerances can be loosened and which must be tightened in order to meet customer needs while producing a cost-effective product.

As with Taguchi's concept of parameter design, DOE is used to determine what is significant. We know where to go because we have already defined the ideal transfer function, so we know what the best result must be. Now we use the DOE to help move us closer to the ideal function. We will have constructed a p-diagram (or the more detailed noise diagram) to discern the potential noise sources affecting the product. We will use the orthogonal arrays during the DOE to efficiently (fractional factorial) analyze the significance of various components and tolerances, and we will perform an economic analysis using the Quality Loss Function.

Some Statistical Methods

Equation (X.2) shows the standard formula for the root sum of the squares:

$$\sigma_{adjusted} = \frac{Tolerance}{3C_{pk}} \tag{X.2}$$

The Z-value (remember Z from the standard normal distribution?) is:

$$Z_F = \frac{F - \sum_{i=1}^{n} N_i V_i B_i}{\sqrt{\sum_{i=1}^{n} \left(\frac{T_i B_i}{3C_{pk_i}} \right)^2}},$$

where V is the direction vector, B is the correction factor for true position, and F is the gap constraint.

Expect to see the term tolerance stackup. What is wrong with this formula? The $3Cpk$ value is not a Six Sigma way of looking at things!

Figure X.2 shows the workflow for calculating the tolerances. "GD&T" is geometric dimensioning and tolerancing.

4. TOLERANCE AND PROCESS CAPABILITY

The Z transformation we have already described uses the process capability information to calculate tolerances. It also follows from the formula that as the Cp or Cpk increases (higher capability), the probability of exceeding a specific gap constraint diminishes; that is, they are inversely proportional.

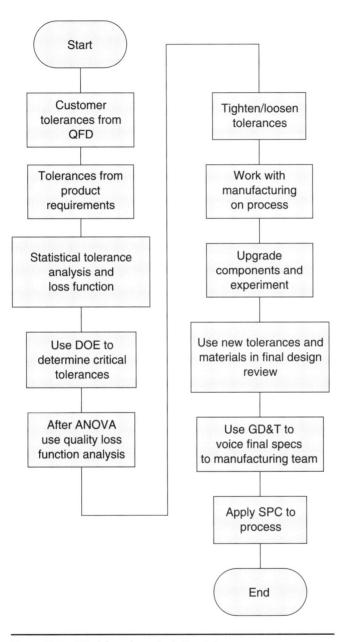

Figure X.2   Workflow for calculating tolerances.

So what is a tolerance stack? Here is where we really see the root sum of the squares:

$$T = \sqrt{T_1^2 + T_2^2 + T_3^2 + \cdots} = T_n^2 \tag{X.3}$$

Unfortunately, this formula only works in an ideal world where no process shifts exist. Motorola initiated the use of Cpk in the Z formula we have already seen as a way to force the concept of centering into the calculation. Motorola's method for treating Cpk uses it as a long-term process capability number. If the tolerancing equations still say the product and the process are going to fly, then the product has been designed for manufacturability and robustness.

What about Nonlinear Root Sum of the Squares (RSS)?

In the real world, we make adjustments for multi-dimensional variations:

$$tol_y = \sqrt{\left(\frac{df}{dx_1}\right)tol_1^2 + \left(\frac{df}{dx_2}\right)tol_2^2 + \left(\frac{df}{dx_3}\right)tol_3^2 + \cdots + \left(\frac{df}{dxn}\right)tol_n^2} \qquad (X.4)$$

Replace the terms with an adjustment:

$$\sigma_{adjusted} = \frac{Tol_i}{3C_{pk}}, \therefore Tol_i = 3C_{pk} \times \sigma_{adjusted}$$

The equation for this situation takes into account potential nonlinearity.
Equation (X.5) gives us the formula for sensitivity analysis in tolerancing.
The overall sensitivity (standard deviation) can be calculated from the root of sum of the variances:

$$s = \sqrt{s_1^2 + s_2^2 + s_3^2 + \cdots + s_n^2} \qquad (X.5)$$

The overall proportional summation is

$$1 = \sum_{i=1}^{n} P_i,$$

where

$$P_i = \frac{t_i^2}{t_{total}^2},$$

or individual component tolerance atop overall assembly tolerance.

At this point the practitioner can use one or more of the following methods:

- ANOVA techniques

- Empirical analysis

- One-at-a-time factor analysis

FURTHER READING

Stamatis, D. H. 2001. *Six Sigma and Beyond: Design for Six Sigma.* Vol. 6. Boca Raton, FL: St. Lucie Press.

C. Failure Mode and Effects Analysis (FMEA)

TERMINOLOGY[60]

Item and Function Description

In most failure mode and effects analysis (FMEA) formats, the item appears in the very first column. It is as simple as defining the item under failure mode analysis. If we are developing an electronic or mechanical design FMEA (DFMEA), the item may refer to a drawing, a schematic, or a layout diagram. Entering the item alone is probably not sufficient: the description should also have a definition of the function of the item. Because it is the function that fails and not the item, we have to list each item's functions separately while making it clear that they relate to the same item.

Cause

If we can accept that failure modes are always the product of unplanned behavior at the outputs, then the causes come from one of two sources:

1. Unplanned behavior at an input

2. Incorrect behavior at a transformation

When we are dealing strictly with hardware, we can expect that the bulk of the causes will fall into the class of an input or inputs mated with an output or outputs. In some cases, however, we can treat the hardware as a form of program, where the input triggers a set of internal behaviors that, in turn, lead to an output. The collection of internal behaviors constitutes a transformation. If we use the DFMEA to analyze software, every program is the relationship of inputs to outputs through some kind of transformation. In the DFMEA layout, we should create a new row for each cause. This suggests that in the FMEA method of analysis, all untoward effects ultimately resolve down to one cause. This is a weakness of the FMEA method. If it is clear to us that multiple causes, independently or jointly, lead to a failure, then we can use another tool—the fault tree—to analyze the failure mode. We do not want to use fault trees in every situation because they are labor-intensive, typically much more so than the FMEA.

General Information about the FMEA

What?

- Failure mode and effects analysis
- Industrial tool used for:
  - Process
  - Design
- Can be used by anybody dealing with things that just don't work out right!

Why?

- Explaining the primary purpose for the FMEA
- Anticipating failure
- Prioritizing different failures
- Doing it right the first time

Who?

- Anybody who wants to look smart and be smart
- Engineers
- Planners
- Anyone who values "pro-action"

When?

- As early as possible
- *Before* the failure occurs!
- Frequently document your issues
- Update it with every change

Where?

- Industry
- Education
- Health
- Business
- In fact, anywhere

Severity

The concept of severity in the DFMEA is significant for several reasons:

- We use it to calculate a "significance" using a combined value called "RPN."

- We can designate items that present safety issues, which should receive analysis regardless of their RPN.

- We establish a baseline against which we can compare our action results.

- We start off with a list recommended by SAE J1739.

We should note that the SAE J1739 list is *not* the final word on severity. MIL-STD-1629A, for example, uses the MIL-STD-882 (Safety and Hazard Analysis) four-category classification system to judge severity: Category I = Catastrophic, Category II = Critical, Category III = Marginal, and Category IV = Minor. The government recognizes that categories I and II are significant regardless of their occurrence or detection and requires that these items be explicitly called out. SAE set up the J1739 format for a granularity of 10 categories; this is probably the most common arrangement. A DFMEA may elaborate on the definitions contained in the standard. If these documents are subject to customer review, all parties should agree on the meanings in the severity categories.

Classification

The concept of classification is peculiar to the SAE J1739 and QS-9000 way of looking at DFMEA work. The DFMEA and/or design team can use the classification column to mark items that require process controls during manufacturing. If the team is using the DFMEA for software test-case generation, this column is not necessary. Classification is *not* used in the calculation of the RPN value.

Occurrence

In the DFMEA, "occurrence" relates to how often the failure mode occurs and uses a scale from 1 to 10. SAE J1739 recommends a set of ranking criteria in a relatively straightforward table. However, the DFMEA team can set any standard they want; for example, in some cases the criteria for establishing occurrence are simply unavailable. In many cases, the team will *not* have empirical data to support their estimates, especially if they are working on a new product. Another case occurs in a situation where the DFMEA becomes a tool for software. With a given software version and a given failure mode, the event will occur in all products that have that software. In most cases, it makes more sense to simply set the occurrence value at "5" and eliminate it from the calculation.

Other Types of Failure Mode Tools

Fault Tree Analysis

- In many ways stronger than FMEA
- Accounts for multiple causes

- Accounts for precipitating cause and setup cause

- Based on pure logic

- Cut Sets can be analyzed

Failure Mode, Effects, and Criticality Analysis (FMECA)
- Considers rare but very severe failure modes (a wing falling off an airplane, for example)

Management Oversight and Risk Tree Analysis (MORT)

- Similar to fault tree analysis, except analysts work from a preexisting template tree

- Used mainly for Nuclear Regulatory Commission issues

- The full version has 1500 questions

- A version called "mini-MORT" exists for quick studies

Safety and Hazard Analyses

- Similar to FMEA

- Only highly severe issues are considered

Design Controls

For a DFMEA, design controls are typically one, some, or all of the following:

- Reviews

- Computer-aided tools

- Testing

- Inspection

- Standards

The point is that we control designs by performing a collection of best practices that we believe result in better designs. In some cases—inspections, for example—we know empirically that the design control does in fact lead to a more defect-free design. When the design control is a test, the FMEA team should call out the specific test document or test that is relevant to the particular failure mode. This way, the DFMEA becomes not only an anticipatory tool, but a means for specifying test cases. The related test document should show how the test cases flow from the DFMEA to the test description.

Detection Description

The detection description, or detection value, provides a way to subjectively evaluate the capability of a design control to detect a defect in the product.

Risk Priority Number (RPN)

The RPN value is the product of the severity, occurrence, and detection values determined after "actions taken":

$$RPN = severity \times occurrence \times detection$$

The higher the RPN, the more significant the failure mode. It is also important to remember criticality, which ties in most strongly with the idea of severity. For example, safety issues are significant regardless of the final RPN.

Recommended Actions

In a DFMEA, recommended actions usually revolve around design modifications that lower the RPN value. It is also possible that the team may come up with *no* recommendations. Recommendations may also be procedural; that is, the problem may be so intractable that the team recommends the problem be handled in the instruction manual for the product or a data sheet.

Responsibility and Target Completion Date

This column tries to establish ownership of issues as well as define a time at which the problem will come to resolution. Where there is no ownership, nobody does the design and detection work necessary to improve the product and the FMEA fails. Where there is no completion date, we have no way to audit the FMEA to determine whether the engineer ever took the recommended action. Again, the FMEA fails.

Let's look at a list of potential failure modes:

- Burned connector
- Burned relay
- Melted printed circuit board
- Too loud
- Too quiet
- Too bright
- Too dark
- Open circuit (not enough solder)
- Short circuit (too much solder)
- Malodorous
- Too cold
- Too hot
- Failed to meet schedule

Note that these are all *observable behaviors*.

Actions Taken

This column implies that either the FMEA team or the responsible engineer or engineers have taken the steps necessary to improve the product. If the box is empty, then presumably no action has occurred and the product has not improved. This portion of the FMEA can also serve to record decisions *not* to act and point to an external document that defines that decision. Remember, the FMEA is a tool to help us work better, not a bureaucratic, go-through-the-motions waste of time. We have seen the FMEA treated like a checklist in order to provide documentation for a Production Part Approval Process (PPAP) notebook. Doing this kind of paper-wrestling misses the point! The technique is potentially a massive money-saver because we are terminating problems before they really become issues. The Actions Taken column helps document the activities we actually did in order to make a better product.

Sev, Occ, and Det

After we take action, we recalculate the severity, occurrence, and detection values. All of the comments made in previous sections still apply. If we have done our job well, the new values should be decidedly lower than the old.

Final RPN

This value is the product of the new severity, occurrence, and detection values determined after "actions taken":

$$RPN = severity \times occurrence \times detection$$

Tables X.1 and X.2 show typical criteria for occurrence and severity.

Table X.1   FMEA occurrence values.

Probability	Likely failure rates	Ppk	Ranking
Very high—persistent failures	≥ 100,000 ppm	< 0.55	10
	50,000 ppm	≥ 0.55	9
High—frequent failures	20,000 ppm	≥ 0.78	8
	10,000 ppm	≥ 0.86	7
Moderate—occasional failures	5000 ppm	≥ 0.94	6
	2000 ppm	≥ 1.00	5
	1000 ppm	≥ 1.10	4
Low—relatively few failures	500 ppm	≥ 1.20	3
	100 ppm	≥ 1.30	2
Remote—failure unlikely	10 ppm	≥ 1.67	1

Table X.2   FMEA severity criteria.

Effect	Customer effect	Manufacturing effect	Ranking
Hazardous, no warning	Safety issue; noncompliance with government regulations	Endangers operator without warning	10
Hazardous, warning	Safety issue; noncompliance with government regulations	Endangers operator with warning	9
Very high	Inoperable	100% scrapped	8
High	Operable but reduced performance	Sorted, < 100% scrapped	7
Moderate	Operable, but convenience/ comfort items inoperable	< 100% may have to be scrapped	6
Low	Operable, convenience/comfort items operable, but reduced performance	100% product reworked but no repair department	5
Very low	Fit/finish noticeable by > 75% of customers	Sorting, no scrap, rework	4
Minor	Fit/finish noticeable by > 50% of customers	No scrap but < 100% needs rework out-of-station	3
Very minor	Fit/finish noticeable by > 25% of customers	No scrap but < 100% needs rework in-station	2
None	No noticeable effect	Slight inconvenience to operator	1

When creating an FMEA, we need to remember that the work is a team effort. No absolute RPN values exist. The team will have to decide ahead of time what values are to be considered significant. Additionally, all severity values in the range of 8 to 10 should be reviewed for criticality; in other words, they may not happen often and they may be readily detectable, but their potential for large-scale damage is enough to merit special attention.

PURPOSE

Anticipation

One of the most significant benefits of the FMEA lies in the anticipation of failure. This does not mean we are compiling self-fulfilling prophecies—it means we are making deliberate and systematic efforts to manage potential problems and risks before they can become problems and risks. And we capture our efforts in a compact format useful for quick study and conducive to terse descriptions.

Problems

If and when problems occur, the Black Belt can return to the FMEA to see if a particular problem has already been considered. If not, then the FMEA should be updated; if so, then find out why the issue was not dealt with from the beginning.

Documentation

The FMEA can also serve as documentation of "due diligence." That is, should we have to go to court during a litigation, a well-formulated FMEA can serve as evidence that we have worked diligently to design or manufacture a high-quality product.

QS-9000 and TS 16949

The FMEA is a requirement for automotive suppliers. QS-9000 is the automotive (AIAG) standard based on the ISO 9000:1994 set of standards. TS 16949 is the descendant of QS-9000 and represents the ISO understanding of automotive systems as based on the ISO 9000:2000 set of standards.

Product Improvement

The DFMEA is a tool for product improvement. When created with the right attitude, it can serve as a large part of a quality function deployment (QFD). Theoretically, if all potential failure modes have already been considered, then they should have all been dealt with during the action phase of the FMEA.

Process Improvement

The PFMEA is a tool for process improvement. When created with the right attitude, it can be used to eliminate all significant line problems from the very beginning. Any process can be analyzed, including front office business processes.

Types of Design Controls

If we understand the mechanism that produces the failure mode, we should be able to prevent all but intractable situations. Clearly, prevention is preferable to detection, because prevention is proactive and detection is reactive. Some examples of prevention are the following:

- Add a grounding plane to a printed circuit board to prevent EMI issues.
- Use a printed circuit board with a higher glass transition temperature to prevent board softness.
- Autocalibrate gages so calibration issues disappear.
- Add a redundant system as a backup.
- Use diodes, resistors, and capacitors to regulate and protect the microprocessor.
- Add poka-yoke to processes to prevent failure.
- Add autonomation to processes to stop failure.
- Use visual aids on line to illustrate proper assembly.

Detection

Some examples of detection are:

- Perform design verification testing.
- Perform product validation testing.
- Use an andon on the manufacturing line to inform about line situations.
- Use control charts.
- Use sensors in the system to inform about the state of the system.
- Send messages informing about state of the system.

USE OF RPN

RPN

The details:

- Risk priority number
- RPN = severity × occurrence × detection
- 1 < RPN < 1000

    Note: we have 10 numbers, which we take three at a time. If we use the formula for combinations (since order is not significant), we see:

$$\binom{10}{3} = \frac{10!}{3!(10-3)!} = \frac{10 \cdot 9 \cdot 8 \cdot 7 \cdot 6 \cdot 5 \cdot 4 \cdot 3 \cdot 2 \cdot 1}{(3 \cdot 2 \cdot 1)(7 \cdot 6 \cdot 5 \cdot 4 \cdot 3 \cdot 2 \cdot 1)} = \frac{10 \cdot 9 \cdot 8}{3 \cdot 2 \cdot 1} = \frac{720}{6} = 120 \qquad (X.6)$$

    Tip: use cancellation whenever possible to simplify factorial arithmetic. Calculators provide satisfactory solutions only for relatively small numbers!

- Used to rank failure modes.
- Bad news: a low occurrence and a low detection may cause the rank to be low enough that a significant severity is ignored (criticality).

Table X.3 shows part of the header row for an FMEA (design or process type).

Table X.3 The header information for an FMEA table showing the position of the RPN.

SEV	Class	Potential cause(s)/ mechanism(s) of failure	Occurrence	Current controls		Detection	RPN
				Prevention	Detection		

The RPNs may be sorted, and the examination of problems can start with the worst and work its way down to some arbitrary point where the RPN is no longer considered to be an issue. The addition of a column for prevention was an innovation of the third edition of the AIAG FMEA book. An outstanding poka-yoke is a form of prevention because it does not allow error to occur; automated inspection equipment is a form of detection and frequently generates scrap or rework in a manufacturing facility.

Frequently, the detection column in a DFMEA points to some kind of testing, whether laboratory or production. If the testing used for detection will be performed in the laboratory, the FMEA should point to a reference in a test plan so that the two documents are bound together. This linkage can be readily achieved if we are using a spreadsheet to create the FMEA. In the case where we are creating a PFMEA, the detection column needs to point to examples of poka-yoke or automated test equipment. A high numerical value in the detection column of a PFMEA could serve as a flag to the manufacturing organization that process control may be nonexistent at that specific operation.

An enterprise can decide to become FMEA-centric and link many of its controlling documents into the FMEA or link the FMEA to other significant documents. In automotive manufacturing, one of the most significant documents is the process control plan (PCP). The PFMEA and the PCP are linked by work center activity number (they are related in the database sense). Although not customary, any process—including those in accounting and human resources departments—can be defined and then assessed with a PFMEA. Additionally, these FMEAs and PCPs can cascade into more detailed levels, providing significant evidence of forethought applied to eliminate issues in processes before those issues can become serious problems.

Why Do This?

- Separates the significant few from the trivial many.

- Selects design blocks for further decomposition.

- Documents diligence at managing critical failures.

Resolving Arguments

- Don't waste time nitpicking the values.

- Reduce the granularity of the rankings (for example, 1, 3, 5, 7, 9).

- The goal is to illuminate failure modes of significance for further study and resolution.

Criticality

- Criticality = severity × occurrence.

- Add another column to the matrix if safety is a special concern.

DFMEA

The DFMEA is the design version of the FMEA.

Output Primacy

Most inadequate and unintelligible FMEAs result from starting on the wrong part of the document. The analyst needs to put *outputs first*. When constructing any FMEA, but especially a DFMEA, we always start with the outputs. A failure of an output is a *failure mode*. This choice has the benefits of simplicity, consistency, sense, and customer-orientation.

Outputs are behaviors. Behaviors are what the customer (or the consumer of the activity) ultimately sees. Use the following thought experiment: Input fails, but output continues to function. Is there a failure mode? We can say "no," because the customer/consumer sees no failure. True, this event doesn't happen in the reality, but it highlights the argument for output primacy. The same rules apply for PFMEAs. Any given step in the process has an input and an output. The rule about outputs applies just the same. Let's look at a speedometer as an example. Typical failure modes for a gage are the following:

- Pointer (needle) stuck in one position

- Pointer stuck at maximum value

- Pointer stuck at minimum value

- Pointer oscillating periodically

- Pointer oscillating aperiodically

- Pointer has different behavior in down direction than up direction

We can further subdivide the oscillation mal-behaviors into massive oscillations, small oscillations, and so on. We can now say that *inputs are causes*. How can output be a cause? A cause is nearly always an input or combination of inputs that exhibit an undesirable action leading to the observable behavior we have called an output.

In the FMEA world, *effects are sense-able*. Usually, we describe the effect by describing how the external entity observing the system will see it. For example, if the failure mode is a speedometer that always shows a zero value, the effect is that the driver does not know the speed of the vehicle, which in turn leads to safety issues.

The people preparing an FMEA frequently confuse the effect with the output failure mode. The preparer must understand that the failure mode occurs at the output of the device under analysis, and the effect occurs in the observer of the device (the observer could be a sensor or a human being).

Section X.C

Figure X.3 shows the sequence of events for performing a DFMEA. Note that we iterate the RPN calculation because the second set of columns allows for RPN recalculation after we have taken action to deal with critical RPNs.

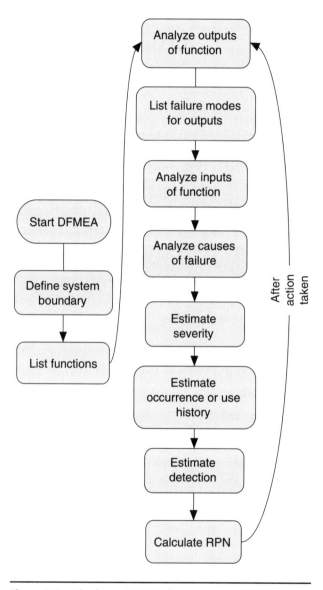

Figure X.3   The basic DFMEA flow.

PFMEA

Where the DFMEA is structured around design function, the PFMEA is structured around a manufacturing process (actually, it is applicable to any process).

The Numbers

In some ways, the PFMEA may be more tractable with regard to RPN than is the DFMEA:

- Occurrence can be related to historical capability in the form of Ppk.
- Occurrence can be related to PPM.
- Occurrence can be related to the Six Sigma value.
- Severity can be tied to line stoppage.
- Detection has already been explicitly defined in the process control plan (if an automotive supplier).
- Prevention can be applied just like the DFMEA.
- Outputs and inputs are obvious from the workflow.
- Usually an abstract line diagram exists that explicitly shows the workflow, so the process is already documented.

Prevention and Detection

If anything, prevention is more significant than detection here. Line stoppages are deadly, unprofitable, and some customers will fine a supplier for downtime. Forms of prevention in the process are:

- Poka-yoke
- 5S
- Total productive maintenance
- Kaizen

Some forms of detection are:

- Dock audits
- Process audits
- In-circuit testing
- End-of-line testing

Figure X.4 shows the slightly different sequence for the PFMEA.

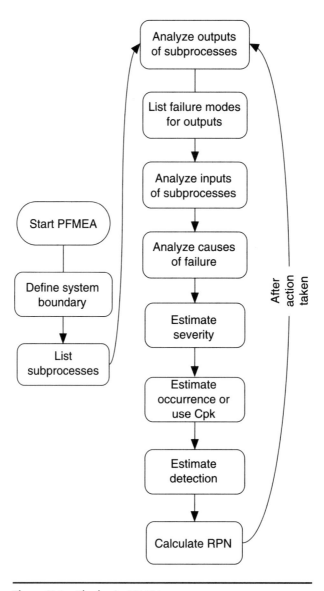

Figure X.4   The basic PFMEA sequence.

FURTHER READING

Stamatis, D. H. 2003. *Failure Mode and Effect Analysis: FMEA from Theory to Execution.* 2nd ed. Milwaukee, WI: ASQ Quality Press.

D. Design for X (DFX)

DESIGN CONSTRAINTS[61]

Cost (DFC)

In previous years, the U.S. government has called this "value engineering." Cost is a constraint because we cannot design without considering pricing limitations. Activity Based Costing (ABC) can help provide detailed analyses of the real cost of making a product.

Manufacturability (DFM)

If we can't build it, we already have a problem. Screws are usually more difficult to work with than snaps, two-sided reflow solder is an issue, component location is an issue, and the use of lead in the process can affect health. The design must consider manufacturability from the very beginning of the design process.

Produceability (DFP)

In DFP, we can look at the reduction of unique components, the reduction of suppliers, the structure of the bill of materials—anything that affects our ability to get the product out the door.

Test (DFT)

A common example of design for test (DFT) is the use of built-in test points on the printed circuit board, allowing in-circuit testers to easily verify the integrity of the electrical connections. Another example is the use of software to provide built-in testing (BIT) accessible by a special triggering command. Consideration of line testing up front in the process makes life easier for everybody.

Maintainability (DFMain)

The designer needs to design the product so it can be serviced. Even though many modular products are simply sent back for warranty issues, a lot of servicing occurs—consider your car. If access to critical areas of the product is secure yet simple, servicing is that much easier. Maintainability is a significant means for reducing customer warranty and diminishing complaints.

Quality (DFQ)

In DFQ, we would expect that all elements that are Critical to Quality (CTQ) had been defined and managed. CTQ analysis is an important technique in Six Sigma for precisely this reason. Furthermore, it makes sense to use solid components rather than eat the warranty from using borderline products.

Some Software Design Constraints

Software presents its own body of peculiar problems. Yet it is clearly part of the Six Sigma universe. Here are some typical software design constraints:

- Microprocessor choice
- Operating system choice (or no operating system)
- Interface definition
- Signal integrity expectations
- Programming language
- System memory
  - Volatile
  - Nonvolatile
- Processor speed
- Bus architectures
- Built-in testing requirements
- Storage redundancy for critical information (for example, odometer)

DFT and DFM Comments

It is not uncommon to see mechanical/electronic designs with many screws to hold a housing together, to position the printed circuit board, or to affix other paraphernalia. Anything that reduces takt time on the line is bad:

- Screws
- "Daughter" printed circuit boards
- Flimsy, warped printed circuit boards
- Through-hole components instead of surface-mount parts

Production testing is another overlooked issue during design. Best practices include:

- As many test points for in-circuit testing as possible

- Good spacing for test points

- Reduction in "tall" components

- Access to testing areas

- Built-in self test (let the product test itself if it has enough "brains")

FURTHER READING

Stamatis, D. H. 2001. *Six Sigma and Beyond: Design for Six Sigma.* Vol. 6. Boca Raton, FL: St. Lucie Press.

E. Special Design Tools

TRIZ[62]

TRIZ is a systematic approach to innovation developed by G. S. Altshuller based on his study of two million patents (inventions). Four hundred thousand of these patents were defined as innovative and used for the study. Out of Altshuller's study came several significant concepts.

Levels of Innovation

1. *Basic problem solving by individuals or small teams.* Almost a third of all innovations use this level.

2. *More complex problem solving using specialists from within the same company, industry, or technology.* Accounts for a little less than half of all the innovations.

3. *Fundamental changes in how "it" operates.* Innovator goes to other fields and technologies (outside the box!). This method accounts for about a fifth of all innovations.

4. *Radical change.* Scientific paradigm may change. Only 4 percent of innovations go this route.

5. *Discovery.* Totally new concept, technology, or science. A fraction of a percent of all innovations use this level.

Ideality

When the ideal solution occurs, (1) the shortcomings of the original system are gone, (2) the positive characteristics of the old system are retained, (3) the system does not become more complicated, (4) no new disadvantages are introduced, and (5) the ideal solution adds no new mechanism.

Patterns of Evolution

- Ideality
- Uneven system development
- Complexity increase, then simplicity
- Matching/mismatching of parts
- Increased automation, decreased human interaction
- Stages of evolution (S curves)
- Increased dynamism and controllability
- Transition to micro-level

Mindsets

This concept is largely a matter of overcoming mental constipation or psychological inertia—"resistance." It is very easy to reject new ideas; it is much more difficult to generate the new idea in the first place.

Table X.4 illustrates some of the tools and ideas used in TRIZ analysis.

Table X.4   The TRIZ 40 principles.

Segmentation	Be prepared	Rushing through	Porous material
Extraction	Equipotentiality	Convert harm to benefit	Changing color
Localized characteristics	Reverse	Feedback	Homogeneity
Asymmetry	Spheroidality	Mediator	Rejecting and regenerating parts
Consolidation	Dynamicity	Self-service	Transform physical/chemical properties
Universality	Partial or excessive action	Copying	Phase transition
Nesting	Transition to new dimension	Inexpensive replacement object	Using thermal expansion
Counterweight	Mechanical vibrations	Replace mechanical system	Use strong oxidizers
Preloading tension	Periodic action	Pneumatic or hydraulic construction	Inert environment
Prior action	Continuity of useful action	Flexible film or thin membrane	Composite materials

Contradictions

Contradictions are determined using the contradiction matrix, which is too large to reproduce here. Technical contradictions lead to trade-offs. Physical contradictions appear to be impossible to solve.

Scientific Effects

Include diverse experience and knowledge on the problem-solving team to increase chances for serendipity (fortuitous discovery).

S-field Analysis

1. Define the problem (*define!*).
2. Diagram the problem.
3. Identify sources of the problem.
4. Compare to standard problems.
5. Find a solution.

Functional Value Analysis

1. Describe the product or service as separate parts or functions.
2. Assess the cost of each part or function.
3. Assess the relative value of each part or function in relation to function of final product.
4. Develop new approach for any items too high in cost relative to value.

AXIOMATIC DESIGN[63]

Axiomatic design is the brainchild of Dr. Nam Suh of MIT. He has said that the goals of the process are to:

- Increase creativity in the human designer.
- Reduce the random search process.
- Minimize the iterative trial-and-error process.
- Determine the best design among choices.

The First Axiom

Maintain the independence of the functional requirements (the "what"). A given set of functional requirements can be decomposed into other functional requirements, and so on. This leads to a customary zigzag as the requirements and design team explores all the domains, culminating in a set of functional requirements, design parameters, and process parameters. In short, the designer must identify design parameters that do not cause a functional requirement to affect any other functional requirement. A good design with this axiom is *de-coupled* (a term used for good software also); a perfect design is said to be *uncoupled* (that is, the design parameters are utterly independent).

The Second Axiom

Minimize the information content of the design (the "how"). Given the equation

$$I = \sum_{i=1}^{n} \left[\log_2 \frac{1}{p_i} \right], \text{ units in bits,} \tag{X.7}$$

where p_i is the probability of the ith design parameter satisfying the ith functional requirement. Suh uses $\log_2$ to convert the results to binary (bits).

The Information Axiom states that the design with the smallest I (note that I is in *bits*) is the best design, because it requires the least amount of information to achieve the functional requirements of the design.

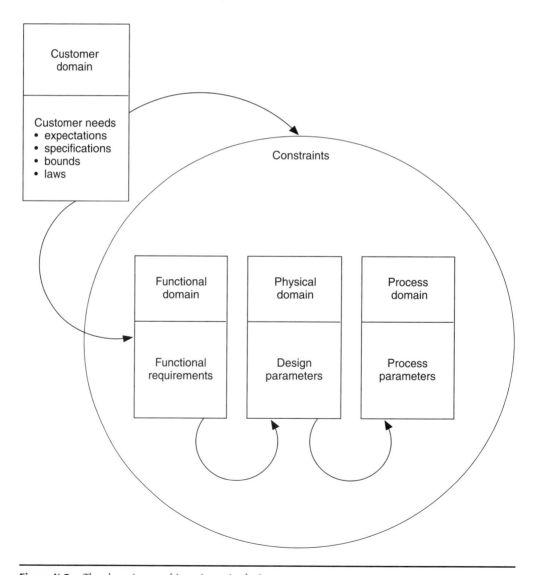

Figure X.5   The domains used in axiomatic design.

Axiomatic design is much more objective than techniques like QFD; on the other hand, axiomatic design requires significantly more mathematical maturity than does QFD. A complementary technique is the Taguchi robust design method. Axiomatic design clears up or reduces the relationships and compensates the greatest weakness of the Taguchi, which is the examination of one variable at a time. Figure X.5 shows the general phasing among the axiomatic design domains. Note how the process follows a logical progression from one domain to another.

FURTHER READING

The TRIZ Journal. http://www.triz-journal.com. Accessed July 17, 2005.
Technical Innovation Center. http://www.triz.org. Accessed July 17, 2005.

Concluding Comments

W e are at the end of our walk through the Six Sigma Black Belt Body of Knowledge. We have covered material that has ranged from teams and leadership to probability and statistics, as well as the concepts of lean manufacturing and Design for Six Sigma. The Body of Knowledge covers an immense amount of material and no book available today can pretend to include all there is to cover. At the end of each subsection I have listed books and material that have worked for me, both on the job and when I took the Certified Six Sigma Black Belt examination.

ASQ Quality Press offers substantial support for the individual reading for the examination, *The Certified Six Sigma Black Belt Handbook*[64] being a prime example. The ASQ Quality Press catalog offers many other books to support the intense study required to pass the examination.

WHAT YOU SHOULD HAVE LEARNED

In a sense, the Black Belt Body of Knowledge is a conflation of the practices associated with certified quality engineers and certified quality managers. This idea makes sense because part of the Black Belt's job is to manage the activities of Green Belts and other supporting workers during Six Sigma projects. What follows is a quick two-level overview of the body of knowledge as described in the ASQ test book for 2005:

I. Enterprise-Wide Deployment (9 Questions)
   A. Enterprise view
   B. Leadership
   C. Organizational goals and objectives
   D. History of organizational improvement/foundations of Six Sigma
II. Business Process Management (9 Questions)
   A. Process vs. functional view
   B. Voice of the customer
   C. Business results

III. Project Management (15 Questions)
    A. Project charter and plan
    B. Team leadership
    C. Team dynamics and performance
    D. Change agent
    E. Management and planning tools
IV. Six Sigma Improvement Methodology and Tools—*Define* (9 Questions)
    A. Project scope
    B. Metrics
    C. Problem statement
V. Six Sigma Improvement Methodology and Tools—*Measure* (30 Questions)
    A. Process analysis and documentation
    B. Probability and statistics
    C. Collecting and summarizing data
    D. Properties and applications of probability distributions
    E. Measurement systems
    F. Analyzing process capability
VI. Six Sigma Improvement Methodology and Tools—*Analyze* (23 Questions)
    A. Exploratory data analysis
    B. Hypothesis testing
VII. Six Sigma Improvement Methodology and Tools—*Improve* (22 Questions)
    A. Design of experiments (DOE)
    B. Response surface methodology
    C. Evolutionary operations (EVOP)
VIII. Six Sigma Improvement Methodology and Tools—*Control* (15 Questions)
    A. Statistical process control
    B. Advanced statistical process control
    C. Lean tools for control
    D. Measurement system re-analysis
IX. Lean Enterprise (9 Questions)
    A. Lean concepts
    B. Lean tools
    C. Total productive maintenance (TPM)
X. Design for Six Sigma (DFSS) (9 Questions)
    A. Quality function deployment (QFD)
    B. Robust design and process
    C. Failure mode and effects analysis (FMEA)
    D. Design for X (DFX)
    E. Special design tools

The ASQ test book also refers to the six levels of Cognition based on Bloom's Taxonomy[65]:

- Knowledge Level (also commonly referred to as recognition, recall, or rote knowledge): Being able to remember or recognize terminology, definitions, facts, ideas, materials, patterns, sequences, methodologies, principles, and so on.

- Comprehension Level: Being able to read and understand descriptions, communications, reports, tables, diagrams, directions, regulations, and so on.

- Application Level: Being able to apply ideas, procedures, methods, formulas, principles, theories, and so on, in job-related situations.

- Analysis: Being able to break down information into its constituent parts and recognize the relationships between parts and how parts are organized; identify sublevel factors or salient data from a complex scenario.

- Synthesis: Being able to put parts or elements together in such a way as to show a pattern or structure not clearly there before; identify which data or information from a complex set is appropriate to examine further or from which supported conclusions can be drawn.

- Evaluation: Being able to make judgments regarding the value of proposed ideas, solutions, methodologies, and so on, by using appropriate criteria or standards to estimate accuracy, effectiveness, economic benefits, and so on.

WHERE YOU SHOULD GO NEXT

I have passed every certification examination I have taken on the first try. I don't think this is a testimony to intelligence as much as it is a testimony to hard work and preparation. This book gives a very broad coverage of the topics in the Body of Knowledge. Readers who need to explore some areas of the BoK more fully can refer to the Further Reading sections. I used every one of these resources in preparation for the ASQ Certified Six Sigma Black Belt Examination.

You should have two projects completed and signed off by a supervisor when you apply to take the examination. You can find information on the requirements in the certification section of ASQ's Web site, http://www.asq.org.

BEING A SIX SIGMA BLACK BELT

A Black Belt is a chimera: a combination of manager, quality engineer, auditor, mathematician, and team leader. For people who enjoy different challenges and new encounters every day, the Black Belt endeavor can be extremely rewarding.

In my own case, I have become a management executive directing every facet of testing and evaluation for the transportation electronics division of Stoneridge Corporation. I use every bit of the knowledge gained during Black Belt preparation every day to pursue problems and solve them. Additionally, the background and experience have put me in a position to pass on the benefits of experience and training to my fellow engineers, managers, and technicians—a consummation that is truly rewarding!

COMMENTS ON MINITAB

As indicated at the beginning of the book, MINITAB (Windows only) is a powerful weapon in the armamentarium of the Six Sigma Black Belt. Other products of similar power exist: Statistica, Systat, SAS, and SPSS, to name a few. Any of these products is capable of supporting the quantitative side of the Black Belt effort. MINITAB, however, is the tool that I use to do my work, both in support of Six Sigma projects and in support of reliability engineering. With some assistance from MINITAB's help system and additions of my own, here is a quick and by no means exhaustive overview of the capabilities of this program.

File Menu

New	Opens new worksheet or project
Open Project	Opens project file. A project contains worksheets, graphs, and other objects
Save Project	Saves current project
Save Project As	Saves current project with different name
Project Description	Edits description of current project
Open Worksheet	Copies (imports) data from file (MINITAB, Excel, Lotus, text, and others) and replaces current worksheet
Save Current Worksheet	Saves current worksheet in an existing MTW or MTP file (these are MINITAB-specific file extensions)
Save Current Worksheet As	Saves worksheet data in file, with choice of many different file formats (export mode)
Worksheet Description	Edits description of current worksheet
Close Worksheet	Closes current worksheet
Query Database (ODBC)	Imports data from a *database file*— Microsoft Access, Oracle, Sybase, or SAS—into MINITAB worksheet
Open Graph	Opens MINITAB graph (MGF) file
Other Files	Displays commands for importing and exporting special text files, and for running an Exec
Save Session Window As	Saves Session window content to file
Save History As	Saves History folder content to file
Save Graph As	Saves current Graph window to file
Print Session Window	Prints Session window
Print History	Prints History (MINITAB shows the script mode in one of its screens—this menu item allows the user to print out the history for future script writing)

Print Graph Window	Prints current Graph window
Print Worksheet	Prints contents of current Data window
Print Setup	Defines printer specifications
Exit	Exits MINITAB
Most Recently Used Worksheets	The bottom of the File menu lists the most recently used worksheets and projects. Click any item to open it.

Edit Menu

Undo	Reverses most recent editing operation
Redo	Repeats most recent editing operation
Clear/Clear Cells	Erases contents of highlighted cells, without moving rows up or columns left
Delete/Delete Cells	Deletes highlighted text or data
Copy/Copy Cells	Copies highlighted text or data to the Clipboard
Cut/Cut Cells	Removes highlighted text or data and copies it to Clipboard
Paste/Paste Cells	Copies contents of the Clipboard to the current position in the active window
Paste Link	Creates new Dynamic Data Exchange (DDE) link by pasting an existing link into Data window (DDE is a way for different files to exchange data with each other)
Worksheet Links	Creates new Dynamic Data Exchange (DDE) links, changes or removes existing links, gets external data, or executes an external command
Select All/Select All Cells	Highlights everything in active window
Edit Last Dialog	Opens the most recently used dialog box, with same selections from last time used
Command Line Editor	Allows one to execute session commands and/or edit and resubmit previously executed commands

Data Menu

Subset Worksheet	Copies specified rows from the active worksheet to a new worksheet
Split Worksheet	Splits or unstacks the active worksheet into two or more new worksheets based on one or more "By" variables
Merge Worksheets	Combines two worksheets into one new worksheet
Sort	Sorts one or more columns of data
Rank	Assigns rank scores to values in column
Delete Rows	Deletes specified rows from columns in the worksheet
Erase Variables	Erases any combination of columns, stored constants, and matrices
Copy	Copies selections from one position in the worksheet to another; can copy entire selections or subset
Stack	Stacks columns on top of each other to make longer columns
Unstack	Unstacks (or splits) columns into shorter columns
Transpose Columns	Switches columns to rows
Concatenate	Combines two or more text columns side by side into one new column
Code	Recodes values in columns
Change Data Type	Changes columns from one data type (such as numeric, text, or date/time) to another
Display Data	Displays data from the current worksheet in the Session window
Extract from Date/Time to Numeric/Text	Extracts one or more parts of date/time column, such as the year, the quarter, or the hour, and saves that data in numeric or text column

Calc Menu

Calculator	Performs various arithmetic operations
Column Statistics	Performs column-based calculations

Row Statistics	Performs row-based calculations
Standardize	Centers and scales columns of data
Make Patterned Data	Allows the filling of a column with numbers or date/time values that follow a pattern
Make Mesh Data	Creates mesh to use for drawing contour, 3-D surface, and wireframe plots
Make Indicator Variables	Creates indicator (dummy) variables that you can use in regression analysis—a very sophisticated option
Set Base	Fixes a starting point for the random number generator
Random Data	Provides substantial control for generating random data from columns of the worksheet or from a variety of distributions
Probability Distributions	Computes probabilities, probability densities, cumulative probabilities, and inverse cumulative probabilities for continuous and discrete distributions
Matrices	Commands for doing matrix operations

Stat Menu

Basic Statistics	Similar to the descriptive statistics function in spreadsheets, but more powerful
Regression	Various kinds of regression (linear, power law, and so on)
ANOVA (Analysis of Variance)	Non-design of experiments (DOE) ANOVA
DOE (Design of Experiments)	Various models including classical (Fisher), Taguchi, response surface, and mixtures
Control Charts	Control charts for subgroups, individuals, time-weighted, and more. The CuSum chart is particularly well done
Quality Tools	Tools that are particularly useful in manufacturing facilities

Reliability/Survival	Weibull analyses, other distributions, hazard functions, and more
Multivariate	Allows for analysis of variables in multiple dimensions
Time Series	Can perform Box-Jenkins and other signal-based analyses of time series
Tables	Contingency tables and variants thereof
Nonparametrics	A collection of many of the non-parametric tests
EDA (Exploratory Data Analysis)	Specialty plots like stem-and-leaf and others
Power and Sample Size	Assists in analysis of hypothesis tests, where the "p" or "power" value defines the probability of rejecting the null hypothesis

Graph Menu

Scatterplot	Various scatterplots
Matrix Plot	A matrix plot is like a window with multiple panes
Marginal Plot	Assesses the relationship between two variables and examines their distributions. The distributions are displayed on the margins of the graph, providing a lot of bivariate information in one plot
Histogram	With various groupings and a choice of fit to a distribution
Dotplot	Plots the data in vertical columns of dots, which readily allows the user to see potential striations in the data; also allows for categorical groupings
Stem-and-Leaf	As in the book
Probability Plot	Linearized fit of a probability distribution
Empirical CDF	Empirical cumulative distribution function
Boxplot	The box-and-whisker plot showing twenty-fifth percentile, seventy-fifth percentile, median, and outlier

Interval Plot	Often called a candlestick plot because the highs and lows resemble a candlestick
Individual Value Plot	Like a dot plot, but compares sample distributions
Bar Chart	True categorical version of the histogram
Pie Chart	As expected; it is rare that a pie chart cannot be improved by converting it to a Pareto chart
Time Series Plot	Sometimes called a run chart, with sophisticated options
Area Graph	The run chart is filled in from the data down to the abscissa—the data often look like a mountain range
Contour Plot	Two-dimensional projection of three-dimensional data
3D Surface Plot	Three-dimensional data treated as a surface
3D Scatterplot	Three-dimensional data not treated as a surface

Editor Menu

The Editor Menu commands are dynamic—they depend on which window is active:

- Session window
- Data window
- Graph window
- Graph window while brushing

Tools Menu

Use the Tools menu to:

- Add new user-defined tools
- Display and hide tool and status bars
- Customize MINITAB's menus, toolbars, and shortcut keys
- Change MINITAB's default options
- Create user profiles to store multiple MINITAB configurations

Additionally . . .

Microsoft Calculator	Opens Microsoft Calculator
Notepad	Opens Windows Notepad
Windows Explorer	Opens Windows Explorer
Answers Database	Links to the Answers Database at MINITAB's official Web site for extra support
Contact Us	Displays MINITAB's contact numbers

MINITAB Tools Menu

Toolbars	Displays or hides available default toolbars in user interface
Status Bar	Displays or hides the Status Bar
Customize	Customizes and creates toolbars, menus, shortcut keys, and more
Options	Changes your default options for MINITAB commands and functionality
Manage Profiles	Manages, imports, and exports profiles of MINITAB options and customization settings

Windows Menu

Cascade	Arranges all open MINITAB windows so that they overlap with each title bar visible (if possible)
Tile	Arranges all open MINITAB windows so they fit next to each other on the desktop and do not overlap (if possible)
Minimize All	Reduces all open windows to icons and places them at the bottom of the screen
Restore Icons	Opens all icons into windows, sized as they were when last reduced to icons within the session
Arrange Icons	Arranges icons along the bottom of the MINITAB window
Refresh	Redraws the graph in the active window

Close All Graphs	Closes all Graph windows
Update All Graphs Now	Updates all Graph windows
Session [Ctrl]+[M]	Switches to Session window, which is the MINITAB script/command-line environment
Project Manager	Switches to the Project Manager window, for management of windows, graphs, worksheets, related documents, and project information
Worksheets and Graphs	Provides ready access to all worksheets and graphs through a menu interface

Help Menu

Help	Displays table of contents of information in the Help system
How to Use Help	Explains how to use the Windows Help system, including how to print, copy, and paste Help text
StatGuide	Displays welcome page
Search the StatGuide	Opens table of contents
How to Use the StatGuide	Opens How to Use the StatGuide Help file
Tutorials	Opens Tutorials, which are extensive
Session Command Help	Opens Session Command Help, containing documentation on each session command, including syntax and examples
Macros Help	Opens Macros Help, containing documentation on how to write macros, including syntax and examples, as well as list of macro commands by function
MINITAB on the Web	Access http://www.minitab.com and follow the support links
Keyboard Map	Displays lists of assigned keyboard shortcuts for commands
About MINITAB	Displays the serial number, product name, release number, and other information

Appendix A

Table of Control Chart Parameters

Subgroup size	A	A2	A3	c2	c4	B3	B4	B5	B6
2	2.1213	1.8800	2.6587	0.5642	0.7979	0.0000	3.2665	0.0000	2.6063
3	1.7321	1.0233	1.9544	0.7236	0.8862	0.0000	2.5682	0.0000	2.2760
4	1.5000	0.7286	1.6281	0.7979	0.9213	0.0000	2.2660	0.0000	2.0877
5	1.3416	0.5768	1.4273	0.8407	0.9400	0.0000	2.0890	0.0000	1.9636
6	1.2247	0.4832	1.2871	0.8686	0.9515	0.0304	1.9696	0.0289	1.8742
7	1.1339	0.4193	1.1819	0.8882	0.9594	0.1177	1.8823	0.1129	1.8058
8	1.0607	0.3725	1.0991	0.9027	0.9650	0.1851	1.8149	0.1786	1.7514
9	1.0000	0.3367	1.0317	0.9139	0.9693	0.2391	1.7609	0.2318	1.7068
10	0.9487	0.3083	0.9754	0.9227	0.9727	0.2837	1.7163	0.2759	1.6694
11	0.9045	0.2851	0.9274	0.9300	0.9754	0.3213	1.6787	0.3134	1.6373
12	0.8660	0.2658	0.8859	0.9359	0.9776	0.3535	1.6465	0.3456	1.6095
13	0.8321	0.2494	0.8495	0.9410	0.9794	0.3816	1.6184	0.3737	1.5851
14	0.8018	0.2354	0.8173	0.9453	0.9810	0.4062	1.5938	0.3985	1.5634
15	0.7746	0.2231	0.7885	0.9490	0.9823	0.4282	1.5718	0.4206	1.5440
16	0.7500	0.2123	0.7626	0.9523	0.9835	0.4479	1.5521	0.4405	1.5265
17	0.7276	0.2028	0.7391	0.9551	0.9845	0.4657	1.5343	0.4585	1.5106
18	0.7071	0.1943	0.7176	0.9576	0.9854	0.4818	1.5182	0.4748	1.4960
19	0.6882	0.1866	0.6979	0.9599	0.9862	0.4966	1.5034	0.4898	1.4826
20	0.6708	0.1796	0.6797	0.9619	0.9869	0.5102	1.4898	0.5036	1.4703

Subgroup size	d2	Standard deviation for d2	D1	D2	D3	D4
2	1.1284	0.8525	0.0000	3.6859	0.0000	3.2665
3	1.6926	0.8884	0.0000	4.3578	0.0000	2.5746
4	2.0588	0.8798	0.0000	4.6982	0.0000	2.2820
5	2.3259	0.8641	0.0000	4.9182	0.0000	2.1145
6	2.5344	0.8480	0.0000	5.0784	0.0000	2.0038
7	2.7044	0.8332	0.2048	5.2040	0.0757	1.9243
8	2.8472	0.8198	0.3878	5.3066	0.1362	1.8638
9	2.9700	0.8078	0.5466	5.3934	0.1840	1.8160
10	3.0775	0.7971	0.6862	5.4688	0.2230	1.7770
11	3.1729	0.7873	0.8110	5.5348	0.2556	1.7444
12	3.2585	0.7785	0.9230	5.5940	0.2833	1.7167
13	3.3360	0.7704	1.0248	5.6472	0.3072	1.6928
14	3.4068	0.7630	1.1178	5.6958	0.3281	1.6719
15	3.4718	0.7562	1.2032	5.7404	0.3466	1.6534
16	3.5320	0.7499	1.2823	5.7817	0.3630	1.6370
17	3.5879	0.7441	1.3556	5.8202	0.3778	1.6222
18	3.6401	0.7386	1.4243	5.8559	0.3913	1.6087
19	3.6890	0.7335	1.4885	5.8895	0.4035	1.5965
20	3.7350	0.7287	1.5489	5.9211	0.4147	1.5853

Appendix B

Chi-Squared Values

Degrees of freedom		
	0.05	0.01
1	3.8415	6.6349
2	5.9915	9.2103
3	7.8147	11.3449
4	9.4877	13.2767
5	11.0705	15.0863
6	12.5916	16.8119
7	14.0671	18.4753
8	15.5073	20.0902
9	16.9190	21.6660
10	18.3070	23.2093
11	19.6751	24.7250
12	21.0261	26.2170
13	22.3620	27.6882
14	23.6848	29.1412
15	24.9958	30.5779
16	26.2962	31.9999
17	27.5871	33.4087
18	28.8693	34.8053
19	30.1435	36.1909
20	31.4104	37.5662
21	32.6706	38.9322
22	33.9244	40.2894
23	35.1725	41.6384
24	36.4150	42.9798
25	37.6525	44.3141
26	38.8851	45.6417
27	40.1133	46.9629
28	41.3371	48.2782
29	42.5570	49.5879
30	43.7730	50.8922
40	55.7585	63.6907
50	67.5048	76.1539
60	79.0819	88.3794

Appendix C

F-Test Values

	nu1	1	2	3	4	5	6	7
nu2								
2		18.5128	19.0000	19.1643	19.2468	19.2964	19.3295	19.3532
3		10.1280	9.5521	9.2766	9.1172	9.0135	8.9406	8.8867
4		7.7086	6.9443	6.5914	6.3882	6.2561	6.1631	6.0942
5		6.6079	5.7861	5.4095	5.1922	5.0503	4.9503	4.8759
6		5.9874	5.1433	4.7571	4.5337	4.3874	4.2839	4.2067
7		5.5914	4.7374	4.3468	4.1203	3.9715	3.8660	3.7870
8		5.3177	4.4590	4.0662	3.8379	3.6875	3.5806	3.5005
9		5.1174	4.2565	3.8625	3.6331	3.4817	3.3738	3.2927
10		4.9646	4.1028	3.7083	3.4780	3.3258	3.2172	3.1355
12		4.7472	3.8853	3.4903	3.2592	3.1059	2.9961	2.9134
14		4.6001	3.7389	3.3439	3.1122	2.9582	2.8477	2.7642
16		4.4940	3.6337	3.2389	3.0069	2.8524	2.7413	2.6572
18		4.4139	3.5546	3.1599	2.9277	2.7729	2.6613	2.5767
20		4.3512	3.4928	3.0984	2.8661	2.7109	2.5990	2.5140
22		4.3009	3.4434	3.0491	2.8167	2.6613	2.5491	2.4638
24		4.2597	3.4028	3.0088	2.7763	2.6207	2.5082	2.4226
26		4.2252	3.3690	2.9752	2.7426	2.5868	2.4741	2.3883
28		4.1960	3.3404	2.9467	2.7141	2.5581	2.4453	2.3593
30		4.1709	3.3158	2.9223	2.6896	2.5336	2.4205	2.3343
40		4.0847	3.2317	2.8387	2.6060	2.4495	2.3359	2.2490
50		4.0343	3.1826	2.7900	2.5572	2.4004	2.2864	2.1992
60		4.0012	3.1504	2.7581	2.5252	2.3683	2.2541	2.1665

8	9	10	15	20	25	30	40	60
19.3710	19.3848	19.3959	19.4291	19.4458	19.4558	19.4624	19.4707	19.4791
8.8452	8.8123	8.7855	8.7029	8.6602	8.6341	8.6166	8.5944	8.5720
6.0410	5.9988	5.9644	5.8578	5.8025	5.7687	5.7459	5.7170	5.6877
4.8183	4.7725	4.7351	4.6188	4.5581	4.5209	4.4957	4.4638	4.4314
4.1468	4.0990	4.0600	3.9381	3.8742	3.8348	3.8082	3.7743	3.7398
3.7257	3.6767	3.6365	3.5107	3.4445	3.4036	3.3758	3.3404	3.3043
3.4381	3.3881	3.3472	3.2184	3.1503	3.1081	3.0794	3.0428	3.0053
3.2296	3.1789	3.1373	3.0061	2.9365	2.8932	2.8637	2.8259	2.7872
3.0717	3.0204	2.9782	2.8450	2.7740	2.7298	2.6996	2.6609	2.6211
2.8486	2.7964	2.7534	2.6169	2.5436	2.4977	2.4663	2.4259	2.3842
2.6987	2.6458	2.6022	2.4630	2.3879	2.3407	2.3082	2.2664	2.2229
2.5911	2.5377	2.4935	2.3522	2.2756	2.2272	2.1938	2.1507	2.1058
2.5102	2.4563	2.4117	2.2686	2.1906	2.1413	2.1071	2.0629	2.0166
2.4471	2.3928	2.3479	2.2033	2.1242	2.0739	2.0391	1.9938	1.9464
2.3965	2.3419	2.2967	2.1508	2.0707	2.0196	1.9842	1.9380	1.8894
2.3551	2.3002	2.2547	2.1077	2.0267	1.9750	1.9390	1.8920	1.8424
2.3205	2.2655	2.2197	2.0716	1.9898	1.9375	1.9010	1.8533	1.8027
2.2913	2.2360	2.1900	2.0411	1.9586	1.9057	1.8687	1.8203	1.7689
2.2662	2.2107	2.1646	2.0148	1.9317	1.8782	1.8409	1.7918	1.7396
2.1802	2.1240	2.0772	1.9245	1.8389	1.7835	1.7444	1.6928	1.6373
2.1299	2.0734	2.0261	1.8714	1.7841	1.7273	1.6872	1.6337	1.5757
2.0970	2.0401	1.9926	1.8364	1.7480	1.6902	1.6491	1.5943	1.5343

Appendix D

Standard Normal Values

Z	0	0.01	0.02	0.03	0.04	0.05	0.06	0.07	0.08	0.09
0	0.5000	0.5040	0.5080	0.5120	0.5160	0.5199	0.5239	0.5279	0.5319	0.5359
0.1	0.5398	0.5438	0.5478	0.5517	0.5557	0.5596	0.5636	0.5675	0.5714	0.5753
0.2	0.5793	0.5832	0.5871	0.5910	0.5948	0.5987	0.6026	0.6064	0.6103	0.6141
0.3	0.6179	0.6217	0.6255	0.6293	0.6331	0.6368	0.6406	0.6443	0.6480	0.6517
0.4	0.6554	0.6591	0.6628	0.6664	0.6700	0.6736	0.6772	0.6808	0.6844	0.6879
0.5	0.6915	0.6950	0.6985	0.7019	0.7054	0.7088	0.7123	0.7157	0.7190	0.7224
0.6	0.7257	0.7291	0.7324	0.7357	0.7389	0.7422	0.7454	0.7486	0.7517	0.7549
0.7	0.7580	0.7611	0.7642	0.7673	0.7704	0.7734	0.7764	0.7794	0.7823	0.7852
0.8	0.7881	0.7910	0.7939	0.7967	0.7995	0.8023	0.8051	0.8078	0.8106	0.8133
0.9	0.8159	0.8186	0.8212	0.8238	0.8264	0.8289	0.8315	0.8340	0.8365	0.8389
1	0.8413	0.8438	0.8461	0.8485	0.8508	0.8531	0.8554	0.8577	0.8599	0.8621
1.1	0.8643	0.8665	0.8686	0.8708	0.8729	0.8749	0.8770	0.8790	0.8810	0.8830
1.2	0.8849	0.8869	0.8888	0.8907	0.8925	0.8944	0.8962	0.8980	0.8997	0.9015
1.3	0.9032	0.9049	0.9066	0.9082	0.9099	0.9115	0.9131	0.9147	0.9162	0.9177
1.4	0.9192	0.9207	0.9222	0.9236	0.9251	0.9265	0.9279	0.9292	0.9306	0.9319
1.5	0.9332	0.9345	0.9357	0.9370	0.9382	0.9394	0.9406	0.9418	0.9429	0.9441
1.6	0.9452	0.9463	0.9474	0.9484	0.9495	0.9505	0.9515	0.9525	0.9535	0.9545
1.7	0.9554	0.9564	0.9573	0.9582	0.9591	0.9599	0.9608	0.9616	0.9625	0.9633
1.8	0.9641	0.9649	0.9656	0.9664	0.9671	0.9678	0.9686	0.9693	0.9699	0.9706
1.9	0.9713	0.9719	0.9726	0.9732	0.9738	0.9744	0.9750	0.9756	0.9761	0.9767
2	0.9772	0.9778	0.9783	0.9788	0.9793	0.9798	0.9803	0.9808	0.9812	0.9817
2.1	0.9821	0.9826	0.9830	0.9834	0.9838	0.9842	0.9846	0.9850	0.9854	0.9857
2.2	0.9861	0.9864	0.9868	0.9871	0.9875	0.9878	0.9881	0.9884	0.9887	0.9890
2.3	0.9893	0.9896	0.9898	0.9901	0.9904	0.9906	0.9909	0.9911	0.9913	0.9916
2.4	0.9918	0.9920	0.9922	0.9925	0.9927	0.9929	0.9931	0.9932	0.9934	0.9936
2.5	0.9938	0.9940	0.9941	0.9943	0.9945	0.9946	0.9948	0.9949	0.9951	0.9952
2.6	0.9953	0.9955	0.9956	0.9957	0.9959	0.9960	0.9961	0.9962	0.9963	0.9964
2.7	0.9965	0.9966	0.9967	0.9968	0.9969	0.9970	0.9971	0.9972	0.9973	0.9974
2.8	0.9974	0.9975	0.9976	0.9977	0.9977	0.9978	0.9979	0.9979	0.9980	0.9981
2.9	0.9981	0.9982	0.9982	0.9983	0.9984	0.9984	0.9985	0.9985	0.9986	0.9986
3	0.9987	0.9987	0.9987	0.9988	0.9988	0.9989	0.9989	0.9989	0.9990	0.9990

Appendix E

T-Test Values

Degrees of freedom				
	0.1	0.05	0.02	0.01
1	6.3138	12.7062	31.8205	63.6567
2	2.9200	4.3027	6.9646	9.9248
3	2.3534	3.1824	4.5407	5.8409
4	2.1318	2.7764	3.7469	4.6041
5	2.0150	2.5706	3.3649	4.0321
6	1.9432	2.4469	3.1427	3.7074
7	1.8946	2.3646	2.9980	3.4995
8	1.8595	2.3060	2.8965	3.3554
9	1.8331	2.2622	2.8214	3.2498
10	1.8125	2.2281	2.7638	3.1693
11	1.7959	2.2010	2.7181	3.1058
12	1.7823	2.1788	2.6810	3.0545
13	1.7709	2.1604	2.6503	3.0123
14	1.7613	2.1448	2.6245	2.9768
15	1.7531	2.1314	2.6025	2.9467
16	1.7459	2.1199	2.5835	2.9208
17	1.7396	2.1098	2.5669	2.8982
18	1.7341	2.1009	2.5524	2.8784
19	1.7291	2.0930	2.5395	2.8609
20	1.7247	2.0860	2.5280	2.8453
21	1.7207	2.0796	2.5176	2.8314
22	1.7171	2.0739	2.5083	2.8188
23	1.7139	2.0687	2.4999	2.8073
24	1.7109	2.0639	2.4922	2.7969
25	1.7081	2.0595	2.4851	2.7874
26	1.7056	2.0555	2.4786	2.7787
27	1.7033	2.0518	2.4727	2.7707
28	1.7011	2.0484	2.4671	2.7633
29	1.6991	2.0452	2.4620	2.7564
30	1.6973	2.0423	2.4573	2.7500
40	1.6839	2.0211	2.4233	2.7045
50	1.6759	2.0086	2.4033	2.6778
60	1.6706	2.0003	2.3901	2.6603

Appendix F
Binomial Distribution

	Binomial cumulative density function, 0.01–0.09								
n	x	0.01	0.02	0.03	0.04	0.05	0.06	0.07	0.08	0.09
1	0	0.9900	0.9800	0.9700	0.9600	0.9500	0.9400	0.9300	0.9200	0.9100
1	1	1.0000	1.0000	1.0000	1.0000	1.0000	1.0000	1.0000	1.0000	1.0000
2	0	0.9801	0.9604	0.9409	0.9216	0.9025	0.8836	0.8649	0.8464	0.8281
2	1	0.9999	0.9996	0.9991	0.9984	0.9975	0.9964	0.9951	0.9936	0.9919
2	2	1.0000	1.0000	1.0000	1.0000	1.0000	1.0000	1.0000	1.0000	1.0000
3	0	0.9703	0.9412	0.9127	0.8847	0.8574	0.8306	0.8044	0.7787	0.7536
3	1	0.9997	0.9988	0.9974	0.9953	0.9928	0.9896	0.9860	0.9818	0.9772
3	2	1.0000	1.0000	1.0000	0.9999	0.9999	0.9998	0.9997	0.9995	0.9993
3	3	1.0000	1.0000	1.0000	1.0000	1.0000	1.0000	1.0000	1.0000	1.0000
4	0	0.9606	0.9224	0.8853	0.8493	0.8145	0.7807	0.7481	0.7164	0.6857
4	1	0.9994	0.9977	0.9948	0.9909	0.9860	0.9801	0.9733	0.9656	0.9570
4	2	1.0000	1.0000	0.9999	0.9998	0.9995	0.9992	0.9987	0.9981	0.9973
4	3	1.0000	1.0000	1.0000	1.0000	1.0000	1.0000	1.0000	1.0000	0.9999
4	4	1.0000	1.0000	1.0000	1.0000	1.0000	1.0000	1.0000	1.0000	1.0000
5	0	0.9510	0.9039	0.8587	0.8154	0.7738	0.7339	0.6957	0.6591	0.6240
5	1	0.9990	0.9962	0.9915	0.9852	0.9774	0.9681	0.9575	0.9456	0.9326
5	2	1.0000	0.9999	0.9997	0.99t94	0.9988	0.9980	0.9969	0.9955	0.9937
5	3	1.0000	1.0000	1.0000	1.0000	1.0000	0.9999	0.9999	0.9998	0.9997
5	4	1.0000	1.0000	1.0000	1.0000	1.0000	1.0000	1.0000	1.0000	1.0000
5	5	1.0000	1.0000	1.0000	1.0000	1.0000	1.0000	1.0000	1.0000	1.0000
6	0	0.9415	0.8858	0.8330	0.7828	0.7351	0.6899	0.6470	0.6064	0.5679
6	1	0.9985	0.9943	0.9875	0.9784	0.9672	0.9541	0.9392	0.9227	0.9048
6	2	1.0000	0.9998	0.9995	0.9988	0.9978	0.9962	0.9942	0.9915	0.9882
6	3	1.0000	1.0000	1.0000	1.0000	0.9999	0.9998	0.9997	0.9995	0.9992
6	4	1.0000	1.0000	1.0000	1.0000	1.0000	1.0000	1.0000	1.0000	1.0000
6	5	1.0000	1.0000	1.0000	1.0000	1.0000	1.0000	1.0000	1.0000	1.0000
6	6	1.0000	1.0000	1.0000	1.0000	1.0000	1.0000	1.0000	1.0000	1.0000
7	0	0.9321	0.8681	0.8080	0.7514	0.6983	0.6485	0.6017	0.5578	0.5168
7	1	0.9980	0.9921	0.9829	0.9706	0.9556	0.9382	0.9187	0.8974	0.8745
7	2	1.0000	0.9997	0.9991	0.9980	0.9962	0.9937	0.9903	0.9860	0.9807
7	3	1.0000	1.0000	1.0000	0.9999	0.9998	0.9996	0.9993	0.9988	0.9982

	**Binomial cumulative density function, 0.01–0.09**
7	4	1.0000	1.0000	1.0000	1.0000	1.0000	1.0000	1.0000	0.9999	0.9999
7	5	1.0000	1.0000	1.0000	1.0000	1.0000	1.0000	1.0000	1.0000	1.0000
7	6	1.0000	1.0000	1.0000	1.0000	1.0000	1.0000	1.0000	1.0000	1.0000
7	7	1.0000	1.0000	1.0000	1.0000	1.0000	1.0000	1.0000	1.0000	1.0000
8	0	0.9227	0.8508	0.7837	0.7214	0.6634	0.6096	0.5596	0.5132	0.4703
8	1	0.9973	0.9897	0.9777	0.9619	0.9428	0.9208	0.8965	0.8702	0.8423
8	2	0.9999	0.9996	0.9987	0.9969	0.9942	0.9904	0.9853	0.9789	0.9711
8	3	1.0000	1.0000	0.9999	0.9998	0.9996	0.9993	0.9987	0.9978	0.9966
8	4	1.0000	1.0000	1.0000	1.0000	1.0000	1.0000	0.9999	0.9999	0.9997
8	5	1.0000	1.0000	1.0000	1.0000	1.0000	1.0000	1.0000	1.0000	1.0000
8	6	1.0000	1.0000	1.0000	1.0000	1.0000	1.0000	1.0000	1.0000	1.0000
8	7	1.0000	1.0000	1.0000	1.0000	1.0000	1.0000	1.0000	1.0000	1.0000
8	8	1.0000	1.0000	1.0000	1.0000	1.0000	1.0000	1.0000	1.0000	1.0000
9	0	0.9135	0.8337	0.7602	0.6925	0.6302	0.5730	0.5204	0.4722	0.4279
9	1	0.9966	0.9869	0.9718	0.9522	0.9288	0.9022	0.8729	0.8417	0.8088
9	2	0.9999	0.9994	0.9980	0.9955	0.9916	0.9862	0.9791	0.9702	0.9595
9	3	1.0000	1.0000	0.9999	0.9997	0.9994	0.9987	0.9977	0.9963	0.9943
9	4	1.0000	1.0000	1.0000	1.0000	1.0000	0.9999	0.9998	0.9997	0.9995
9	5	1.0000	1.0000	1.0000	1.0000	1.0000	1.0000	1.0000	1.0000	1.0000
9	6	1.0000	1.0000	1.0000	1.0000	1.0000	1.0000	1.0000	1.0000	1.0000
9	7	1.0000	1.0000	1.0000	1.0000	1.0000	1.0000	1.0000	1.0000	1.0000
9	8	1.0000	1.0000	1.0000	1.0000	1.0000	1.0000	1.0000	1.0000	1.0000
9	9	1.0000	1.0000	1.0000	1.0000	1.0000	1.0000	1.0000	1.0000	1.0000
10	0	0.9044	0.8171	0.7374	0.6648	0.5987	0.5386	0.4840	0.4344	0.3894
10	1	0.9957	0.9838	0.9655	0.9418	0.9139	0.8824	0.8483	0.8121	0.7746
10	2	0.9999	0.9991	0.9972	0.9938	0.9885	0.9812	0.9717	0.9599	0.9460
10	3	1.0000	1.0000	0.9999	0.9996	0.9990	0.9980	0.9964	0.9942	0.9912
10	4	1.0000	1.0000	1.0000	1.0000	0.9999	0.9998	0.9997	0.9994	0.9990
10	5	1.0000	1.0000	1.0000	1.0000	1.0000	1.0000	1.0000	1.0000	0.9999
10	6	1.0000	1.0000	1.0000	1.0000	1.0000	1.0000	1.0000	1.0000	1.0000
10	7	1.0000	1.0000	1.0000	1.0000	1.0000	1.0000	1.0000	1.0000	1.0000
10	8	1.0000	1.0000	1.0000	1.0000	1.0000	1.0000	1.0000	1.0000	1.0000
10	9	1.0000	1.0000	1.0000	1.0000	1.0000	1.0000	1.0000	1.0000	1.0000
10	10	1.0000	1.0000	1.0000	1.0000	1.0000	1.0000	1.0000	1.0000	1.0000
11	0	0.8953	0.8007	0.7153	0.6382	0.5688	0.5063	0.4501	0.3996	0.3544
11	1	0.9948	0.9805	0.9587	0.9308	0.8981	0.8618	0.8228	0.7819	0.7399

		Binomial cumulative density function, 0.01–0.09								
11	2	0.9998	0.9988	0.9963	0.9917	0.9848	0.9752	0.9630	0.9481	0.9305
11	3	1.0000	1.0000	0.9998	0.9993	0.9984	0.9970	0.9947	0.9915	0.9871
11	4	1.0000	1.0000	1.0000	1.0000	0.9999	0.9997	0.9995	0.9990	0.9983
11	5	1.0000	1.0000	1.0000	1.0000	1.0000	1.0000	1.0000	0.9999	0.9998
11	6	1.0000	1.0000	1.0000	1.0000	1.0000	1.0000	1.0000	1.0000	1.0000
11	7	1.0000	1.0000	1.0000	1.0000	1.0000	1.0000	1.0000	1.0000	1.0000
11	8	1.0000	1.0000	1.0000	1.0000	1.0000	1.0000	1.0000	1.0000	1.0000
11	9	1.0000	1.0000	1.0000	1.0000	1.0000	1.0000	1.0000	1.0000	1.0000
11	10	1.0000	1.0000	1.0000	1.0000	1.0000	1.0000	1.0000	1.0000	1.0000
11	11	1.0000	1.0000	1.0000	1.0000	1.0000	1.0000	1.0000	1.0000	1.0000
12	0	0.8864	0.7847	0.6938	0.6127	0.5404	0.4759	0.4186	0.3677	0.3225
12	1	0.9938	0.9769	0.9514	0.9191	0.8816	0.8405	0.7967	0.7513	0.7052
12	2	0.9998	0.9985	0.9952	0.9893	0.9804	0.9684	0.9532	0.9348	0.9134
12	3	1.0000	0.9999	0.9997	0.9990	0.9978	0.9957	0.9925	0.9880	0.9820
12	4	1.0000	1.0000	1.0000	0.9999	0.9998	0.9996	0.9991	0.9984	0.9973
12	5	1.0000	1.0000	1.0000	1.0000	1.0000	1.0000	0.9999	0.9998	0.9997
12	6	1.0000	1.0000	1.0000	1.0000	1.0000	1.0000	1.0000	1.0000	1.0000
12	7	1.0000	1.0000	1.0000	1.0000	1.0000	1.0000	1.0000	1.0000	1.0000
12	8	1.0000	1.0000	1.0000	1.0000	1.0000	1.0000	1.0000	1.0000	1.0000
12	9	1.0000	1.0000	1.0000	1.0000	1.0000	1.0000	1.0000	1.0000	1.0000
12	10	1.0000	1.0000	1.0000	1.0000	1.0000	1.0000	1.0000	1.0000	1.0000
12	11	1.0000	1.0000	1.0000	1.0000	1.0000	1.0000	1.0000	1.0000	1.0000
12	12	1.0000	1.0000	1.0000	1.0000	1.0000	1.0000	1.0000	1.0000	1.0000
13	0	0.8775	0.7690	0.6730	0.5882	0.5133	0.4474	0.3893	0.3383	0.2935
13	1	0.9928	0.9730	0.9436	0.9068	0.8646	0.8186	0.7702	0.7206	0.6707
13	2	0.9997	0.9980	0.9938	0.9865	0.9755	0.9608	0.9422	0.9201	0.8946
13	3	1.0000	0.9999	0.9995	0.9986	0.9969	0.9940	0.9897	0.9837	0.9758
13	4	1.0000	1.0000	1.0000	0.9999	0.9997	0.9993	0.9987	0.9976	0.9959
13	5	1.0000	1.0000	1.0000	1.0000	1.0000	0.9999	0.9999	0.9997	0.9995
13	6	1.0000	1.0000	1.0000	1.0000	1.0000	1.0000	1.0000	1.0000	0.9999
13	7	1.0000	1.0000	1.0000	1.0000	1.0000	1.0000	1.0000	1.0000	1.0000
13	8	1.0000	1.0000	1.0000	1.0000	1.0000	1.0000	1.0000	1.0000	1.0000
13	9	1.0000	1.0000	1.0000	1.0000	1.0000	1.0000	1.0000	1.0000	1.0000
13	10	1.0000	1.0000	1.0000	1.0000	1.0000	1.0000	1.0000	1.0000	1.0000
13	11	1.0000	1.0000	1.0000	1.0000	1.0000	1.0000	1.0000	1.0000	1.0000
13	12	1.0000	1.0000	1.0000	1.0000	1.0000	1.0000	1.0000	1.0000	1.0000

		Binomial cumulative density function, 0.01–0.09								
13	13	1.0000	1.0000	1.0000	1.0000	1.0000	1.0000	1.0000	1.0000	1.0000
14	0	0.8687	0.7536	0.6528	0.5647	0.4877	0.4205	0.3620	0.3112	0.2670
14	1	0.9916	0.9690	0.9355	0.8941	0.8470	0.7963	0.7436	0.6900	0.6368
14	2	0.9997	0.9975	0.9923	0.9833	0.9699	0.9522	0.9302	0.9042	0.8745
14	3	1.0000	0.9999	0.9994	0.9981	0.9958	0.9920	0.9864	0.9786	0.9685
14	4	1.0000	1.0000	1.0000	0.9998	0.9996	0.9990	0.9980	0.9965	0.9941
14	5	1.0000	1.0000	1.0000	1.0000	1.0000	0.9999	0.9998	0.9996	0.9992
14	6	1.0000	1.0000	1.0000	1.0000	1.0000	1.0000	1.0000	1.0000	0.9999
14	7	1.0000	1.0000	1.0000	1.0000	1.0000	1.0000	1.0000	1.0000	1.0000
14	8	1.0000	1.0000	1.0000	1.0000	1.0000	1.0000	1.0000	1.0000	1.0000
14	9	1.0000	1.0000	1.0000	1.0000	1.0000	1.0000	1.0000	1.0000	1.0000
14	10	1.0000	1.0000	1.0000	1.0000	1.0000	1.0000	1.0000	1.0000	1.0000
14	11	1.0000	1.0000	1.0000	1.0000	1.0000	1.0000	1.0000	1.0000	1.0000
14	12	1.0000	1.0000	1.0000	1.0000	1.0000	1.0000	1.0000	1.0000	1.0000
14	13	1.0000	1.0000	1.0000	1.0000	1.0000	1.0000	1.0000	1.0000	1.0000
14	14	1.0000	1.0000	1.0000	1.0000	1.0000	1.0000	1.0000	1.0000	1.0000
15	0	0.8601	0.7386	0.6333	0.5421	0.4633	0.3953	0.3367	0.2863	0.2430
15	1	0.9904	0.9647	0.9270	0.8809	0.8290	0.7738	0.7168	0.6597	0.6035
15	2	0.9996	0.9970	0.9906	0.9797	0.9638	0.9429	0.9171	0.8870	0.8531
15	3	1.0000	0.9998	0.9992	0.9976	0.9945	0.9896	0.9825	0.9727	0.9601
15	4	1.0000	1.0000	0.9999	0.9998	0.9994	0.9986	0.9972	0.9950	0.9918
15	5	1.0000	1.0000	1.0000	1.0000	0.9999	0.9999	0.9997	0.9993	0.9987
15	6	1.0000	1.0000	1.0000	1.0000	1.0000	1.0000	1.0000	0.9999	0.9998
15	7	1.0000	1.0000	1.0000	1.0000	1.0000	1.0000	1.0000	1.0000	1.0000
15	8	1.0000	1.0000	1.0000	1.0000	1.0000	1.0000	1.0000	1.0000	1.0000
15	9	1.0000	1.0000	1.0000	1.0000	1.0000	1.0000	1.0000	1.0000	1.0000
15	10	1.0000	1.0000	1.0000	1.0000	1.0000	1.0000	1.0000	1.0000	1.0000
15	11	1.0000	1.0000	1.0000	1.0000	1.0000	1.0000	1.0000	1.0000	1.0000
15	12	1.0000	1.0000	1.0000	1.0000	1.0000	1.0000	1.0000	1.0000	1.0000
15	13	1.0000	1.0000	1.0000	1.0000	1.0000	1.0000	1.0000	1.0000	1.0000
15	14	1.0000	1.0000	1.0000	1.0000	1.0000	1.0000	1.0000	1.0000	1.0000
15	15	1.0000	1.0000	1.0000	1.0000	1.0000	1.0000	1.0000	1.0000	1.0000
16	0	0.8515	0.7238	0.6143	0.5204	0.4401	0.3716	0.3131	0.2634	0.2211
16	1	0.9891	0.9601	0.9182	0.8673	0.8108	0.7511	0.6902	0.6299	0.5711
16	2	0.9995	0.9963	0.9887	0.9758	0.9571	0.9327	0.9031	0.8689	0.8306
16	3	1.0000	0.9998	0.9989	0.9968	0.9930	0.9868	0.9779	0.9658	0.9504

Binomial cumulative density function, 0.01–0.09										
16	4	1.0000	1.0000	0.9999	0.9997	0.9991	0.9981	0.9962	0.9932	0.9889
16	5	1.0000	1.0000	1.0000	1.0000	0.9999	0.9998	0.9995	0.9990	0.9981
16	6	1.0000	1.0000	1.0000	1.0000	1.0000	1.0000	0.9999	0.9999	0.9997
16	7	1.0000	1.0000	1.0000	1.0000	1.0000	1.0000	1.0000	1.0000	1.0000
16	8	1.0000	1.0000	1.0000	1.0000	1.0000	1.0000	1.0000	1.0000	1.0000
16	9	1.0000	1.0000	1.0000	1.0000	1.0000	1.0000	1.0000	1.0000	1.0000
16	10	1.0000	1.0000	1.0000	1.0000	1.0000	1.0000	1.0000	1.0000	1.0000
16	11	1.0000	1.0000	1.0000	1.0000	1.0000	1.0000	1.0000	1.0000	1.0000
16	12	1.0000	1.0000	1.0000	1.0000	1.0000	1.0000	1.0000	1.0000	1.0000
16	13	1.0000	1.0000	1.0000	1.0000	1.0000	1.0000	1.0000	1.0000	1.0000
16	14	1.0000	1.0000	1.0000	1.0000	1.0000	1.0000	1.0000	1.0000	1.0000
16	15	1.0000	1.0000	1.0000	1.0000	1.0000	1.0000	1.0000	1.0000	1.0000
16	16	1.0000	1.0000	1.0000	1.0000	1.0000	1.0000	1.0000	1.0000	1.0000
17	0	0.8429	0.7093	0.5958	0.4996	0.4181	0.3493	0.2912	0.2423	0.2012
17	1	0.9877	0.9554	0.9091	0.8535	0.7922	0.7283	0.6638	0.6005	0.5396
17	2	0.9994	0.9956	0.9866	0.9714	0.9497	0.9218	0.8882	0.8497	0.8073
17	3	1.0000	0.9997	0.9986	0.9960	0.9912	0.9836	0.9727	0.9581	0.9397
17	4	1.0000	1.0000	0.9999	0.9996	0.9988	0.9974	0.9949	0.9911	0.9855
17	5	1.0000	1.0000	1.0000	1.0000	0.9999	0.9997	0.9993	0.9985	0.9973
17	6	1.0000	1.0000	1.0000	1.0000	1.0000	1.0000	0.9999	0.9998	0.9996
17	7	1.0000	1.0000	1.0000	1.0000	1.0000	1.0000	1.0000	1.0000	1.0000
17	8	1.0000	1.0000	1.0000	1.0000	1.0000	1.0000	1.0000	1.0000	1.0000
17	9	1.0000	1.0000	1.0000	1.0000	1.0000	1.0000	1.0000	1.0000	1.0000
17	10	1.0000	1.0000	1.0000	1.0000	1.0000	1.0000	1.0000	1.0000	1.0000
17	11	1.0000	1.0000	1.0000	1.0000	1.0000	1.0000	1.0000	1.0000	1.0000
17	12	1.0000	1.0000	1.0000	1.0000	1.0000	1.0000	1.0000	1.0000	1.0000
17	13	1.0000	1.0000	1.0000	1.0000	1.0000	1.0000	1.0000	1.0000	1.0000
17	14	1.0000	1.0000	1.0000	1.0000	1.0000	1.0000	1.0000	1.0000	1.0000
17	15	1.0000	1.0000	1.0000	1.0000	1.0000	1.0000	1.0000	1.0000	1.0000
17	16	1.0000	1.0000	1.0000	1.0000	1.0000	1.0000	1.0000	1.0000	1.0000
17	17	1.0000	1.0000	1.0000	1.0000	1.0000	1.0000	1.0000	1.0000	1.0000
18	0	0.8345	0.6951	0.5780	0.4796	0.3972	0.3283	0.2708	0.2229	0.1831
18	1	0.9862	0.9505	0.8997	0.8393	0.7735	0.7055	0.6378	0.5719	0.5091
18	2	0.9993	0.9948	0.9843	0.9667	0.9419	0.9102	0.8725	0.8298	0.7832
18	3	1.0000	0.9996	0.9982	0.9950	0.9891	0.9799	0.9667	0.9494	0.9277
18	4	1.0000	1.0000	0.9998	0.9994	0.9985	0.9966	0.9933	0.9884	0.9814

Binomial cumulative density function, 0.01–0.09									
18	5	1.0000	1.0000	1.0000	0.9999	0.9998	0.9995	0.9990	0.9979	0.9962
18	6	1.0000	1.0000	1.0000	1.0000	1.0000	1.0000	0.9999	0.9997	0.9994
18	7	1.0000	1.0000	1.0000	1.0000	1.0000	1.0000	1.0000	1.0000	0.9999
18	8	1.0000	1.0000	1.0000	1.0000	1.0000	1.0000	1.0000	1.0000	1.0000
18	9	1.0000	1.0000	1.0000	1.0000	1.0000	1.0000	1.0000	1.0000	1.0000
18	10	1.0000	1.0000	1.0000	1.0000	1.0000	1.0000	1.0000	1.0000	1.0000
18	11	1.0000	1.0000	1.0000	1.0000	1.0000	1.0000	1.0000	1.0000	1.0000
18	12	1.0000	1.0000	1.0000	1.0000	1.0000	1.0000	1.0000	1.0000	1.0000
18	13	1.0000	1.0000	1.0000	1.0000	1.0000	1.0000	1.0000	1.0000	1.0000
18	14	1.0000	1.0000	1.0000	1.0000	1.0000	1.0000	1.0000	1.0000	1.0000
18	15	1.0000	1.0000	1.0000	1.0000	1.0000	1.0000	1.0000	1.0000	1.0000
18	16	1.0000	1.0000	1.0000	1.0000	1.0000	1.0000	1.0000	1.0000	1.0000
18	17	1.0000	1.0000	1.0000	1.0000	1.0000	1.0000	1.0000	1.0000	1.0000
18	18	1.0000	1.0000	1.0000	1.0000	1.0000	1.0000	1.0000	1.0000	1.0000
19	0	0.8262	0.6812	0.5606	0.4604	0.3774	0.3086	0.2519	0.2051	0.1666
19	1	0.9847	0.9454	0.8900	0.8249	0.7547	0.6829	0.6121	0.5440	0.4798
19	2	0.9991	0.9939	0.9817	0.9616	0.9335	0.8979	0.8561	0.8092	0.7585
19	3	1.0000	0.9995	0.9978	0.9939	0.9868	0.9757	0.9602	0.9398	0.9147
19	4	1.0000	1.0000	0.9998	0.9993	0.9980	0.9956	0.9915	0.9853	0.9765
19	5	1.0000	1.0000	1.0000	0.9999	0.9998	0.9994	0.9986	0.9971	0.9949
19	6	1.0000	1.0000	1.0000	1.0000	1.0000	0.9999	0.9998	0.9996	0.9991
19	7	1.0000	1.0000	1.0000	1.0000	1.0000	1.0000	1.0000	0.9999	0.9999
19	8	1.0000	1.0000	1.0000	1.0000	1.0000	1.0000	1.0000	1.0000	1.0000
19	9	1.0000	1.0000	1.0000	1.0000	1.0000	1.0000	1.0000	1.0000	1.0000
19	10	1.0000	1.0000	1.0000	1.0000	1.0000	1.0000	1.0000	1.0000	1.0000
19	11	1.0000	1.0000	1.0000	1.0000	1.0000	1.0000	1.0000	1.0000	1.0000
19	12	1.0000	1.0000	1.0000	1.0000	1.0000	1.0000	1.0000	1.0000	1.0000
19	13	1.0000	1.0000	1.0000	1.0000	1.0000	1.0000	1.0000	1.0000	1.0000
19	14	1.0000	1.0000	1.0000	1.0000	1.0000	1.0000	1.0000	1.0000	1.0000
19	15	1.0000	1.0000	1.0000	1.0000	1.0000	1.0000	1.0000	1.0000	1.0000
19	16	1.0000	1.0000	1.0000	1.0000	1.0000	1.0000	1.0000	1.0000	1.0000
19	17	1.0000	1.0000	1.0000	1.0000	1.0000	1.0000	1.0000	1.0000	1.0000
19	18	1.0000	1.0000	1.0000	1.0000	1.0000	1.0000	1.0000	1.0000	1.0000
19	19	1.0000	1.0000	1.0000	1.0000	1.0000	1.0000	1.0000	1.0000	1.0000
20	0	0.8179	0.6676	0.5438	0.4420	0.3585	0.2901	0.2342	0.1887	0.1516
20	1	0.9831	0.9401	0.8802	0.8103	0.7358	0.6605	0.5869	0.5169	0.4516

Binomial cumulative density function, 0.01–0.09									
20	2	0.9990	0.9929	0.9790	0.9561	0.9245	0.8850	0.8390	0.7879	0.7334
20	3	1.0000	0.9994	0.9973	0.9926	0.9841	0.9710	0.9529	0.9294	0.9007
20	4	1.0000	1.0000	0.9997	0.9990	0.9974	0.9944	0.9893	0.9817	0.9710
20	5	1.0000	1.0000	1.0000	0.9999	0.9997	0.9991	0.9981	0.9962	0.9932
20	6	1.0000	1.0000	1.0000	1.0000	1.0000	0.9999	0.9997	0.9994	0.9987
20	7	1.0000	1.0000	1.0000	1.0000	1.0000	1.0000	1.0000	0.9999	0.9998
20	8	1.0000	1.0000	1.0000	1.0000	1.0000	1.0000	1.0000	1.0000	1.0000
20	9	1.0000	1.0000	1.0000	1.0000	1.0000	1.0000	1.0000	1.0000	1.0000
20	10	1.0000	1.0000	1.0000	1.0000	1.0000	1.0000	1.0000	1.0000	1.0000
20	11	1.0000	1.0000	1.0000	1.0000	1.0000	1.0000	1.0000	1.0000	1.0000
20	12	1.0000	1.0000	1.0000	1.0000	1.0000	1.0000	1.0000	1.0000	1.0000
20	13	1.0000	1.0000	1.0000	1.0000	1.0000	1.0000	1.0000	1.0000	1.0000
20	14	1.0000	1.0000	1.0000	1.0000	1.0000	1.0000	1.0000	1.0000	1.0000
20	15	1.0000	1.0000	1.0000	1.0000	1.0000	1.0000	1.0000	1.0000	1.0000
20	16	1.0000	1.0000	1.0000	1.0000	1.0000	1.0000	1.0000	1.0000	1.0000
20	17	1.0000	1.0000	1.0000	1.0000	1.0000	1.0000	1.0000	1.0000	1.0000
20	18	1.0000	1.0000	1.0000	1.0000	1.0000	1.0000	1.0000	1.0000	1.0000
20	19	1.0000	1.0000	1.0000	1.0000	1.0000	1.0000	1.0000	1.0000	1.0000
20	20	1.0000	1.0000	1.0000	1.0000	1.0000	1.0000	1.0000	1.0000	1.0000

Binomial cumulative density function, 0.10–0.50									
n	x	0.10	0.15	0.20	0.25	0.30	0.35	0.40	0.45	0.50
1	0	0.9000	0.8500	0.8000	0.7500	0.7000	0.6500	0.6000	0.5500	0.5000
1	1	1.0000	1.0000	1.0000	1.0000	1.0000	1.0000	1.0000	1.0000	1.0000
2	0	0.8100	0.7225	0.6400	0.5625	0.4900	0.4225	0.3600	0.3025	0.2500
2	1	0.9900	0.9775	0.9600	0.9375	0.9100	0.8775	0.8400	0.7975	0.7500
2	2	1.0000	1.0000	1.0000	1.0000	1.0000	1.0000	1.0000	1.0000	1.0000
3	0	0.7290	0.6141	0.5120	0.4219	0.3430	0.2746	0.2160	0.1664	0.1250
3	1	0.9720	0.9393	0.8960	0.8438	0.7840	0.7183	0.6480	0.5748	0.5000
3	2	0.9990	0.9966	0.9920	0.9844	0.9730	0.9571	0.9360	0.9089	0.8750
3	3	1.0000	1.0000	1.0000	1.0000	1.0000	1.0000	1.0000	1.0000	1.0000
4	0	0.6561	0.5220	0.4096	0.3164	0.2401	0.1785	0.1296	0.0915	0.0625
4	1	0.9477	0.8905	0.8192	0.7383	0.6517	0.5630	0.4752	0.3910	0.3125
4	2	0.9963	0.9880	0.9728	0.9492	0.9163	0.8735	0.8208	0.7585	0.6875
4	3	0.9999	0.9995	0.9984	0.9961	0.9919	0.9850	0.9744	0.9590	0.9375
4	4	1.0000	1.0000	1.0000	1.0000	1.0000	1.0000	1.0000	1.0000	1.0000
5	0	0.5905	0.4437	0.3277	0.2373	0.1681	0.1160	0.0778	0.0503	0.0313
5	1	0.9185	0.8352	0.7373	0.6328	0.5282	0.4284	0.3370	0.2562	0.1875
5	2	0.9914	0.9734	0.9421	0.8965	0.8369	0.7648	0.6826	0.5931	0.5000
5	3	0.9995	0.9978	0.9933	0.9844	0.9692	0.9460	0.9130	0.8688	0.8125
5	4	1.0000	0.9999	0.9997	0.9990	0.9976	0.9947	0.9898	0.9815	0.9688
5	5	1.0000	1.0000	1.0000	1.0000	1.0000	1.0000	1.0000	1.0000	1.0000
6	0	0.5314	0.3771	0.2621	0.1780	0.1176	0.0754	0.0467	0.0277	0.0156
6	1	0.8857	0.7765	0.6554	0.5339	0.4202	0.3191	0.2333	0.1636	0.1094
6	2	0.9842	0.9527	0.9011	0.8306	0.7443	0.6471	0.5443	0.4415	0.3438
6	3	0.9987	0.9941	0.9830	0.9624	0.9295	0.8826	0.8208	0.7447	0.6563
6	4	0.9999	0.9996	0.9984	0.9954	0.9891	0.9777	0.9590	0.9308	0.8906
6	5	1.0000	1.0000	0.9999	0.9998	0.9993	0.9982	0.9959	0.9917	0.9844
6	6	1.0000	1.0000	1.0000	1.0000	1.0000	1.0000	1.0000	1.0000	1.0000
7	0	0.4783	0.3206	0.2097	0.1335	0.0824	0.0490	0.0280	0.0152	0.0078
7	1	0.8503	0.7166	0.5767	0.4449	0.3294	0.2338	0.1586	0.1024	0.0625
7	2	0.9743	0.9262	0.8520	0.7564	0.6471	0.5323	0.4199	0.3164	0.2266
7	3	0.9973	0.9879	0.9667	0.9294	0.8740	0.8002	0.7102	0.6083	0.5000
7	4	0.9998	0.9988	0.9953	0.9871	0.9712	0.9444	0.9037	0.8471	0.7734

Binomial cumulative density function, 0.10–0.50									
7	5	1.0000	0.9999	0.9996	0.9987	0.9962	0.9910	0.9812	0.9643	0.9375
7	6	1.0000	1.0000	1.0000	0.9999	0.9998	0.9994	0.9984	0.9963	0.9922
7	7	1.0000	1.0000	1.0000	1.0000	1.0000	1.0000	1.0000	1.0000	1.0000
8	0	0.4305	0.2725	0.1678	0.1001	0.0576	0.0319	0.0168	0.0084	0.0039
8	1	0.8131	0.6572	0.5033	0.3671	0.2553	0.1691	0.1064	0.0632	0.0352
8	2	0.9619	0.8948	0.7969	0.6785	0.5518	0.4278	0.3154	0.2201	0.1445
8	3	0.9950	0.9786	0.9437	0.8862	0.8059	0.7064	0.5941	0.4770	0.3633
8	4	0.9996	0.9971	0.9896	0.9727	0.9420	0.8939	0.8263	0.7396	0.6367
8	5	1.0000	0.9998	0.9988	0.9958	0.9887	0.9747	0.9502	0.9115	0.8555
8	6	1.0000	1.0000	0.9999	0.9996	0.9987	0.9964	0.9915	0.9819	0.9648
8	7	1.0000	1.0000	1.0000	1.0000	0.9999	0.9998	0.9993	0.9983	0.9961
8	8	1.0000	1.0000	1.0000	1.0000	1.0000	1.0000	1.0000	1.0000	1.0000
9	0	0.3874	0.2316	0.1342	0.0751	0.0404	0.0207	0.0101	0.0046	0.0020
9	1	0.7748	0.5995	0.4362	0.3003	0.1960	0.1211	0.0705	0.0385	0.0195
9	2	0.9470	0.8591	0.7382	0.6007	0.4628	0.3373	0.2318	0.1495	0.0898
9	3	0.9917	0.9661	0.9144	0.8343	0.7297	0.6089	0.4826	0.3614	0.2539
9	4	0.9991	0.9944	0.9804	0.9511	0.9012	0.8283	0.7334	0.6214	0.5000
9	5	0.9999	0.9994	0.9969	0.9900	0.9747	0.9464	0.9006	0.8342	0.7461
9	6	1.0000	1.0000	0.9997	0.9987	0.9957	0.9888	0.9750	0.9502	0.9102
9	7	1.0000	1.0000	1.0000	0.9999	0.9996	0.9986	0.9962	0.9909	0.9805
9	8	1.0000	1.0000	1.0000	1.0000	1.0000	0.9999	0.9997	0.9992	0.9980
9	9	1.0000	1.0000	1.0000	1.0000	1.0000	1.0000	1.0000	1.0000	1.0000
10	0	0.3487	0.1969	0.1074	0.0563	0.0282	0.0135	0.0060	0.0025	0.0010
10	1	0.7361	0.5443	0.3758	0.2440	0.1493	0.0860	0.0464	0.0233	0.0107
10	2	0.9298	0.8202	0.6778	0.5256	0.3828	0.2616	0.1673	0.0996	0.0547
10	3	0.9872	0.9500	0.8791	0.7759	0.6496	0.5138	0.3823	0.2660	0.1719
10	4	0.9984	0.9901	0.9672	0.9219	0.8497	0.7515	0.6331	0.5044	0.3770
10	5	0.9999	0.9986	0.9936	0.9803	0.9527	0.9051	0.8338	0.7384	0.6230
10	6	1.0000	0.9999	0.9991	0.9965	0.9894	0.9740	0.9452	0.8980	0.8281
10	7	1.0000	1.0000	0.9999	0.9996	0.9984	0.9952	0.9877	0.9726	0.9453
10	8	1.0000	1.0000	1.0000	1.0000	0.9999	0.9995	0.9983	0.9955	0.9893
10	9	1.0000	1.0000	1.0000	1.0000	1.0000	1.0000	0.9999	0.9997	0.9990
10	10	1.0000	1.0000	1.0000	1.0000	1.0000	1.0000	1.0000	1.0000	1.0000
11	0	0.3138	0.1673	0.0859	0.0422	0.0198	0.0088	0.0036	0.0014	0.0005
11	1	0.6974	0.4922	0.3221	0.1971	0.1130	0.0606	0.0302	0.0139	0.0059
11	2	0.9104	0.7788	0.6174	0.4552	0.3127	0.2001	0.1189	0.0652	0.0327

Binomial cumulative density function, 0.10–0.50									
11	3	0.9815	0.9306	0.8389	0.7133	0.5696	0.4256	0.2963	0.1911	0.1133
11	4	0.9972	0.9841	0.9496	0.8854	0.7897	0.6683	0.5328	0.3971	0.2744
11	5	0.9997	0.9973	0.9883	0.9657	0.9218	0.8513	0.7535	0.6331	0.5000
11	6	1.0000	0.9997	0.9980	0.9924	0.9784	0.9499	0.9006	0.8262	0.7256
11	7	1.0000	1.0000	0.9998	0.9988	0.9957	0.9878	0.9707	0.9390	0.8867
11	8	1.0000	1.0000	1.0000	0.9999	0.9994	0.9980	0.9941	0.9852	0.9673
11	9	1.0000	1.0000	1.0000	1.0000	1.0000	0.9998	0.9993	0.9978	0.9941
11	10	1.0000	1.0000	1.0000	1.0000	1.0000	1.0000	1.0000	0.9998	0.9995
11	11	1.0000	1.0000	1.0000	1.0000	1.0000	1.0000	1.0000	1.0000	1.0000
12	0	0.2824	0.1422	0.0687	0.0317	0.0138	0.0057	0.0022	0.0008	0.0002
12	1	0.6590	0.4435	0.2749	0.1584	0.0850	0.0424	0.0196	0.0083	0.0032
12	2	0.8891	0.7358	0.5583	0.3907	0.2528	0.1513	0.0834	0.0421	0.0193
12	3	0.9744	0.9078	0.7946	0.6488	0.4925	0.3467	0.2253	0.1345	0.0730
12	4	0.9957	0.9761	0.9274	0.8424	0.7237	0.5833	0.4382	0.3044	0.1938
12	5	0.9995	0.9954	0.9806	0.9456	0.8822	0.7873	0.6652	0.5269	0.3872
12	6	0.9999	0.9993	0.9961	0.9857	0.9614	0.9154	0.8418	0.7393	0.6128
12	7	1.0000	0.9999	0.9994	0.9972	0.9905	0.9745	0.9427	0.8883	0.8062
12	8	1.0000	1.0000	0.9999	0.9996	0.9983	0.9944	0.9847	0.9644	0.9270
12	9	1.0000	1.0000	1.0000	1.0000	0.9998	0.9992	0.9972	0.9921	0.9807
12	10	1.0000	1.0000	1.0000	1.0000	1.0000	0.9999	0.9997	0.9989	0.9968
12	11	1.0000	1.0000	1.0000	1.0000	1.0000	1.0000	1.0000	0.9999	0.9998
12	12	1.0000	1.0000	1.0000	1.0000	1.0000	1.0000	1.0000	1.0000	1.0000
13	0	0.2542	0.1209	0.0550	0.0238	0.0097	0.0037	0.0013	0.0004	0.0001
13	1	0.6213	0.3983	0.2336	0.1267	0.0637	0.0296	0.0126	0.0049	0.0017
13	2	0.8661	0.6920	0.5017	0.3326	0.2025	0.1132	0.0579	0.0269	0.0112
13	3	0.9658	0.8820	0.7473	0.5843	0.4206	0.2783	0.1686	0.0929	0.0461
13	4	0.9935	0.9658	0.9009	0.7940	0.6543	0.5005	0.3530	0.2279	0.1334
13	5	0.9991	0.9925	0.9700	0.9198	0.8346	0.7159	0.5744	0.4268	0.2905
13	6	0.9999	0.9987	0.9930	0.9757	0.9376	0.8705	0.7712	0.6437	0.5000
13	7	1.0000	0.9998	0.9988	0.9944	0.9818	0.9538	0.9023	0.8212	0.7095
13	8	1.0000	1.0000	0.9998	0.9990	0.9960	0.9874	0.9679	0.9302	0.8666
13	9	1.0000	1.0000	1.0000	0.9999	0.9993	0.9975	0.9922	0.9797	0.9539
13	10	1.0000	1.0000	1.0000	1.0000	0.9999	0.9997	0.9987	0.9959	0.9888
13	11	1.0000	1.0000	1.0000	1.0000	1.0000	1.0000	0.9999	0.9995	0.9983
13	12	1.0000	1.0000	1.0000	1.0000	1.0000	1.0000	1.0000	1.0000	0.9999
13	13	1.0000	1.0000	1.0000	1.0000	1.0000	1.0000	1.0000	1.0000	1.0000

Binomial cumulative density function, 0.10–0.50									
14	0	0.2288	0.1028	0.0440	0.0178	0.0068	0.0024	0.0008	0.0002	0.0001
14	1	0.5846	0.3567	0.1979	0.1010	0.0475	0.0205	0.0081	0.0029	0.0009
14	2	0.8416	0.6479	0.4481	0.2811	0.1608	0.0839	0.0398	0.0170	0.0065
14	3	0.9559	0.8535	0.6982	0.5213	0.3552	0.2205	0.1243	0.0632	0.0287
14	4	0.9908	0.9533	0.8702	0.7415	0.5842	0.4227	0.2793	0.1672	0.0898
14	5	0.9985	0.9885	0.9561	0.8883	0.7805	0.6405	0.4859	0.3373	0.2120
14	6	0.9998	0.9978	0.9884	0.9617	0.9067	0.8164	0.6925	0.5461	0.3953
14	7	1.0000	0.9997	0.9976	0.9897	0.9685	0.9247	0.8499	0.7414	0.6047
14	8	1.0000	1.0000	0.9996	0.9978	0.9917	0.9757	0.9417	0.8811	0.7880
14	9	1.0000	1.0000	1.0000	0.9997	0.9983	0.9940	0.9825	0.9574	0.9102
14	10	1.0000	1.0000	1.0000	1.0000	0.9998	0.9989	0.9961	0.9886	0.9713
14	11	1.0000	1.0000	1.0000	1.0000	1.0000	0.9999	0.9994	0.9978	0.9935
14	12	1.0000	1.0000	1.0000	1.0000	1.0000	1.0000	0.9999	0.9997	0.9991
14	13	1.0000	1.0000	1.0000	1.0000	1.0000	1.0000	1.0000	1.0000	0.9999
14	14	1.0000	1.0000	1.0000	1.0000	1.0000	1.0000	1.0000	1.0000	1.0000
15	0	0.2059	0.0874	0.0352	0.0134	0.0047	0.0016	0.0005	0.0001	0.0000
15	1	0.5490	0.3186	0.1671	0.0802	0.0353	0.0142	0.0052	0.0017	0.0005
15	2	0.8159	0.6042	0.3980	0.2361	0.1268	0.0617	0.0271	0.0107	0.0037
15	3	0.9444	0.8227	0.6482	0.4613	0.2969	0.1727	0.0905	0.0424	0.0176
15	4	0.9873	0.9383	0.8358	0.6865	0.5155	0.3519	0.2173	0.1204	0.0592
15	5	0.9978	0.9832	0.9389	0.8516	0.7216	0.5643	0.4032	0.2608	0.1509
15	6	0.9997	0.9964	0.9819	0.9434	0.8689	0.7548	0.6098	0.4522	0.3036
15	7	1.0000	0.9994	0.9958	0.9827	0.9500	0.8868	0.7869	0.6535	0.5000
15	8	1.0000	0.9999	0.9992	0.9958	0.9848	0.9578	0.9050	0.8182	0.6964
15	9	1.0000	1.0000	0.9999	0.9992	0.9963	0.9876	0.9662	0.9231	0.8491
15	10	1.0000	1.0000	1.0000	0.9999	0.9993	0.9972	0.9907	0.9745	0.9408
15	11	1.0000	1.0000	1.0000	1.0000	0.9999	0.9995	0.9981	0.9937	0.9824
15	12	1.0000	1.0000	1.0000	1.0000	1.0000	0.9999	0.9997	0.9989	0.9963
15	13	1.0000	1.0000	1.0000	1.0000	1.0000	1.0000	1.0000	0.9999	0.9995
15	14	1.0000	1.0000	1.0000	1.0000	1.0000	1.0000	1.0000	1.0000	1.0000
15	15	1.0000	1.0000	1.0000	1.0000	1.0000	1.0000	1.0000	1.0000	1.0000
16	0	0.1853	0.0743	0.0281	0.0100	0.0033	0.0010	0.0003	0.0001	0.0000
16	1	0.5147	0.2839	0.1407	0.0635	0.0261	0.0098	0.0033	0.0010	0.0003
16	2	0.7892	0.5614	0.3518	0.1971	0.0994	0.0451	0.0183	0.0066	0.0021
16	3	0.9316	0.7899	0.5981	0.4050	0.2459	0.1339	0.0651	0.0281	0.0106
16	4	0.9830	0.9209	0.7982	0.6302	0.4499	0.2892	0.1666	0.0853	0.0384

		Binomial cumulative density function, 0.10–0.50							
16	5	0.9967	0.9765	0.9183	0.8103	0.6598	0.4900	0.3288	0.1976	0.1051
16	6	0.9995	0.9944	0.9733	0.9204	0.8247	0.6881	0.5272	0.3660	0.2272
16	7	0.9999	0.9989	0.9930	0.9729	0.9256	0.8406	0.7161	0.5629	0.4018
16	8	1.0000	0.9998	0.9985	0.9925	0.9743	0.9329	0.8577	0.7441	0.5982
16	9	1.0000	1.0000	0.9998	0.9984	0.9929	0.9771	0.9417	0.8759	0.7728
16	10	1.0000	1.0000	1.0000	0.9997	0.9984	0.9938	0.9809	0.9514	0.8949
16	11	1.0000	1.0000	1.0000	1.0000	0.9997	0.9987	0.9951	0.9851	0.9616
16	12	1.0000	1.0000	1.0000	1.0000	1.0000	0.9998	0.9991	0.9965	0.9894
16	13	1.0000	1.0000	1.0000	1.0000	1.0000	1.0000	0.9999	0.9994	0.9979
16	14	1.0000	1.0000	1.0000	1.0000	1.0000	1.0000	1.0000	0.9999	0.9997
16	15	1.0000	1.0000	1.0000	1.0000	1.0000	1.0000	1.0000	1.0000	1.0000
16	16	1.0000	1.0000	1.0000	1.0000	1.0000	1.0000	1.0000	1.0000	1.0000
17	0	0.1668	0.0631	0.0225	0.0075	0.0023	0.0007	0.0002	0.0000	0.0000
17	1	0.4818	0.2525	0.1182	0.0501	0.0193	0.0067	0.0021	0.0006	0.0001
17	2	0.7618	0.5198	0.3096	0.1637	0.0774	0.0327	0.0123	0.0041	0.0012
17	3	0.9174	0.7556	0.5489	0.3530	0.2019	0.1028	0.0464	0.0184	0.0064
17	4	0.9779	0.9013	0.7582	0.5739	0.3887	0.2348	0.1260	0.0596	0.0245
17	5	0.9953	0.9681	0.8943	0.7653	0.5968	0.4197	0.2639	0.1471	0.0717
17	6	0.9992	0.9917	0.9623	0.8929	0.7752	0.6188	0.4478	0.2902	0.1662
17	7	0.9999	0.9983	0.9891	0.9598	0.8954	0.7872	0.6405	0.4743	0.3145
17	8	1.0000	0.9997	0.9974	0.9876	0.9597	0.9006	0.8011	0.6626	0.5000
17	9	1.0000	1.0000	0.9995	0.9969	0.9873	0.9617	0.9081	0.8166	0.6855
17	10	1.0000	1.0000	0.9999	0.9994	0.9968	0.9880	0.9652	0.9174	0.8338
17	11	1.0000	1.0000	1.0000	0.9999	0.9993	0.9970	0.9894	0.9699	0.9283
17	12	1.0000	1.0000	1.0000	1.0000	0.9999	0.9994	0.9975	0.9914	0.9755
17	13	1.0000	1.0000	1.0000	1.0000	1.0000	0.9999	0.9995	0.9981	0.9936
17	14	1.0000	1.0000	1.0000	1.0000	1.0000	1.0000	0.9999	0.9997	0.9988
17	15	1.0000	1.0000	1.0000	1.0000	1.0000	1.0000	1.0000	1.0000	0.9999
17	16	1.0000	1.0000	1.0000	1.0000	1.0000	1.0000	1.0000	1.0000	1.0000
17	17	1.0000	1.0000	1.0000	1.0000	1.0000	1.0000	1.0000	1.0000	1.0000
18	0	0.1501	0.0536	0.0180	0.0056	0.0016	0.0004	0.0001	0.0000	0.0000
18	1	0.4503	0.2241	0.0991	0.0395	0.0142	0.0046	0.0013	0.0003	0.0001
18	2	0.7338	0.4797	0.2713	0.1353	0.0600	0.0236	0.0082	0.0025	0.0007
18	3	0.9018	0.7202	0.5010	0.3057	0.1646	0.0783	0.0328	0.0120	0.0038
18	4	0.9718	0.8794	0.7164	0.5187	0.3327	0.1886	0.0942	0.0411	0.0154
18	5	0.9936	0.9581	0.8671	0.7175	0.5344	0.3550	0.2088	0.1077	0.0481

Binomial cumulative density function, 0.10–0.50									
18	6	0.9988	0.9882	0.9487	0.8610	0.7217	0.5491	0.3743	0.2258	0.1189
18	7	0.9998	0.9973	0.9837	0.9431	0.8593	0.7283	0.5634	0.3915	0.2403
18	8	1.0000	0.9995	0.9957	0.9807	0.9404	0.8609	0.7368	0.5778	0.4073
18	9	1.0000	0.9999	0.9991	0.9946	0.9790	0.9403	0.8653	0.7473	0.5927
18	10	1.0000	1.0000	0.9998	0.9988	0.9939	0.9788	0.9424	0.8720	0.7597
18	11	1.0000	1.0000	1.0000	0.9998	0.9986	0.9938	0.9797	0.9463	0.8811
18	12	1.0000	1.0000	1.0000	1.0000	0.9997	0.9986	0.9942	0.9817	0.9519
18	13	1.0000	1.0000	1.0000	1.0000	1.0000	0.9997	0.9987	0.9951	0.9846
18	14	1.0000	1.0000	1.0000	1.0000	1.0000	1.0000	0.9998	0.9990	0.9962
18	15	1.0000	1.0000	1.0000	1.0000	1.0000	1.0000	1.0000	0.9999	0.9993
18	16	1.0000	1.0000	1.0000	1.0000	1.0000	1.0000	1.0000	1.0000	0.9999
18	17	1.0000	1.0000	1.0000	1.0000	1.0000	1.0000	1.0000	1.0000	1.0000
18	18	1.0000	1.0000	1.0000	1.0000	1.0000	1.0000	1.0000	1.0000	1.0000
19	0	0.1351	0.0456	0.0144	0.0042	0.0011	0.0003	0.0001	0.0000	0.0000
19	1	0.4203	0.1985	0.0829	0.0310	0.0104	0.0031	0.0008	0.0002	0.0000
19	2	0.7054	0.4413	0.2369	0.1113	0.0462	0.0170	0.0055	0.0015	0.0004
19	3	0.8850	0.6841	0.4551	0.2631	0.1332	0.0591	0.0230	0.0077	0.0022
19	4	0.9648	0.8556	0.6733	0.4654	0.2822	0.1500	0.0696	0.0280	0.0096
19	5	0.9914	0.9463	0.8369	0.6678	0.4739	0.2968	0.1629	0.0777	0.0318
19	6	0.9983	0.9837	0.9324	0.8251	0.6655	0.4812	0.3081	0.1727	0.0835
19	7	0.9997	0.9959	0.9767	0.9225	0.8180	0.6656	0.4878	0.3169	0.1796
19	8	1.0000	0.9992	0.9933	0.9713	0.9161	0.8145	0.6675	0.4940	0.3238
19	9	1.0000	0.9999	0.9984	0.9911	0.9674	0.9125	0.8139	0.6710	0.5000
19	10	1.0000	1.0000	0.9997	0.9977	0.9895	0.9653	0.9115	0.8159	0.6762
19	11	1.0000	1.0000	1.0000	0.9995	0.9972	0.9886	0.9648	0.9129	0.8204
19	12	1.0000	1.0000	1.0000	0.9999	0.9994	0.9969	0.9884	0.9658	0.9165
19	13	1.0000	1.0000	1.0000	1.0000	0.9999	0.9993	0.9969	0.9891	0.9682
19	14	1.0000	1.0000	1.0000	1.0000	1.0000	0.9999	0.9994	0.9972	0.9904
19	15	1.0000	1.0000	1.0000	1.0000	1.0000	1.0000	0.9999	0.9995	0.9978
19	16	1.0000	1.0000	1.0000	1.0000	1.0000	1.0000	1.0000	0.9999	0.9996
19	17	1.0000	1.0000	1.0000	1.0000	1.0000	1.0000	1.0000	1.0000	1.0000
19	18	1.0000	1.0000	1.0000	1.0000	1.0000	1.0000	1.0000	1.0000	1.0000
19	19	1.0000	1.0000	1.0000	1.0000	1.0000	1.0000	1.0000	1.0000	1.0000
20	0	0.1216	0.0388	0.0115	0.0032	0.0008	0.0002	0.0000	0.0000	0.0000
20	1	0.3917	0.1756	0.0692	0.0243	0.0076	0.0021	0.0005	0.0001	0.0000
20	2	0.6769	0.4049	0.2061	0.0913	0.0355	0.0121	0.0036	0.0009	0.0002

Binomial cumulative density function, 0.10–0.50									
20	3	0.8670	0.6477	0.4114	0.2252	0.1071	0.0444	0.0160	0.0049	0.0013
20	4	0.9568	0.8298	0.6296	0.4148	0.2375	0.1182	0.0510	0.0189	0.0059
20	5	0.9887	0.9327	0.8042	0.6172	0.4164	0.2454	0.1256	0.0553	0.0207
20	6	0.9976	0.9781	0.9133	0.7858	0.6080	0.4166	0.2500	0.1299	0.0577
20	7	0.9996	0.9941	0.9679	0.8982	0.7723	0.6010	0.4159	0.2520	0.1316
20	8	0.9999	0.9987	0.9900	0.9591	0.8867	0.7624	0.5956	0.4143	0.2517
20	9	1.0000	0.9998	0.9974	0.9861	0.9520	0.8782	0.7553	0.5914	0.4119
20	10	1.0000	1.0000	0.9994	0.9961	0.9829	0.9468	0.8725	0.7507	0.5881
20	11	1.0000	1.0000	0.9999	0.9991	0.9949	0.9804	0.9435	0.8692	0.7483
20	12	1.0000	1.0000	1.0000	0.9998	0.9987	0.9940	0.9790	0.9420	0.8684
20	13	1.0000	1.0000	1.0000	1.0000	0.9997	0.9985	0.9935	0.9786	0.9423
20	14	1.0000	1.0000	1.0000	1.0000	1.0000	0.9997	0.9984	0.9936	0.9793
20	15	1.0000	1.0000	1.0000	1.0000	1.0000	1.0000	0.9997	0.9985	0.9941
20	16	1.0000	1.0000	1.0000	1.0000	1.0000	1.0000	1.0000	0.9997	0.9987
20	17	1.0000	1.0000	1.0000	1.0000	1.0000	1.0000	1.0000	1.0000	0.9998
20	18	1.0000	1.0000	1.0000	1.0000	1.0000	1.0000	1.0000	1.0000	1.0000
20	19	1.0000	1.0000	1.0000	1.0000	1.0000	1.0000	1.0000	1.0000	1.0000
20	20	1.0000	1.0000	1.0000	1.0000	1.0000	1.0000	1.0000	1.0000	1.0000

Appendix G

Cumulative Poisson Distribution

x	0.1	0.2	0.3	0.4	0.5	0.6	0.7	0.8	0.9	1.0
0	0.9048	0.8187	0.7408	0.6703	0.6065	0.5488	0.4966	0.4493	0.4066	0.3679
1	0.9953	0.9825	0.9631	0.9384	0.9098	0.8781	0.8442	0.8088	0.7725	0.7358
2	0.9998	0.9989	0.9964	0.9921	0.9856	0.9769	0.9659	0.9526	0.9371	0.9197
3	1.0000	0.9999	0.9997	0.9992	0.9982	0.9966	0.9942	0.9909	0.9865	0.9810
4	1.0000	1.0000	1.0000	0.9999	0.9998	0.9996	0.9992	0.9986	0.9977	0.9963
5	1.0000	1.0000	1.0000	1.0000	1.0000	1.0000	0.9999	0.9998	0.9997	0.9994
6	1.0000	1.0000	1.0000	1.0000	1.0000	1.0000	1.0000	1.0000	1.0000	0.9999
7	1.0000	1.0000	1.0000	1.0000	1.0000	1.0000	1.0000	1.0000	1.0000	1.0000
8	1.0000	1.0000	1.0000	1.0000	1.0000	1.0000	1.0000	1.0000	1.0000	1.0000
9	1.0000	1.0000	1.0000	1.0000	1.0000	1.0000	1.0000	1.0000	1.0000	1.0000
10	1.0000	1.0000	1.0000	1.0000	1.0000	1.0000	1.0000	1.0000	1.0000	1.0000
11	1.0000	1.0000	1.0000	1.0000	1.0000	1.0000	1.0000	1.0000	1.0000	1.0000
12	1.0000	1.0000	1.0000	1.0000	1.0000	1.0000	1.0000	1.0000	1.0000	1.0000
13	1.0000	1.0000	1.0000	1.0000	1.0000	1.0000	1.0000	1.0000	1.0000	1.0000
14	1.0000	1.0000	1.0000	1.0000	1.0000	1.0000	1.0000	1.0000	1.0000	1.0000
15	1.0000	1.0000	1.0000	1.0000	1.0000	1.0000	1.0000	1.0000	1.0000	1.0000
16	1.0000	1.0000	1.0000	1.0000	1.0000	1.0000	1.0000	1.0000	1.0000	1.0000
17	1.0000	1.0000	1.0000	1.0000	1.0000	1.0000	1.0000	1.0000	1.0000	1.0000
18	1.0000	1.0000	1.0000	1.0000	1.0000	1.0000	1.0000	1.0000	1.0000	1.0000
19	1.0000	1.0000	1.0000	1.0000	1.0000	1.0000	1.0000	1.0000	1.0000	1.0000
20	1.0000	1.0000	1.0000	1.0000	1.0000	1.0000	1.0000	1.0000	1.0000	1.0000
21	1.0000	1.0000	1.0000	1.0000	1.0000	1.0000	1.0000	1.0000	1.0000	1.0000
22	1.0000	1.0000	1.0000	1.0000	1.0000	1.0000	1.0000	1.0000	1.0000	1.0000
23	1.0000	1.0000	1.0000	1.0000	1.0000	1.0000	1.0000	1.0000	1.0000	1.0000

x	1.1	1.2	1.3	1.4	1.5	1.6	1.7	1.8	1.9	2.0
0	0.3329	0.3012	0.2725	0.2466	0.2231	0.2019	0.1827	0.1653	0.1496	0.1353
1	0.6990	0.6626	0.6268	0.5918	0.5578	0.5249	0.4932	0.4628	0.4337	0.4060
2	0.9004	0.8795	0.8571	0.8335	0.8088	0.7834	0.7572	0.7306	0.7037	0.6767
3	0.9743	0.9662	0.9569	0.9463	0.9344	0.9212	0.9068	0.8913	0.8747	0.8571
4	0.9946	0.9923	0.9893	0.9857	0.9814	0.9763	0.9704	0.9636	0.9559	0.9473
5	0.9990	0.9985	0.9978	0.9968	0.9955	0.9940	0.9920	0.9896	0.9868	0.9834
6	0.9999	0.9997	0.9996	0.9994	0.9991	0.9987	0.9981	0.9974	0.9966	0.9955

7	1.0000	1.0000	0.9999	0.9999	0.9998	0.9997	0.9996	0.9994	0.9992	0.9989
8	1.0000	1.0000	1.0000	1.0000	1.0000	1.0000	0.9999	0.9999	0.9998	0.9998
9	1.0000	1.0000	1.0000	1.0000	1.0000	1.0000	1.0000	1.0000	1.0000	1.0000
10	1.0000	1.0000	1.0000	1.0000	1.0000	1.0000	1.0000	1.0000	1.0000	1.0000
11	1.0000	1.0000	1.0000	1.0000	1.0000	1.0000	1.0000	1.0000	1.0000	1.0000
12	1.0000	1.0000	1.0000	1.0000	1.0000	1.0000	1.0000	1.0000	1.0000	1.0000
13	1.0000	1.0000	1.0000	1.0000	1.0000	1.0000	1.0000	1.0000	1.0000	1.0000
14	1.0000	1.0000	1.0000	1.0000	1.0000	1.0000	1.0000	1.0000	1.0000	1.0000
15	1.0000	1.0000	1.0000	1.0000	1.0000	1.0000	1.0000	1.0000	1.0000	1.0000
16	1.0000	1.0000	1.0000	1.0000	1.0000	1.0000	1.0000	1.0000	1.0000	1.0000
17	1.0000	1.0000	1.0000	1.0000	1.0000	1.0000	1.0000	1.0000	1.0000	1.0000
18	1.0000	1.0000	1.0000	1.0000	1.0000	1.0000	1.0000	1.0000	1.0000	1.0000
19	1.0000	1.0000	1.0000	1.0000	1.0000	1.0000	1.0000	1.0000	1.0000	1.0000
20	1.0000	1.0000	1.0000	1.0000	1.0000	1.0000	1.0000	1.0000	1.0000	1.0000
21	1.0000	1.0000	1.0000	1.0000	1.0000	1.0000	1.0000	1.0000	1.0000	1.0000
22	1.0000	1.0000	1.0000	1.0000	1.0000	1.0000	1.0000	1.0000	1.0000	1.0000
23	1.0000	1.0000	1.0000	1.0000	1.0000	1.0000	1.0000	1.0000	1.0000	1.0000

x	2.2	2.4	2.6	2.8	3.0	3.2	3.4	3.6	3.8	4.0
0	0.1108	0.0907	0.0743	0.0608	0.0498	0.0408	0.0334	0.0273	0.0224	0.0183
1	0.3546	0.3084	0.2674	0.2311	0.1991	0.1712	0.1468	0.1257	0.1074	0.0916
2	0.6227	0.5697	0.5184	0.4695	0.4232	0.3799	0.3397	0.3027	0.2689	0.2381
3	0.8194	0.7787	0.7360	0.6919	0.6472	0.6025	0.5584	0.5152	0.4735	0.4335
4	0.9275	0.9041	0.8774	0.8477	0.8153	0.7806	0.7442	0.7064	0.6678	0.6288
5	0.9751	0.9643	0.9510	0.9349	0.9161	0.8946	0.8705	0.8441	0.8156	0.7851
6	0.9925	0.9884	0.9828	0.9756	0.9665	0.9554	0.9421	0.9267	0.9091	0.8893
7	0.9980	0.9967	0.9947	0.9919	0.9881	0.9832	0.9769	0.9692	0.9599	0.9489
8	0.9995	0.9991	0.9985	0.9976	0.9962	0.9943	0.9917	0.9883	0.9840	0.9786
9	0.9999	0.9998	0.9996	0.9993	0.9989	0.9982	0.9973	0.9960	0.9942	0.9919
10	1.0000	1.0000	0.9999	0.9998	0.9997	0.9995	0.9992	0.9987	0.9981	0.9972
11	1.0000	1.0000	1.0000	1.0000	0.9999	0.9999	0.9998	0.9996	0.9994	0.9991
12	1.0000	1.0000	1.0000	1.0000	1.0000	1.0000	0.9999	0.9999	0.9998	0.9997
13	1.0000	1.0000	1.0000	1.0000	1.0000	1.0000	1.0000	1.0000	1.0000	0.9999
14	1.0000	1.0000	1.0000	1.0000	1.0000	1.0000	1.0000	1.0000	1.0000	1.0000
15	1.0000	1.0000	1.0000	1.0000	1.0000	1.0000	1.0000	1.0000	1.0000	1.0000
16	1.0000	1.0000	1.0000	1.0000	1.0000	1.0000	1.0000	1.0000	1.0000	1.0000
17	1.0000	1.0000	1.0000	1.0000	1.0000	1.0000	1.0000	1.0000	1.0000	1.0000

18	1.0000	1.0000	1.0000	1.0000	1.0000	1.0000	1.0000	1.0000	1.0000	1.0000
19	1.0000	1.0000	1.0000	1.0000	1.0000	1.0000	1.0000	1.0000	1.0000	1.0000
20	1.0000	1.0000	1.0000	1.0000	1.0000	1.0000	1.0000	1.0000	1.0000	1.0000
21	1.0000	1.0000	1.0000	1.0000	1.0000	1.0000	1.0000	1.0000	1.0000	1.0000
22	1.0000	1.0000	1.0000	1.0000	1.0000	1.0000	1.0000	1.0000	1.0000	1.0000
23	1.0000	1.0000	1.0000	1.0000	1.0000	1.0000	1.0000	1.0000	1.0000	1.0000

x	4.2	4.4	4.6	4.8	5.0	5.2	5.4	5.6	5.8	6.0
0	0.0150	0.0123	0.0101	0.0082	0.0067	0.0055	0.0045	0.0037	0.0030	0.0025
1	0.0780	0.0663	0.0563	0.0477	0.0404	0.0342	0.0289	0.0244	0.0206	0.0174
2	0.2102	0.1851	0.1626	0.1425	0.1247	0.1088	0.0948	0.0824	0.0715	0.0620
3	0.3954	0.3594	0.3257	0.2942	0.2650	0.2381	0.2133	0.1906	0.1700	0.1512
4	0.5898	0.5512	0.5132	0.4763	0.4405	0.4061	0.3733	0.3422	0.3127	0.2851
5	0.7531	0.7199	0.6858	0.6510	0.6160	0.5809	0.5461	0.5119	0.4783	0.4457
6	0.8675	0.8436	0.8180	0.7908	0.7622	0.7324	0.7017	0.6703	0.6384	0.6063
7	0.9361	0.9214	0.9049	0.8867	0.8666	0.8449	0.8217	0.7970	0.7710	0.7440
8	0.9721	0.9642	0.9549	0.9442	0.9319	0.9181	0.9027	0.8857	0.8672	0.8472
9	0.9889	0.9851	0.9805	0.9749	0.9682	0.9603	0.9512	0.9409	0.9292	0.9161
10	0.9959	0.9943	0.9922	0.9896	0.9863	0.9823	0.9775	0.9718	0.9651	0.9574
11	0.9986	0.9980	0.9971	0.9960	0.9945	0.9927	0.9904	0.9875	0.9841	0.9799
12	0.9996	0.9993	0.9990	0.9986	0.9980	0.9972	0.9962	0.9949	0.9932	0.9912
13	0.9999	0.9998	0.9997	0.9995	0.9993	0.9990	0.9986	0.9980	0.9973	0.9964
14	1.0000	0.9999	0.9999	0.9999	0.9998	0.9997	0.9995	0.9993	0.9990	0.9986
15	1.0000	1.0000	1.0000	1.0000	0.9999	0.9999	0.9998	0.9998	0.9996	0.9995
16	1.0000	1.0000	1.0000	1.0000	1.0000	1.0000	0.9999	0.9999	0.9999	0.9998
17	1.0000	1.0000	1.0000	1.0000	1.0000	1.0000	1.0000	1.0000	1.0000	0.9999
18	1.0000	1.0000	1.0000	1.0000	1.0000	1.0000	1.0000	1.0000	1.0000	1.0000
19	1.0000	1.0000	1.0000	1.0000	1.0000	1.0000	1.0000	1.0000	1.0000	1.0000
20	1.0000	1.0000	1.0000	1.0000	1.0000	1.0000	1.0000	1.0000	1.0000	1.0000
21	1.0000	1.0000	1.0000	1.0000	1.0000	1.0000	1.0000	1.0000	1.0000	1.0000
22	1.0000	1.0000	1.0000	1.0000	1.0000	1.0000	1.0000	1.0000	1.0000	1.0000
23	1.0000	1.0000	1.0000	1.0000	1.0000	1.0000	1.0000	1.0000	1.0000	1.0000

x	6.5	7.0	7.5	8.0	8.5	9.0	9.5	10.0	10.5	11.0
0	0.0015	0.0009	0.0006	0.0003	0.0002	0.0001	0.0001	0.0000	0.0000	0.0000
1	0.0113	0.0073	0.0047	0.0030	0.0019	0.0012	0.0008	0.0005	0.0003	0.0002
2	0.0430	0.0296	0.0203	0.0138	0.0093	0.0062	0.0042	0.0028	0.0018	0.0012

3	0.1118	0.0818	0.0591	0.0424	0.0301	0.0212	0.0149	0.0103	0.0071	0.0049
4	0.2237	0.1730	0.1321	0.0996	0.0744	0.0550	0.0403	0.0293	0.0211	0.0151
5	0.3690	0.3007	0.2414	0.1912	0.1496	0.1157	0.0885	0.0671	0.0504	0.0375
6	0.5265	0.4497	0.3782	0.3134	0.2562	0.2068	0.1649	0.1301	0.1016	0.0786
7	0.6728	0.5987	0.5246	0.4530	0.3856	0.3239	0.2687	0.2202	0.1785	0.1432
8	0.7916	0.7291	0.6620	0.5925	0.5231	0.4557	0.3918	0.3328	0.2794	0.2320
9	0.8774	0.8305	0.7764	0.7166	0.6530	0.5874	0.5218	0.4579	0.3971	0.3405
10	0.9332	0.9015	0.8622	0.8159	0.7634	0.7060	0.6453	0.5830	0.5207	0.4599
11	0.9661	0.9467	0.9208	0.8881	0.8487	0.8030	0.7520	0.6968	0.6387	0.5793
12	0.9840	0.9730	0.9573	0.9362	0.9091	0.8758	0.8364	0.7916	0.7420	0.6887
13	0.9929	0.9872	0.9784	0.9658	0.9486	0.9261	0.8981	0.8645	0.8253	0.7813
14	0.9970	0.9943	0.9897	0.9827	0.9726	0.9585	0.9400	0.9165	0.8879	0.8540
15	0.9988	0.9976	0.9954	0.9918	0.9862	0.9780	0.9665	0.9513	0.9317	0.9074
16	0.9996	0.9990	0.9980	0.9963	0.9934	0.9889	0.9823	0.9730	0.9604	0.9441
17	0.9998	0.9996	0.9992	0.9984	0.9970	0.9947	0.9911	0.9857	0.9781	0.9678
18	0.9999	0.9999	0.9997	0.9993	0.9987	0.9976	0.9957	0.9928	0.9885	0.9823
19	1.0000	1.0000	0.9999	0.9997	0.9995	0.9989	0.9980	0.9965	0.9942	0.9907
20	1.0000	1.0000	1.0000	0.9999	0.9998	0.9996	0.9991	0.9984	0.9972	0.9953
21	1.0000	1.0000	1.0000	1.0000	0.9999	0.9998	0.9996	0.9993	0.9987	0.9977
22	1.0000	1.0000	1.0000	1.0000	1.0000	0.9999	0.9999	0.9997	0.9994	0.9990
23	1.0000	1.0000	1.0000	1.0000	1.0000	1.0000	0.9999	0.9999	0.9998	0.9995

List of Acronyms

APQP—Advanced Product Quality Planning. A product launch process used in the American automotive industry.

ATP—Available to Promise. Manufacturing master planners, using MRP or ERP software, can determine if enough capacity is available to handle dropped-in work.

CFM—continuous flow manufacturing

CONWIP—continuous work in process

CRP—capacity resource planning

CTQ—critical to quality. Frequently expressed as a graphical tree, it helps to define which measurements, features, and design issues are critical to quality.

DFM—Design for Manufacturing

DFMaint—Design for Maintenance

DFQ—Design for Quality

DFT—Design for Testing

DFX—Design for X. X can be "quality," "testing," or whatever component of design and production needs to be emphasized.

DMAIC—Define, Measure, Analyze, Improve, Control

DPMO—defects per million opportunities. Originally pioneered to allow apples-to-apples comparisons of different processes, plants, businesses, and so on, it is open to abuse—increasing the number of opportunities makes the defect level look better. Use with care.

DPO—defects per opportunity

DPU—defects per unit

DRP—distribution resource planning

EMI—electromagnetic interference

ERP—Enterprise Resource Planning

FMEA—Failure Mode and Effects Analysis

FMECA—failure mode, effects, and criticality analysis

GD&T—geometric dimensioning and tolerancing

IDEF0—a graphical technique for documenting processes; it is, in effect, a grammar

ISO 9000—an international quality system standard. The current version is ISO 9000:2000.

KPI—key process input

KPIV—key process input variable
KPO—key process output
KPOV—key process output variable
MRP—material requirements planning
MRP—manufacturing resource planning
OTED—one-touch exchange of die
PDPC—process decision program chart
PPAP—product part approval process. A collection of documents supporting the release of a product to a customer.
PPM—parts per million
QFD—quality function deployment. A matrix-oriented tool for discerning customer-supplier interactions.
RCCP—rough-cut capacity planning
RMA—return merchandise authorization
RTY—rolling throughput yield
SIPOC—supplier-input-process-output-customer. Usually a diagram technique.
SMED—single-minute exchange of die
SOW—statement of work
SWOT—strengths, weaknesses, opportunities, threats
TOC—Theory of Constraints
TPM—Total Productive Maintenance
TQM—Total Quality Management
WBS—work breakdown structure. Projects can be broken down by deliverable product, resource, or process task.
WIP—work in process. A form of inventory between raw goods and finished goods.

Notes

1. AIAG, *ISO/TS 16949: 2002 Implementation Guide* (Southfield, MI: Automotive Industry Action Group, 2003), 182.
2. Masaaki Imai, *Gemba Kaizen: A Commonsense, Low-Cost Approach to Management* (New York: McGraw-Hill, 1997), 14.
3. Peter Senge, *The Fifth Discipline: The Art and Practice of the Learning Organization* (New York: Doubleday, 1990), 378–391.
4. Robert S. Kaplan and David P. Norton, *The Balanced Scorecard: Translating Strategy into Action* (Boston: Harvard Business School Press, 1996), 24–38.
5. H. Chernoff, "Using Faces to Represent Points in K-dimensional Space Graphically," *Journal of American Statistical Association* 68 (1973): 361–368.
6. W. Edwards Deming, *Out of the Crisis* (Cambridge, MA: Massachusetts Institute of Technology, 1986), 23–24.
7. See note 6, pp. 97–98.
8. Joseph M. Juran, *Managerial Breakthrough,* 2nd ed. (New York: McGraw-Hill, 1995), 401–424.
9. See note 8.
10. See note 8.
11. Genichi Taguchi, Subir Chowdhury, and Yuin Wu, *Taguchi's Quality Engineering Handbook* (Hoboken, NJ: John Wiley & Sons, 2005), 127–131.
12. Japanese Management Association, Eds., *Kanban: Just in Time at Toyota* (Portland, OR: Productivity Press, 1989), 16–17.
13. National Institute of Standards and Technology, *Federal Information Processing Standard 183: Integration Definition for Function Modeling (IDEF0)* (Washington, DC: NIST, 1994), 44–58.
14. Project Management Institute, *A Guide to the Project Management Body of Knowledge—2000 Edition* (Newtown Square, PA: Project Management Institute, 2000), 29.
15. See note 14, p. 8.
16. Guy Kawasaki, *The Art of the Start* (New York: Portfolio, 2004), 173–178.
17. Peter S. Pande, Robert P. Neuman, and Roland R. Cavanagh, *The Six Sigma Way: How GE, Motorola, and Other Top Companies Are Honing Their Performance* (New York: McGraw-Hill, 2000), 220–228.
18. William Y. Fowlkes and Clyde Creveling, *Engineering Methods for Robust Product Design: Using Taguchi Methods in Technology and Product Development* (Reading, MA: Addison-Wesley Longman, 1995), 29–52.
19. Roger M. Schwarz, *The Skilled Facilitator: A Comprehensive Resource for Consultants, Facilitators, Managers, Trainers, and Coaches,* 2nd ed. (San Francisco: Jossey-Bass, 2002), 96–135.

20. Richard G. Weaver and John D. Farrell, *Managers as Facilitators: A Practical Guide to Getting Work Done in a Changing Workplace* (San Francisco: Berrett-Koehler Publishers, 1997), 67–71.

21. Irving Janis, *Victims of Groupthink* (Boston: Houghton Mifflin, 1972), 174–198.

22. Peter Scholtes, Brian Joiner, and Barbara Streibel, *The Team Handbook*, 2nd ed. (Madison, WI: Oriel Incorporated, 1996), 6–15.

23. Michael Brassard and Diane Ritter, *The Memory Jogger II* (Salem, NH: Goal/QPC, 1994), 91–93.

24. See note 8, p. 163.

25. See note 8, pp. 165–167.

26. Steven Covey, *The Seven Habits of Highly Successful People: Restoring the Character Ethic* (New York: Simon and Schuster, 1989), 151–154.

27. Roger Fisher, William Ury, and Bruce Patton, *Getting to Yes*, 2nd ed. (New York: Penguin, 1991), 15–95.

28. F. Herzberg, B. Mausner, and B. Snyderman, *The Motivation to Work* (New York: John Wiley & Sons, 1959), 68.

29. Abraham Maslow, "A Theory of Human Motivation," *Psychological Review* 50 (1943): 370–396.

30. Sharon A. Bower and Gordon H. Bower, *Asserting Yourself: A Practical Guide for Positive Change,* Update ed. (Reading, MA: Perseus Books, 1991), 87–102.

31. See note 23, pp. 12–18. Note: *The Memory Jogger II* shows examples and provides explanation. The explanations here are my interpretation of how to proceed.

32. Wallace J. Hopp and Mark L. Spearman, *Factory Physics*, 2nd ed. (New York: McGraw-Hill, 2000), inside cover.

33. Rajan Suri, *Quick Response Manufacturing: A Companywide Approach to Reducing Lead Times* (Portland, OR: Productivity Press, 1998), 303–334.

34. Rudyard Kipling, "The Elephant's Child," in *Classics of Children's Literature*, 3rd ed., ed. John W. Griffith and Charles H. Frey (New York: Macmillan Publishing Company, 1992), 1245.

35. James M. Higgins, *101 Creative Problem Solving Techniques: The Handbook of New Ideas for Business* (New York: New Management Publishing Company, 1994), 51.

36. Charles H. Kepner and Benjamin B. Tregoe, *The New Rational Manager: An Updated Edition for a New World* (Princeton, NJ: Princeton Research Press, 1997), 31–32.

37. AIAG, *Measurement Systems Analysis*, 2nd printing (Southfield, MI: Automotive Industry Action Group, 1998), 13–19.

38. ISO, *International Vocabulary of Basic and General Terms in Metrology*, 2nd ed. (Geneva, Switzerland: International Organization for Standardization, 1993).

39. Keki R. Bhote, *World Class Quality: Using Design of Experiments to Make It Happen* (New York: AMACOM, 2000), 107–146.

40. W. J. Conover, *Practical Nonparametric Statistics* (New York: John Wiley & Sons, 1999), inside cover.

41. Douglas C. Montgomery, *Design and Analysis of Experiments*, 5th ed. (New York: John Wiley & Sons, 2000), 1–30.

42. Clyde M. Creveling, J. L. Slutsky, and D. Antis, *Design for Six Sigma: In Technology and Product Development* (Upper Saddle River, NJ: Prentice Hall, 2003), 200–201.

43. Douglas C. Montgomery, *Response Surface Methodology: Process and Product Optimization Using Designed Experiments*, 2nd ed. (New York: John Wiley & Sons, 2002), 235–302.

44. George E. P. Box and Norman R. Draper, *Evolutionary Operation: A Statistical Method for Process Improvement* (New York: John Wiley & Sons, 1998), 12.

45. George Box and Alberto Luceño, *Statistical Control by Monitoring and Feedback Adjustment* (New York: John Wiley & Sons, 1997), 128–153.

46. AIAG, *Statistical Process Control*, 2nd printing (Southfield, MI: Automotive Industry Action Group, 1995), 131–136.

47. See note 39, pp. 399–420.

48. Douglas C. Montgomery, *Introduction to Statistical Quality Control*, 5th ed. (New York: John Wiley & Sons, 2004), 424–427.

49. Gwendolyn D. Galsworth, *Visual Systems* (New York: AMACOM, 1997), 3–20.

50. Masaaki Imai, *Kaizen: The Key to Japan's Competitive Success* (New York: Random House, 1986), 24–29.

51. U.S. Department of Defense, "Form DD-1723" (Washington, DC: Defense Technical Information Center, 1976), 1.

52. See note 37, p. 60.

53. Eliyahu Goldratt, *What Is This Thing Called Theory of Constraints and How Should It Be Implemented?* (Croton-on-Hudson: North River Press, 1990), 5–6.

54. Wallace J. Hopp and Mark L. Spearman, *Factory Physics: Foundations of Manufacturing Management*, 2nd ed. (Boston, MA: McGraw-Hill, 2000), 654.

55. James P. Womack and Daniel T. Jones, *Lean Thinking: Banish Waste and Create Wealth in Your Corporation*, Rev. ed. (New York: Free Press, 2003), 15–90.

56. See note 54, pp. 349–362.

57. Shigeru Mizuno and Yoshi Akao, Eds., *QFD: The Customer-Driven Approach to Quality Planning and Deployment* (Tokyo: Asian Productivity Organization, 1994), 3–49.

58. Genichi Taguchi, Subir Chowdhury, and Shin Taguchi, *Robust Engineering* (New York: McGraw-Hill, 1999), 10–15.

59. Clyde M. Creveling, *Tolerance Design: A Handbook for Developing Optimal Specifications* (Upper Saddle River, NJ: Prentice Hall, 1999), 124–131.

60. AIAG, *Potential Failure Mode and Effects Analysis,* 3rd printing (Southfield, MI: Automotive Industry Action Group, 2001), 13–31.

61. D. H. Stamatis, *Six Sigma and Beyond: Design for Six Sigma,* vol. 6 (Boca Raton, FL: CRC Press, 2001), 187–222.

62. Bob King, Ellen Domb, and Karen Tate, *TRIZ: An Approach to Systematic Innovation* (Salem, NH: Goal/QPC, 1997), 10–47.

63. Nam P. Suh, *The Principles of Design* (New York: Oxford University Press, 1990), 46–67.

64. Donald Benbow and T. M. Kubiak, *The Certified Six Sigma Black Belt Handbook* (Milwaukee, WI: ASQ Quality Press, 2005).

65. Benjamin Bloom, *Taxonomy of Educational Objectives, Handbook I: The Cognitive Domain* (New York: David McKay, 1956).

Bibliography

AIAG. 1995. *Statistical Process Control.* 2nd printing. Southfield, MI: Automotive Industry Action Group.

———. 1998. *Measurement Systems Analysis.* 2nd printing. Southfield, MI: Automotive Industry Action Group.

———. 2001. *Potential Failure Mode and Effects Analysis.* 3rd printing. Southfield, MI: Automotive Industry Action Group.

———. 2003. *ISO/TS 16949: 2002 Implementation Guide.* Southfield, MI: Automotive Industry Action Group.

Bhote, Keki R. 2000. *World Class Quality: Using Design of Experiments to Make It Happen.* New York: AMACOM.

Bower, Sharon A., and Gordon H. Bower. 1991. *Asserting Yourself: A Practical Guide for Positive Change.* Update ed. Reading, MA: Perseus Books.

Box, George E. P., and Norman R. Draper. 1998. *Evolutionary Operation: A Statistical Method for Process Improvement.* New York: John Wiley & Sons.

Brassard, Michael, and Diane Ritter. 1994. *The Memory Jogger II.* Salem, NH: Goal/QPC.

Chernoff, H. 1973. "Using Faces to Represent Points in K-dimensional Space Graphically." *Journal of American Statistical Association* 68:361–368.

Conover, W. J. 1999. *Practical Nonparametric Statistics.* New York: John Wiley & Sons.

Covey, Steven. 1989. *The Seven Habits of Highly Successful People: Restoring the Character Ethic.* New York: Simon and Schuster.

Creveling, Clyde M. 1999. *Tolerance Design: A Handbook for Developing Optimal Specifications.* Upper Saddle River, NJ: Prentice Hall.

Creveling, Clyde M., J. L. Slutsky, and D. Antis. 2003. *Design for Six Sigma: In Technology and Product Development.* Upper Saddle River, NJ: Prentice Hall.

Deming, W. Edwards. 1986. *Out of the Crisis.* Cambridge, MA: MIT Press.

Fisher, Roger, William Ury, and Bruce Patton. 1991. *Getting to Yes.* 2nd ed. New York: Penguin.

Fowlkes, William Y., and Clyde Creveling. 1995. *Engineering Methods for Robust Product Design: Using Taguchi Methods in Technology and Product Development.* Reading, MA: Addison-Wesley Longman.

Galsworth, Gwendolyn D. 1997. *Visual Systems.* New York: AMACOM.

Goldratt, Eliyahu. 1990. *What Is This Thing Called Theory of Constraints and How Should It Be Implemented?* Croton-on-Hudson: North River Press.

Herzberg, Frederick. 1959. *The Motivation to Work.* New York: John Wiley & Sons.

Higgins, James M. 1994. *101 Creative Problem Solving Techniques: The Handbook of New Ideas for Business*. New York: New Management Publishing Company.

Hopp, Wallace J., and Mark L. Spearman. 2000. *Factory Physics: Foundations of Manufacturing Management*. 2nd ed. New York: McGraw-Hill.

Imai, Masaaki. 1986. *Kaizen: The Key to Japan's Competitive Success*. New York: Random House.

———. 1997. *Gemba Kaizen: A Commonsense, Low-Cost Approach to Management*. New York: McGraw-Hill.

Ishikawa, Kaoru. 1982. *Guide to Quality Control*. Hong Kong: Asian Productivity Organization.

ISO. 1993. *International Vocabulary of Basic and General Terms in Metrology*. 2nd ed. Geneva, Switzerland: International Organization for Standardization.

Janis, Irving. 1972. *Victims of Groupthink*. Boston: Houghton Mifflin.

Japanese Management Association, Eds. 1989. *Kanban: Just in Time at Toyota*. Portland, OR: Productivity Press.

Juran, Joseph M. 1995. *Managerial Breakthrough. The Classic Book on Improving Management Performance*. 2nd ed. New York: McGraw-Hill.

Kaplan, Robert S., and David P. Norton. 1996. *The Balanced Scorecard: Translating Strategy into Action*. Boston: Harvard Business School Press.

Kawasaki, Guy. 2004. *The Art of the Start*. New York: Portfolio.

Kepner, Charles H., and Benjamin B. Tregoe. 1997. *The New Rational Manager: An Updated Edition for a New World*. Princeton, NJ: Princeton Research Press.

King, Bob, Ellen Domb, and Karen Tate. 1997. *TRIZ: An Approach to Systematic Innovation*. Salem, NH: Goal/QPC.

Kipling, Rudyard. 1992. "The Elephant's Child." In *Classics of Children's Literature*. 3rd ed., edited by John W. Griffith and Charles H. Frey. New York: Macmillan Publishing Company.

Maslow, Abraham H. 1970. *Motivation and Personality*. 2nd. ed. New York: Harper & Row.

Mizuo, Shigeru, and Yoshi Akao. 1994. *QFD: The Customer-Driven Approach to Quality Planning & Deployment*. Hong Kong: Asian Productivity Organization.

Montgomery, Douglas C. 2000. *Design and Analysis of Experiments*. 5th ed. New York: John Wiley & Sons.

———. 2002. *Response Surface Methodology: Process and Product Optimization Using Designed Experiments*. 2nd ed. New York: John Wiley & Sons.

———. 2004. *Introduction to Statistical Quality Control*. 5th ed. New York: John Wiley & Sons.

National Institute of Standards and Technology. 1994. *Federal Information Processing Standard 183: Integration Definition for Function Modeling (IDEF0)*. Washington, DC: NIST.

Ohno, Taiichi. 1988. *Toyota Production System: Beyond Large-Scale Production*. Portland, OR: Productivity Press.

Pande, Peter S., Robert P. Neuman, and Roland R. Cavanagh. 2000. *The Six Sigma Way: How GE, Motorola, and Other Top Companies Are Honing Their Performance*. New York: McGraw-Hill.

Peace, Glen Stuart. 1993. *Taguchi Methods: A Hands-On Approach to Quality Engineering*. Reading, MA: Addison-Wesley Publishing Company.

Philip Crosby and Associates. 2002. "Biography." http://www.philipcrosby.com/pca/C.Articles/articles/year.2002/philsbio.htm.

Project Management Institute. 2000. *A Guide to the Project Management Body of Knowledge—2000 Edition*. Newtown Square, PA: Project Management Institute.

Scholtes, Peter. 1998. *The Leader's Handbook: Making Things Happen, Getting Things Done*. New York: McGraw-Hill.

Scholtes, Peter, Brian Joiner, and Barbara Streibel. 1996. *The Team Handbook*, 2nd ed. Madison, WI: Oriel Incorporated.

Schwarz, Roger M. 2002. *The Skilled Facilitator: A Comprehensive Resource for Consultants, Facilitators, Managers, Trainers, and Coaches*. 2nd ed. San Francisco: Jossey-Bass.

Senge, Peter. 1990. *The Fifth Discipline: The Art and Practice of the Learning Organization*. New York: Doubleday.

Shewhart, Walter. 1986. *Statistical Method from the Viewpoint of Quality Control.* Mineola, NY: Dover Publications.

Shingo, Shigeo. 1986. *Zero Quality Control: Source Inspection and the Poka-Yoke System.* Portland, OR: Productivity Press.

Stamatis, D. H. 2001. *Six Sigma and Beyond: Design for Six Sigma.* Vol. 6. Boca Raton, FL: St. Lucie Press.

Suh, Nam P. 1990. *The Principles of Design.* New York: Oxford University Press.

Suri, Rajan. 1998. *Quick Response Manufacturing: A Companywide Approach to Reducing Lead Times.* Portland, OR: Productivity Press.

Taguchi, Genichi, Subir Chowdhury, and Shin Taguchi. 1999. *Robust Engineering.* New York: McGraw-Hill.

Taguchi, Genichi, Subir Chowdhury, and Yuin Wu. 2005. *Taguchi's Quality Engineering Handbook.* Hoboken, NJ: John Wiley & Sons.

Weaver, Richard G., and John D. Farrell. 1997. *Managers as Facilitators: A Practical Guide to Getting Work Done in a Changing Workplace.* San Francisco: Berrett-Koehler Publishers.

Womack, James P., and Daniel T. Jones. 2003. *Lean Thinking: Banish Waste and Create Wealth in Your Corporation.* Rev. ed. New York: Free Press.

Index